Passion in the Wind
Dream, Believe, and Achieve the Extraordinary

Alan M. Leduc

Copyright © 2011 Alan M. Leduc

ISBN-10: 0984792201
ISBN-13: 978-0-9847922-0-7

No part of this publication may be reproduced, stored in a restricted system, or transmitted in any form or by any means, electronic, mechanical, photocopying, scanning, or otherwise, except as permitted under Section 107 and 108 of the 1976 United States Copyright Act, without permission of the publisher.

Published by: Extraordinary Press
Printed in the United States of America by
Quality Printing Company, Anderson, Indiana

The Great Discovery® is a registered trademark of Mikel J. Harry, Ltd.

Six Sigma® is a registered trademark of Motorola, Inc.

Table of Contents

Chapter 1:	Why strive for the extraordinary?	1
Chapter 2:	Alan's Story	5
Chapter 3:	Tim's Story	21
Chapter 4:	What is a Long-Distance Rider?	39
Chapter 5:	Developing an Epic Ride	43
Chapter 6:	The Equipment and Preparation	55
Chapter 7:	Getting to the Start	65
Chapter 8	Southern Bay by Bay	71
Chapter 9:	Western Bay by Bay	97
Chapter 10:	Western Bay by Bay Plus	113
Chapter 11:	Western Bay by Bay Adventure	135
Chapter 12:	Northern Bay by Bay Part I	153
Chapter 13:	Northern Bay by Bay Part II	183
Chapter 14:	Northern Bay by Bay Part III	209
Chapter 15:	Eastern Bay by Bay	239
Chapter 16:	What a Ride	263
Appendix A:	Alan's Long-Distance Accomplishments	273
Appendix B:	Tim's Long-Distance Accomplishments	275
Appendix C:	Ride List	277

Forward

I am an 18 year cancer survivor. Losing a kidney to cancer when I was 42 was traumatic. However, I had no idea how it would change my life. It was through this event that I began to think about the fragility of life; how many people waited until they retired to "start living;" and how frequently they were not able to fulfill their dreams due to physical limitations.

I would not wish cancer on anybody. It is a horrible disease, not just physically, but also how it affects you mentally. However, had I not had to deal with life after cancer, I would likely not have had the experiences that I am able to share about my motorcycle riding. A friend of mine phrases it this way, "Are you living or waiting" – Are you living or are you waiting to die. After having cancer, I chose to live.

My wife Brenda has been beyond tolerant of me in our 43 years of marriage. She has never gotten the love she deserved from me, but still stands by my side. I often tell her that we have survived by mutual toleration, but I would not have wanted to live my life without her. She understands my passion for long-distance motorcycling. Although she may worry about its inherent dangers (which I try to minimize through proper training and gear) she also realizes that it is a vital part of my life and helps me to deal with the other parts of my life which are stressful.

I have had the privilege to be mentored by Dr. Mikel Harry, the co-creator of Six Sigma – the well-known business management system. I came to know Mike after taking a Lean Six Sigma Black Belt program he was teaching at the University of Arizona. Six Sigma was, at that time, primarily used for "big business" and my background was in "small business." I emailed Mike asking how a certain element of Six Sigma related to "small business." The question must have intrigued him and, as Mike says, "We became email buddies." I liked

Mike as much for what he was as a person as I did for his credentials as the foremost leader on Six Sigma.

Mike is a cowboy. Not just a guy from Arizona but a real cowboy. I thought it interesting that we both had rather extreme hobbies: Mine was long-distance motorcycling and his was calf roping. Over the years we have had long telephone conversations and have visited. But the most important honor is that he brought me in on the ground floor of his latest work, The Great Discovery® – a process that creates breakthrough in everything you do. Working with Mike on this project has provided me with tremendous insights, including insights into my own personal life.

I have had terrific support in writing this book. Brenda is an amazing proofreader and has eliminated, hopefully, all of the typos.

Barb Smith of Houston, Texas served as my first editor. Without her input, the book would have been, as my wife said after reading the first draft of the first three chapters, "The most boring thing I've ever read." Barb didn't hold back and she simply made the book much better. Barb taught me that I needed to take a middle school English class and review the grammer and punctuation rules I forgot long ago. Barb's contribution and effort can not be overstated. It was a joy working with her.

Alan Brandon served in the role of editorial overview. Once Barb and I pounded out what we thought was a good draft, Alan would critique our work and Barb and I would flesh out his input.

I cannot go without recognizing my many friends on the Motorcycle Tourer's Forum (MTF). I founded the MTF in 2001. My friends accuse me of enabling them; in truth, I have been the one who has been enabled the most. I would not have done most of the things I have accomplished in motorcycling without their encouragement and support. My best friends are people I have met through the MTF and to all of them I say, "Love ya, man!"

When I decided to write this book, instead of posting a report online, I solicited editing and proofreading help from the MTF. The response was overwhelming. As you read the book, you will see that we relied on our friends from the MTF on many occasions. As one of my friends, Don Kime, said, "I would like these people even if they didn't ride motorcycles."

A special thanks to those who provided feedback.

It is my honor and privilege to share this story with you. I encourage you to think about life: "Are you living or waiting." Now is the time to start living.

Dream, believe, and achieve the extraordinary.

1

Passion in the Wind
Why Strive for the Extraordinary?

Two riders *– one aged 60, the other 68 – traveled more than 23,000 miles circumnavigating the United States and Canada in 48 days. Their families, friends, and indeed most people could not comprehend the magnitude of the trip and the planning needed to accomplish it. However, for these two riders, the trip was possible because it aligns with their core values, giving them the passion and strong spirit to succeed. They approached the 23,000 mile goal simply by riding one day at a time and riding each day, one gas tank at a time. It is too much to be constantly focusing on the overall goal of getting to the end; however, focusing simply on the task at hand is not so difficult.*

Most people live their lives in a state of control by minimizing risk in order to avoid dealing with problems. However, this same modest approach to risk is what restrains them from attempting to fulfill their dreams or striving for the extraordinary.

I had the privilege in recent years to work with Dr. Mikel Harry on The Great Discovery – a process that creates breakthrough in everything that you do. Dr. Harry calls the path which allows ordinary people to achieve extraordinary results "The Proven Path" which is an eight step process:

Chapter 1

1. Clarify Core Values
2. Determine a Catalyst Dream
3. Establish Leading Milestones
4. Select Problematic Milestones
5. Identify Vital Forces
6. Define Enabling Actions
7. Complete Action Plan
8. Check Progress Results

While working on The Great Discovery project and talking to successful people, many of whom had extraordinary accomplishments, I came to understand that, whether they realized it or not, The Proven Path seemed to be a natural process for those who had achieved extraordinary goals. The last six steps in the process are more tool-oriented and familiar to most successful people. These steps are easily taught. However, the real power that causes one to strive for the extraordinary is **passion**. Passion is rooted in the first two steps of The Great Discovery's Proven Path:

1. Clarifying Core Values
2. Determine a Catalyst Dream

Understanding one's core values and aligning those values to a dream provides the spirit and passion to achieve that dream. Many people have dreams but render them impossible. Those who accomplish extraordinary things render virtually everything possible and strive to achieve those things important to them – those things aligned with their core values. The alignment of the dream with their core values is what gives them the spirit to work through difficult barriers.

After working with Dr. Harry on The Great Discovery, I began to analyze my own core values. I found that self-

Why Strive for the Extraordinary?

accomplishment and doing things others found difficult were two of my top core values. Long-distance motorcycle riding aligns with these values.

Prior to my work with Dr. Harry and then applying that work to my personal life, I never really had an answer as to why motorcycling and long-distance motorcycling in particular were so important to me. In the past, when someone asked me why I would do rides that seemed so extreme, I would typically respond, "Because I can." I really didn't have any better answer. Today when asked that question, my answer is less obscure. Planning, executing, and sharing my accomplishment with others satisfies my core values and brings much satisfaction to my life. It satisfies my inner soul.

By breaking extraordinary goals into milestones – smaller tasks – each individual milestone becomes easier to achieve.

My and Tim's story is not just about motorcycling. It is about accomplishing the extraordinary and about two friends doing so together, overcoming personal and mechanical difficulties and celebrating an epic ride.

2

Passion in the Wind
Alan's Story

By the time the medevac helicopter came for me, the adrenaline had worn off and I could feel every one of my cracked ribs and broken collar bone. I don't remember the accident. One minute I was riding along, the next minute I was standing in the middle of Jungo Road staring at my broken Goldwing. If my life passed before my eyes, I imagine the highlights would include regret for not giving my family higher priority, and some of the people who influenced me during my formative years and helped to shape the core values that I have today.

I was raised and still reside in New Castle, Indiana. My wife Brenda and I have lived in Washington, D.C. and Gurnee, Illinois, but New Castle has always been home. We prefer the simple life of a small town.

In order to help you understand the passion and strong spirit that provided the motivation for me to ***dream, believe, and achieve the extraordinary*** with respect to this epic ride, you must know something about me so you will understand how my core values were developed.

Core Values:
Independent – Dreamer – Single Focused

I developed my independence as a very young man. Things were different in the 1950's than they are today. Parents were

Chapter 2

not afraid of allowing their children to roam in "small town Midwest" and most children spent their free time outside as video games had yet to be invented and the television was black and white with limited programming.

To be independent, I needed to earn my own money. I collected bottles alongside the road, picked worms from a manure pile at the packing plant, and had newspaper routes as a young child. I started working as a carhop at 12 years old and later worked as a cook at several restaurants. Child labor laws were largely ignored, so working after school until midnight on a school night and getting in 40 hours per week with weekend work became normal for me. Working long hours not only provided income but also an escape into a different world.

Most of the money I earned was saved to fulfill my adolescent dreams. Even though I had only taken a few drum lessons and was not very good, I bought a $1,000 set of drums, paying for them with money I had saved from working paper routes. I bought my first car when I was 15 and remember driving it up and down the driveway because I didn't have a driver's license to go on the road. Once I identified a dream, I was single focused and could think of little else.

At a very young age my core values were beginning to develop. I was a dreamer and, even then, believed that all dreams were possible. Working and saving money were simply milestones that would allow me to achieve my dreams. Of course I didn't understand this then; I haven't even understood it most of my life.

My work with Dr. Harry, self-analysis during that work, and subsequent conversations with other people who have accomplished extraordinary things have helped me to understand my core values and how they influenced my life. The Great Discovery process, whether known or not, seems to be a natural process for people who have achieved the extraordinary – buying a set of $1,000 drums at age 11, buying

Alan's Story

a first car at age 15, or riding a motorcycle 23,000 miles, circumnavigating the U.S. and Canada in 48 days at age 60.

Core Values:
Recognition – Persistence – Protégé

I did well in elementary school and was placed in classes with the top students in the seventh grade. However, the long hours at work allowed little time for homework and often led to inattentiveness at school. This significantly affected my grades. I was eventually moved to less academically rigorous classes, separating me even further from my friends. Work, not school, had become the basis of my social network, and recognition for being an outstanding worker replaced recognition in the form of academic achievement. I had a strong desire to be recognized for my efforts, so work became my primary focus.

As a junior in high school, I heard about students who worked in retail shops half days during their senior year. I went to my counselor, Mr. Lehr, to ask if I could work half days the next year. Mr. Lehr informed me that this was a special program for students who had taken the retail management classes and that I didn't qualify. I was persistent and pointed out that I had two years of drafting and asked if I found a drafting job would I be allowed to work half days. Mr. Lehr agreed.

I was only sixteen the summer between my junior and senior year of high school. I knocked on a lot of doors with no success, likely due to my youth. I went to Modernfold, a folding door company, and asked for an application. I was given the application and a worn down pencil. There were no seats so I sat on a worn out uneven wooden floor to fill out the application and turned it in to the receptionist. Engineering Manager, Chuck Good, invited me to his office a few minutes later. For a young man, this was very intimidating. Chuck sat on one side of his desk in a big leather chair while I sat on the other side in a wooden chair. It seemed like we were miles apart.

Chapter 2

Chuck placed my application in front of him and said, "Do you see this? This is the most important thing you will ever fill out in your life. Look at it! It is sloppy and almost unreadable." As you can imagine I felt pretty meek. Chuck then changed his tone and said, "I saw you setting out there on the floor with a dull pencil; but this is very important. You should have taken it home and then brought it back." This thought had never occurred to me. Amazingly, just a few days later Chuck called me and offered me a job, likely because of a reference from my drafting teacher, Jack Renner, who worked at Modernfold in the summer.

I went to the high school to tell Mr. Lehr that I had found a job; however, Mr. Lehr had been appointed principal and was no longer my counselor. My new counselor said this was unprecedented and not possible. I was persistent; I made an appointment to see Principal Lehr. True to his word, he allowed me to take only English and Physics my senior year of high school. This gave me enough credits to graduate and allowed me to get out of school by 10:00 a.m. and get in 6-1/2 hours of work daily. With a half day of work on Saturday, I was essentially a full time employee.

At Modernfold, I had a great work mentor, Gale Tarr. Gale expected nothing but hard work and perfection. When I made a mistake, Gale was very tolerant and taught me how to avoid such mistakes in the future, but he made it clear that repeated mistakes of the same nature would not be tolerated. I appreciated Gale's willingness to share his knowledge and his desire to challenge me. He was an excellent mentor and, as a protégé, I tried to mimic his character. I soaked up Gale's teachings and was highly recognized, eventually being placed as a checker, checking work of people much my senior, even before graduating high school. I didn't know it at the time but this job and Gale's mentoring were shaping my life and character.

Alan's Story

Core Values:
Dedication – Self-Initiative – Striver

I figured my destiny was to be a factory worker like my father. Chrysler had a large automotive plant in town and after graduation many of my peers were getting jobs at Chrysler. I applied repeatedly but couldn't get hired. I later found out that there was a gentlemen's agreement that Chrysler would not hire Modernfold employees. I continued to work at Modernfold, advancing in responsibility.

It was the height of the Vietnam War when I graduated high school in 1968. Modernfold was losing a lot of young men to the war. Danny Danielson, President, called in a few young men, including me, and told us about a student deferment. He offered to pay for our college so we could get the deferment. The problem was that we were all living paycheck to paycheck. Mr. Danielson understood our situation and agreed to pay for the college in advance, rather than requiring us to wait for reimbursement after receiving a grade. At Modernfold's request I began studying Industrial Engineering Technology.

Agreeing to go to college was one thing. Getting in was another. My C average in high school and lack of SAT scores meant that I was admitted to college on academic probation. Without extreme dedication, college and the student deferment would be gone. Modernfold required full time employment from those accepting the offer to pay for their college and the government required full time attendance at college in order to maintain the deferment. I worked full time during the day and went to school four nights per week getting home after 10:00 p.m. Homework had to be done on the weekends. It was an exhausting load but I endured and was removed from academic probation, although my grades were nothing to brag about. Student deferments ended two years later. Exhausted, we all dropped out of school but continued to work for Modernfold.

Chapter 2

It would be several years before I returned to school to get my degree. By that time I was doing drafting for structural engineer Robert (Bob) Crooks. Bob was supportive and worked with me from a scheduling stand point, but provided no financial support. Again I worked full time during the day and went to school at night, leading an exhausting life. However, since I was paying the bill, I was much more focused and it was rare for me to get anything other than an "A" grade.

Bob had a tremendous influence on my life. He was a soft disciplinarian like Gale Tarr and expected nothing but the best. The single most important thing I learned from Bob was that, with self-initiative, a person is capable of about anything. The number one reason delegation fails is often said to be "Because it is easier to ask the boss." In other words, instead of trying to work through a problem, it is easier to seek help. However, the real reason delegation fails is that it is easier for the boss to give an answer than to suffer through the process of teaching their employees to think for themselves.

Bob came to me and said, "You are a smart young man. It is time for you to learn design in addition to your drafting." Bob placed several code books on my desk and asked me to design a Little League Scoreboard. I didn't even know where to start. When I would ask Bob a question, Bob would look at his book shelf, pull down a book, and say something like, "I think Chapter 6 will help." It was obvious to me that Bob was not going to answer any questions. It took me two months to complete that job, which Bob could have done in an afternoon. Bob, like Gale Tarr at Modernfold, had been demanding but patient. The lesson that Bob had taught me about searching for my own solutions was a lesson that would shape my life. Bob made me believe that anything was possible if I would strive to achieve it. I worked for Bob for 7 years but still meet with him periodically, some 30 years later. Bob is no doubt the single largest influence in my life and I have told him this on many occasions.

Alan's Story

I eventually earned Associate and Bachelor of Science degrees in Industrial Engineering Technology and left Bob's employment to pursue a job in the field of manufacturing. Bob had taught me that I could do anything, and that knowledge allowed me to be successful as an Industrial Engineer, General Foreman, Engineering Manager, Plant Manager, and Vice-President / General Manager.

Core Values:
Teacher – Challenge – Achievement

Inspired by my excellent life teachers, Gale and Bob, I made an effort to share my knowledge in every position I held. I wanted to challenge my employees and allow them to do things that they may not have thought possible. One of my fondest memories is when an employee of mine said to me, "You have always believed in me and challenged me to do more than I ever thought possible of myself."

Unfortunately, this was such a core part of my character that I expected this from all of my employees. I had the same expectations for my children. At the time, I did not understand that just because challenge and achievement were core values of mine, they were not core values for everybody. In some cases, by being so demanding, I'm sure I did harm.

In 1990, a fellow student in the MBA program I was taking asked me if I had ever considered teaching. This struck a chord with me. Teaching Engineering Technology only required a Master's Degree with real-world experience. I applied and was offered a one year contract at Ball State University. The next year the contract turned into a tenure line position meaning that not only was teaching required but also the need to publish.

I found myself back to working long days for about a third of the money. I had summers off but much of that time had to be spent writing. One benefit was the flexibility of doing the

Chapter 2

work around my sons' activities. Years of neglecting the family by working long hours never allowed a strong relationship to develop between my sons Chad and Ross and me, something that I truly regret. The satisfaction that I received from the challenges and achievement associated with work was well entrenched and family always seemed to be secondary.

My World Changed

In 1992, at age 42, my world changed. I was diagnosed with kidney cancer and lost my right kidney. There was no need for chemotherapy or radiation since it was diagnosed very early. Having the surgery in the middle of the tenure process at Ball State, and teaching a full course load, left me utterly exhausted.

Family and friends had stopped focusing on the cancer once the kidney was removed and there were no signs of recurrence. However, I thought about recurrence constantly. It seemed my life was a matter of making doctor appointments and waiting for results.

It would be years later before I had an official diagnosis, but something wasn't right. While watching television I saw an advertisement about depression. Many of the symptoms seemed to mimic how I was feeling. I did extensive internet research and self-diagnosed this as the primary cause of my exhaustion.

Depression has a stigma, so I chose to deal with it on my own. I elected to quit going for cancer checkups, thinking that the possibility of not living a full life was better than living to wait for news, whether good or bad. The next several years were mentally and physically difficult. I continued to deal with both the pressure of getting tenure and the depression. My depression was aggravated by the feeling that I had deprived my family of a substantial income in order to become closer and that had failed.

Alan's Story

Motorcycles

I have no particular memories of motorcycles as a child except for an occasional story about my father having one as a young man. In the early years of my marriage to Brenda we bought a 1967 Triumph Bonneville which was the hot bike for its day. As anybody who owned a 60's Triumph knows, you couldn't go far from home without a tool kit. The longest ride I can remember taking was about 50 miles round trip, but every ride seemed fun. When Brenda became pregnant, the bike was sold.

After receiving tenure I decided it was time to seek balance in my life. I began to think of that 1967 Triumph Bonneville and the enjoyment that it had brought to Brenda and me. Each Spring the thoughts would occur. It was not until Spring 2000 that I decided to take action. One day I called Brenda from work and said, "I'm going to buy a motorcycle."

"You are?" Brenda replied. "Okay."

2000 Honda 1100 Spirit
Photo by Alan Leduc

Chapter 2

That day I went to Benson's Motorcycles, a Harley/Honda dealership, to look at motorcycles and picked out a new 2000 Honda Shadow 1100 cc Spirit.

The dealer asked if I had a motorcycle endorsement.

"What's that?" I replied.

In Indiana, the motorcycle endorsement requires only a written test to get a learners permit which has limitations: Daylight riding only, helmet required, and no passengers. I passed the test the next day and made arrangement to pick up the motorcycle.

The day I picked up the motorcycle there were severe winds and the dealer tried to discourage me from taking it that day. However, as you might guess, I was determined. They brought it out and asked, "Do you know how to ride it?"

"Of course, it's been a long time but it is like riding a bicycle right? You never forget."

I started to put the bike in neutral but when I pushed on the foot lever on the right side, it didn't seem to do anything, "Why won't this shift into neutral?" I asked.

The salesman said, "The gear shifter is on the left side. It is one down and four up."

"On the left side? My Triumph was on the right side." I'm sure when I left the dealer they were shaking their heads. They called shortly after I arrived home to make sure that I made it. I had, but was scared to death all 18 of those miles. The winds were severe and it was not exactly like riding a bicycle.

Brenda was disappointed because my beginner's permit did not allow passengers. Quite frankly, if I had felt confident, I would have ignored that law. But recognizing the low level of my skills, I used it as an excuse. Every night I would go to the high school parking lot, where the motorcycle test course was painted, and practice. I had to wait 30 days to take my driving test to get a full endorsement, but the practice had paid off. Now it was time for Brenda's first ride. The extra weight seemed to change the handling significantly and I was glad that the state required the 30 day learning period. Brenda and I would go for short rides and it seemed that the motorcycle was providing the balance that I was seeking.

My First Long-Distance Ride

After buying the Honda Shadow Spirit, I began hanging out on an internet group called Shadow Riders Forum (SRF). This was a place where other Honda Shadow riders shared experiences and stories. Bill Rich, aka Bill750 and later Bill1100 because he bought a bigger bike, was the founder of the SRF. Bill posted a message about the Iron Butt Association (IBA) SaddleSore 1000 which required a rider to ride 1,000 miles in 24 hours. I can remember posting, "That is crazy! Who would do something like that?!"

Somebody like me as it turns out.

I already had plans to spend three weeks at my in-laws' in Cocoa Beach, Florida when school was out. I then thought, why not ride my motorcycle? This brought me back to the IBA web site and I began to make plans to take the long way to Florida through New Orleans so I could complete both the Saddle Sore 1000 and the BunBurner 1500 (1,500 miles in 36 hours).

I knew I had to prepare myself and my motorcycle if I wanted to be successful at these two rides. So beginning in March, I began commuting to work daily on the bike and doing longer weekend rides, all to get myself in shape. I used the Internet to research tips on long-distance motorcycle travel, and I enhanced my tool kit and travel gear "just in case."

Chapter 2

Fortunately, the weather was great and I had no problems and completed the rides successfully. I didn't know it at the time but those rides were life-changing. I was hooked.

No More Balance

Those two long-distance rides had upset the balance that motorcycling had brought to my life. Soon, riding around town was no longer enough. It seemed all I could think about was the challenge and satisfaction I had received by completing the SaddleSore 1000 and BunBurner 1500.

2001 Honda GL1800 Goldwing
Photo by Alan Leduc

One day I was at the dealership getting new tires for the Spirit, and on the showroom floor was a beautiful Illusion Red GL1800 Goldwing, considered by many to be the top-of-the-line touring bike. It had every option you could buy and had

Alan's Story

been sitting on the showroom floor for a while, since the dealer sold primarily Harley's. I was looking at it when one of the owners, Steve Benson, said, "You need to buy that." Soon we had a deal and I called Brenda to tell her she didn't need to pick me up.

"Why... aren't you going to get new tires?"

"Yes, I already have them and will be home soon."

I wouldn't recognize it until much later, but my focus now was on long-distance motorcycling and I was about to go at it full force, just like I did with work.

The Motorcycle Tourer's Forum

There was an unexpected consequence from buying the Goldwing. My motorcycling friends were primarily those I had met electronically (not in person) on the Shadow Riders Forum. Now that I no longer had a Shadow, it seemed that I did not have as much to share. I suggested that there needed to be a forum for all kinds of bikes, focused on touring. One of the members agreed and said, "Why don't you start one?"

I didn't know much about how to go about starting a forum, but managed to get one set up, calling it the Motorcycle Tourer's Forum (MTF). I didn't really expect it to grow but the next thing I knew, a couple of people showed up to post messages.

One thing that Bill Rich did on the Shadow Riders Forum was control the bickering so that it was family friendly. I felt it was important to establish this culture for the MTF. I also felt that it was important for it to be open to all brands of motorcycles with no brand bashing allowed. Initially the forum was focused strictly on touring. However, as time passed and the forum grew, the forum developed interest in three styles of motorcycle riding: Touring (which we call Flower Sniffing); Long-Distance

Chapter 2

Riding; and Rough Road Riding. Today the MTF sponsors three or so events annually, held all over the country, for each style of riding. The MTF is usually recognized in Delphi Forums' "Top Forums" webpage.

At the time of this writing, the MTF has over 800,000 messages and over 40,000 members. The MTF is more than a forum. Because of the formal events and informal lunch meetings, many of the members have met in person and the MTF has become a close-knit family.

Hooked on Long-Distance Riding

After I purchased the Goldwing, Brenda and I began to travel on long trips, riding to Florida several times and even a long trip to Montreal and across to Maine. But Brenda had no interest in 1,000 mile days.

On the other hand, I had gotten hooked on the long-distance riding, which I did solo. I completed a BunBurner 1500 Gold (1,500 miles in 24 hours) and several other extreme rides. Long-distance riding fit my introverted personality. Because of the work I have done with Dr. Harry, I now recognize that it also satisfied my core values.

In 2003, I was selected to participate in the Iron Butt Rally (IBR) where riders travel 11,000 miles in 11 days. The IBR only occurs every two years and entry is restricted to elite long-distance riders. It is common for 2000 to 3000 long-distance riders to apply for the 100 or so entry positions.

After the excitement and pride at being selected to participate in the IBR, and after all my planning and preparation for what would surely be my most extreme ride to date, my IBR trip came to end on the Jungo Road between Winnemucca and Gerlach, Nevada. In the early morning hours I was having trouble finding a hardpack track in the loose gravel. I went down hard. The next thing I remember was standing beside my

Alan's Story

wrecked Goldwing, wondering what had happened. My friend, Jason Jonas, had been riding ahead of me. When he hadn't seen me for a while he headed back to look for me. He asked if I could ride the bike. I had tried to start it, but it wouldn't start. We tried again but no luck. Probably a good thing, because adrenaline was making me think I could ride. It ended up that every piece of plastic on the motorcycle was broken. I had a severe concussion, broken ribs, broken collar bone, broken toes, and a lot of bumps and bruises.

Jason punched my coordinates into his GPS and then rode the 28 miles of gravel to Gerlach to call for help. While he was gone I made another attempt to get the bike started. Fortunately I failed, as it was pointed in the wrong direction; and anyway, Jason would have kicked what was left of my ass. Because Jason gave the emergency people my coordinates, they were able to drop a helicopter right on me. By this time the adrenaline had worn off and I was hurting. The EMT's strapped me to a board in the standing position after I refused to lie down at their request. I told Jason, "Love ya, man." This has become an enduring phrase on the MTF today. Jason was already a great friend and this experience bonded us for life.

After the crash in the IBR, I immediately bought another motorcycle without talking to Brenda, except to tell her I had bought it. At one point during my recovery my orthopedic doctor asked, "So are you quitting motorcycling now?" Brenda answered for me and said, "No, that is an important part of his life." After that, Brenda rode less and less with me. She realized how important motorcycling was to me but had come to realize her own mortality and chose a safer path.

Brenda was prudent about her support as she would occasionally ask if my life insurance was current. I think she was kidding!

Chapter 2

Down Again

In December 2008, I was riding with friend Bob (a.k.a. boB, DragRacerBob) Moore. I had a lot of work issues on my mind and got caught daydreaming when traffic stopped in front of us on the interstate just east of San Antonio. When I noticed the stopped traffic ahead, I knew I wouldn't be able to stop in time.

Bob was riding on the right side of the right lane and I was on the left side of the same lane. I had ABS brakes and locked them down. The left lane was open and I thought I had the bike under control and could counter-steer to the left and miss both Bob and the cars in front of me. I released the brake and pushed hard on the left handlebar. BANG! My right saddlebag caught Bob's left saddlebag. I low-sided and ended up sliding down the interstate on my stomach. I was wearing a Kevlar Motoport suit and didn't have a scratch or bruise on me, but the bike flipped a few times and was totaled.

Unlike the 2003 accident in the IBR, this accident made me question whether or not to continue riding. Bob had been in a previous accident where he was tail ended by a car, which resulted in a serious head injury. All I could think about was how almost getting tail ended again might affect my friend. *I was just plain daydreaming and this accident should have never happened.* I made the decision to quit riding until I could move some things off my plate. I sold all of my motorcycles and gave away all of my motorcycle gear to avoid any temptation.

3

Passion in the Wind
Tim's Story

Tim Yow *was my riding partner on this epic adventure. Like me, Tim grew up in small town Midwest: Toledo, Martinsville, and Casey, about 30 miles from the eastern border in central Illinois.*

Tim is very accomplished and has been a friend for several years. During discussions, I realized that he and I had similar childhood upbringings. After beginning the work with Dr. Harry, I soon realized that Tim had followed the "proven path" of The Great Discovery, whether he knew it or not. At that point I started recording several interviews with Tim, thinking someday I might write a book about my friends who seemed to be ordinary people but had accomplished extraordinary things.

This chapter is a synopsis of those interviews with Tim and is written with Tim telling the story with my comments, from the perspective of my work with Dr. Harry and The Great Discovery, in italics.

Early Interest in Motorcycles

As a boy, I would see other boys from the better-to-do families tooling around town on Cushman scooters. Two boys had brand new Harley 125 Hummers and were the stars of the

Chapter 3

town. Being from a family of modest means, I could only dream of what it would be like to have a motorcycle and join the boys in what appeared to be so much fun and such an atention getter.

Zundapp 250

When I was 15 or 16, I spotted a Zundapp 250 while going past Eddie Bolins' dad's Body Shop. The Zundapp was a German motorcycle with horizontally opposed cylinders like a BMW, but most people have never heard of it. In my eye, the Zundapp 250 was a beautiful thing and the vision of it was burned into my mind.

Joining the Army

I dropped out of school at age 16. Jobs were difficult to find and I found myself living on the streets in freezing weather. I clearly recall a conversation while hanging out on the east end of Greenup:

Tommy: "I just joined the Army. I'm going to Hawaii!"

Me: "You're kidding me."

Tim's Story

Tommy: "Nope, that's what they promised me. Matheny is going, too."

Me: "I might as well go with you."

There was a roadblock. I had to have my parent's signature because I was younger than 18. But I found Dad, who agreed to sign the paperwork.

Core Values:
Recognition – Accomplishment

While in the Army, I became the best Communication Chief in Hawaii. Nobody knows that I was the best Commo Chief in Hawaii but me. But I decided I had to do something right. I was 17 years old and didn't have a high school education. You don't get too many times at bat and I had to get something done.

For most, being the best Commo Chief in Hawaii wouldn't mean much. But to this day I consider that small piece of recognition by my commanding officer to be one of the most important accomplishments in my life. It gave me something to build on. There was finally something in my life that I had done right. I might not have a high school education. I might be as poor as Joe's turkey. But I was the Best Commo Chief in Hawaii!

Core Values:
Education – Determination – Persistence

After getting out of the Army, I got a job at a John Deere dealer back in Casey, Illinois. I was making $1.05 per hour and

Chapter 3

working a 52 hour week which works out to $54.60 per week or $2,839.00 per year. The median income for men at that time was about $4,600. I felt like I was in a rut and needed to get out. I went back to my hometown of Toledo, Illinois and walked through town stopping anywhere I thought I could get a job. Jobs were hard to find and I came up empty handed. There were simply no jobs to be found.

My father was a teacher and a minister and his love of learning had shown me the value of an education. If I was going to get out of this rut, I needed to go to college. I had not finished high school but did earn a GED in the Army and had even passed a University of Hawaii entrance exam. The pass rate for the college entrance exam was very low. I was shocked that I passed it. It was on vocabulary and I had no vocabulary. I was in the Army. My vocabulary consisted of cussing.

I thought for sure being an ex-military guy with a GED, and having passed the college entrance exam, I would have no problem getting into college. I called Eastern Illinois University (EIU) in Charleston, Illinois and they confirmed that since I had passed the entrance exam, I would have no problem getting registered. So I hitchhiked to Charleston to register at EIU.

I recall the conversation when I got there vividly; however, I'll try to make a long story short. The clerk told me that while I met the entrance requirement, I would not be considered an in-state student since the rules required that I have an Illinois high school diploma. I insisted that they had told me on the phone I met all of the registration requirements. The clerk responded. "You do meet the registration requirement; but you must pay out-of-state tuition, since you do not have an Illinois high school diploma."

I could barely afford to pay in-state tuition and there was no way I could afford to pay out-of-state tuition. I asked if there was any way I could get an Illinois high school diploma. The

Tim's Story

clerk said, "You will have to wait until you are 21 and take an exam, which means you have to wait about 7 months." I was determined, but they finally convinced me that they were not going to budge, so I went back to looking for a job and finally found one working on the railroad.

I found out that EIU was offering night classes at a grade school in Toledo where I was working on the railroad. I signed up for a 2 credit hour U.S. History class. I would get off work and go straight to class with my face cut up with creosote. Because I was working long days on the railroad and had little time to study, I only got a C. But I passed! Now the dream of getting out of the rut and going to college didn't seem so impossible.

I took the cancelled $12.46 check that I had used to pay for the course in Toledo and headed for the main campus in Charleston, thinking that since I had completed this class, I should now be able to get into EIU. The clerk told me, "The course you took in Toledo was an adult class," and advised me that I still did not meet the criteria for in-state tuition. Frustrated, I ask the clerk, "Who is your boss?" and she sent me to a little old lady who everybody knew was the witch of the Midwest. After getting nowhere with her I said, "Look, I grew up in Illinois; I went and served my country; and I'm a current Illinois resident and you are telling me I'm not entitled to in-state tuition?" She held her ground, so I said, "Who the heck is your boss?" She sent me to Dean Taber, Dean of Registration.

After some extended conversation, Dean Taber said, "I can't do it, Mr. Yow. The rules say you must have an Illinois high school diploma or pay out of state fees."

After more persistence on my part, Dean Taber said, "What is going on here? You are begging me to get into college and I have students out there partying all weekend who don't care if they are in college or not. I'm going to let you in! But if your records are ever checked, I'm going to deny I ever saw you. You better get passing grades!" *Tim's perseverance had paid off.*

Chapter 3

Core Values:
Appreciation – Loyalty – Commitment

My EIU English teacher from that first quarter of classes was Lucinda (Lucy) Gabbard, and she and I became lifelong friends. *This reflects on Tim's character of appreciation and loyalty to those who were willing to help him.*

Lucy was a neat lady but she kept giving me "F's." Knowing that I had to pass English class to satisfy my commitment to Dean Taber and to myself, I went to her and said, "We are partway through this quarter and I have to pass this class. I need you to correct me and tell me what I'm doing wrong." I recall being in a panic and going on and on.

She finally said, "We've been talking for 15 minutes. I thought you were trying to get me to change your grade but it seems like you just want help."

I said, "I deserve an F. I have no background in English and I just need somebody to tell me what I'm doing wrong."

She said, "In all of my years of teaching, nobody has ever asked me to work with them in that way." Lucy agreed to write notes in the margin of the papers and indicate the page number in the text that explained the error. I went from an F to a D to C to a B and aced out the rest of the course. *As Tim related the story, his eyes began to water and he said,* "That woman cared enough to help me. She wrote more on the paper than I did. She gave me help and it changed my life."

After the first quarter, I ended up getting two B's and an A. The C that I had gotten in the "adult class" in Toledo was the only grade lower than B that I would get during my whole college career. Even though I had not done well in high school, I ended up graduating from EIU with honors.

Tim's Story

Core Values:
Need to Finish – Entrepreneur – Loyalty

It took me nine years to graduate from college. I did not have a scholarship and had to work my way through college. By the time I got out, I was running six businesses. Financially the need for a college degree may not even have been important at that point due to my success. However, it was important to me. I felt that my success as a Commo Chief in Hawaii had established a foundation for my future and believed that the college degree would strengthen that foundation and better prepare me for the next challenge. *Tim always seemed to have a need for a dream that served as the next challenge and, unlike the lack of confidence that he had as a youth, he now believed that all dreams were possible.*

I got started in business when I heard that Claude, a friend of mine from back in Martinsville, was looking for me to give him some help. As a result, I soon found myself collecting information on laundry equipment.

It is hard to get started in this world and you have to be willing to give, in order to get. In my case Claude had some money and I had some time. I was also willing to learn as fast as I could to help him out. If he was to call me right now, I would head down to Martinsville to work for $2.00 an hour clearing off his little island. If Claude calls, I'm going. I used to drive to Sullivan, Indiana to do repairs on Claude's laundry equipment and he didn't even pay for my gas. But I owed him. He got me started. *Once again, Tim shows his loyalty to those who were willing to give him a chance.*

Core Values:
Vision – Single-focused – Frugal

Claude wanted me to go around to all of the laundromats in eastern Illinois and write down how many washing machines they had, how old they looked, and the brand. I had two

Chapter 3

months to get the job done. I soon realized that it would not take two months to finish the job and that by working extra hard, I was working myself out of a job, but I didn't slow down. Instead I went to Claude to plant a seed in his ear, "Since I'm working myself out of a job, I'm wondering if there is something I can do when I get this done."

I turned in the report early and Claude said I had done a terrific job. I asked, "Now that I have that job done, what are you going to do with the information?" Claude responded, "Well someday I'm going to hire somebody to go around and sell laundry equipment to the people on the list." I didn't know how good I would be at it but I told Claude, "It won't cost you anything to let me try." Claude agreed, and I found myself selling laundry equipment and ended up being one of Speed Queen's top per capita producers.

Claude helped me buy some Speed Queen washers to put into the fraternity and sorority houses around Eastern Illinois University. That led to us having several partnerships. I was still working on completing my college degree and was typically working 16-18 hours per day. I could do that for a long period of time, but would eventually work to the point of exhaustion and would have to stop and sleep for a weekend.

Patty and I got married while we were in college. She was a waitress and the restaurant let us have the reception there. My Dad performed the ceremony and someone else furnished the cake. We couldn't afford a honeymoon so we stayed in a converted garage where we were planning on living and went to work on Monday. For a couple of years, we both worked all of the time while trying to finish our degrees. *This is typical of Tim today. Even though he is a successful businessman and could be retired, he is frugal and still working to make a future for himself and his family.*

Tim's Story

Core Values:
Desire to be First – Helping Others – Perseverance

I had the opportunity to buy Jiffy Wash, a car wash manufacturer in Bloomington, Indiana. I put the first car wash in the country of Chile. *Tim's desire for a challenge and accomplishment is channeled in his desire to be FIRST.*

I eventually got into real estate, speculating on parcels of land, apartments, and so on. I obtained a real estate license, then broker's license, and a GRI (Graduate of Realtors Institute) designation. My interest in the real estate business led to my doing some commercial real estate and eventually into site development. I've developed sixteen-bed facilities for the disabled, building them all over Illinois and I still own them today. Building those homes was a commercial venture but it was also personal because of my homelessness when I was young. *It was during the difficulties of building the homes for the disabled that Tim developed another core value: perseverance.*

Unfortunately, some people were prejudiced toward the developmentally disabled and didn't want the homes built in their neighborhood. I knew that what I was doing was right and I worked hard to choose appropriate locations. I knew in the end I would get approval to build. But I also learned that sometimes you just have to "outlast the problems and outlast the people who are giving you trouble and keep your cool."

Most business problems are pretty similar. Most of the biggest problems I ever had, I could not solve. I had to find some part of the problem I could solve and work on it. It seemed that, once I got that part of the problem solved, the rest would just seem to go away. Sometimes I would sit around frustrated for a week because I had a problem so big I couldn't do anything about it. Finally, I just learned the pattern and started working on the part of the problem I could solve.

Chapter 3
Getting started in Long-Distance

I remember a conversation with Alan Leduc and Don Kime when Joe Mays was introducing himself:

Tim: "There is another Joe May, without an "s," in Alaska. I stopped at his place on the way to Labrador (Eastern Canada)."

Alan: Laughing, "Do you realize what you just said?"

Tim: With a funny face, "Did I say something wrong?"

Alan: Realizing Tim didn't get it, "You stopped to visit Joe May in Alaska on the way to Labrador and you are from Illinois."

Don: "To a lot of people that would be really unusual."

Tim: "That's like Fletcher, who is from Mississippi, coming up to meet me in Alaska but first taking a side trip through Nova Scotia. I guess we long-distance motorcycle riders live in a different world."

I first started riding when I got out of the Army in 1964. I bought a little Honda 90. It got 125 miles per gallon. I rode the thing winter and summer. When I saw anybody else riding out there in the snow, I thought, I have to meet that guy.

I later bought a 250 Yamaha, 350's, 450's, 750's and just kept getting bigger ones. I did what I would call long-distance riding back then on those little bikes. Gary McCray, a friend of mine, rode a BMW R60 and later an R75, and we used to just take off riding. I went down to Crab Orchard Lake one Friday afternoon after working all day. After I got my tent set up, I called Gary and told him I didn't have any time to call him before I left. Gary asked, "Where are you?" I told him I was down at Crab Orchard Lake planning to ride down through

Tim's Story

Missouri. About 4 hours later a headlight was shining in my tent. He found me and I didn't even tell him exactly where I was. That was the kind of friends we were. Gary and I rode everywhere.

Gary was the person that told me "There is a group of people called Iron Butt."

I said, "What do they do?"

Gary said, "These people ride 1,000 miles in 24 hours."

I said, "Oooooe, I wouldn't want to do that. On my little 350, it would just shake my guts out."

Terry Watson and I rode down to Dallas, Texas in 2003 to a motorcycle get-together. When we got ready to come back, it had been raining cats and dogs and it was going to do it again. I said, "Let's get up real early and beat that rain." We took off from Dallas and were talking on CBs when I told Terry we had done over 800 miles in about 13 hours. As I rode along I started thinking about that deal Gary told me about several years ago of 1,000 miles in a day. I could go to Indianapolis and come back home, but I figured they had some kind of paperwork to verify it. I got home and looked it up and sure enough, there was an Iron Butt Association.

I called Terry and said, "There is an Iron Butt."

Terry said, "When are you leaving?"

I replied, "I'm leaving this weekend for Denver. It is 1,000 miles." That was in 2003 when I did my first Iron Butt ride.

I ran across the Motorcycle Tourer's Forum and talked to Terry and I said, "We did that SS1000, but some of these people go Coast to Coast. I don't know whether I can do it but I want to try."

Dream, Believe, and Achieve the Extraordinary

Chapter 3

Terry said, "Ok, let's check into it."

We didn't really know where to start. I went over to the Iron Butt website to see what the rules were and found that the MTF had a ride planned. The way it was organized seemed so simple that all we had to do was show up in Jacksonville and ride. Terry and I did this on the spur of the moment as the MTF was doing this right away. We didn't know what these folks were going to be like, but they seemed so friendly on the internet. We showed up there as green horns.

It was mainly the MTF that enabled me; they just made it so easy. When you get in with this group of fellas and gals, they become your friends. I saw that other riders were doing big things and I figured I could do it too. Even after I did the Coast to Coast I wasn't sure I could do the Coast to Coast to Coast, but continued to try it because others were doing it. A lot of my most memorable trips have been with the MTF accomplishing something and meeting people and forming friendships that still exist.

The thing that you get along the way is the adventure side. I have always had a little of that in me. I was fortunate that I was stationed in Hawaii, Thailand, and the Philippines while in the Army, and since then I get this wanderlust.

I met a guy in the Army that, before I met him, had hitchhiked from Texas out to the East coast and got a job on a steamer. He had taken a bicycle to Europe to ride up into the Alps and he had watched the sun set on the Great Pyramids. He put something inside of me. I named my son after him. My son is named Timothy Todd. This guy's name was Perry Lynn Todd.

I got to Texas one time and I called his Dad and said, "I'm in Texas and I was thinking of running over to see Perry."

Perry's Dad said, "He is on a bicycle trip to New England."

Tim's Story

I said, "He has talked so much about you; I should just run over and see you."

Perry's Dad said, "Where are you?"

I told him I was in Greenville, Texas.

Perry's Dad said, "Have you had a map out lately?"

I said, "Why?" I had been driving about 12 hours in Texas. Perry's Dad said, "You are closer to home than me."

That was my first realization of the size of Texas. I would recall that moment every time I saw the 874 mile marker on I-10 in Texas. Perry Lynn Todd was an inspiration.

The Record for Most SaddleSores on Different Bikes

It just got so I always wanted to ride a SaddleSore every weekend. When I was on the road I felt good and was clearing my mind. I did a few SaddleSores and I was reading about a guy from Louisiana who had done SaddleSores on four different motorcycles. I thought I'm only a couple away from that. So I got a hold of Mike Kneebone, President of the Iron Butt Association. Mike said, "Let me talk to him first." Mike got back to me and said the other guy was done with it. I thought, "Man, most people just do a SaddleSore and they are done." They might do a couple, but I had these two done and thought, "All I have to do is five to break the record and that will be just a little bit of a stroll." I just started running that number up and it got so that one of my favorite times was when I was out doing a SaddleSore. No ergonomics. Just get on the bike and go.

My friend who has two Honda Helix's said, "Tim, if you think you are such an Iron Butt why don't you take that thing." I left at three o'clock the next morning, running wide open to Mississippi and back. It was a pretty easy ride. I made it in

Chapter 3

about 18 hours but I had to make a lot of gas stops as expected. As soon as I filled up I started looking for the next gas station. The Magna 45 and my Virago 1100 with the thin seat were the most painful. I would just get on a bike I had never seen before in my life and it was just a challenge. All I needed to know was how much gas it would hold.

Did Not Quit

I rode in the 2005 Iron Butt Rally and made it to the finish line but along the way hit a deer carcass and did not get enough points to be considered a finisher.

I was very lucky to come out as well as I did. It was foggy with trucks beside me and trucks behind me; suddenly I saw a deer carcass in the road. There was nowhere to go. Fortunately, I missed the antlers. When I got back from the rally I had a big hump on my back from two vertebrae that were knocked out of place.

It didn't hurt badly at first. But I thought, "I'm going to pay for this." I didn't get a half hour or so down the road and I thought, "Oh, man!" It started feeling like whiplash then. By the time I got to Maine, my head was over to the side and I couldn't straighten it.

The Dusty Butt 1000 is 1,000 miles in 24 hours on gravel, and is a ride developed by Will and Jen Allender, and Dan and Beth Huber. I tried the Dusty Butt and that is my only true DNF (Did Not Finish). I was officially considered a DNF in the Iron Butt Rally, but I got to the finish line – so to me, it is a DNQ (Did Not Quit). During the Dusty Butt I lost my eyesight in one eye before four in the morning. We were riding cow paths. When riding a Dusty Butt, you can't get on pavement except to get to the next dirt. So it was a total of 1,060 miles. The 60 miles were just to get you to filling stations. They don't have filling stations on dirt roads.

Tim's Story

The route had about seven questions we had to answer, such as writing down a certain name at a graveyard, to make sure we didn't cut across or cheat. Other than gas stops, we were in remote areas with wildlife and cows everywhere. It was free range so we had to be very careful.

Like the lessons I learned in business, when you are out on some of the extreme motorcycle rides, you can have a lot of problems. It can be weather, mechanical, a problem at home, or a big moose right in front of you. You put all of those together and just work on the ones you can handle. You just don't give up. You just have to outlast it. You have to keep on until it gives up.

Dreaming of the Epic Ride

In 2009, I completed a ride from Key West, Florida to San Diego, California to Prudhoe Bay, Alaska to Goose Bay, Labrador and back to Key West. I called it the Five Coast ride but the IBA certified it as the Circumnavigation of North America Insanity.

When I completed the ride, Mike Kneebone said, "We will add Inuvik, Northwest Territories and make it a Gold version." So I started planning a ride to include Inuvik. I was talking to my friend Jack Gustafson and he said he had a ride that is based upon bays rather than coasts. After I saw Jack's ride, I thought, "Man, this is something I want to do." I asked Jack if he wanted to do it with me and he said he couldn't right now but it was okay if I did it.

The first time I went to Prudhoe Bay, I was afraid of the Haul Road. The second time I went, I wasn't afraid but later, when I encountered the Trans-Labrador Highway to Goose Bay, I was again afraid because I had never done it. I remember lying in a bed in Labrador City during the 2009 ride. I had heard about a guy who had just gotten hurt. He broke his ribs and clavicle. I'm thinking, "I'm up here by myself. What if the bike breaks?

Chapter 3

What if I break? What if I go off the road?" I laid there and tossed and turned and wondered if I should go on or go home the next day.

I started thinking that if I had gone straight home, I'd have been there by now. I decided that I was not going to quit. I had gotten this far and was going to continue. I was going to keep going until I got so scared that I couldn't go any further. I kept hitting sand and stuff that threw me around. It could have been disastrous. I made it all the way up there and it wasn't as bad as I thought.

Dealing with the Home Front

Fortunately my wife Patty understands, even though she doesn't like it. I finally got her to ride with me and I flipped the bike end over end down in Missouri. That put us in a hospital for treatment. She liked it even less after that. She doesn't like to be by herself, so it is hard on her when I leave for long periods of time.

In addition to not liking motorcycles, she is fearful for me and my safety. Even with the ability to track me through my satellite tracker, she is still fearful. She knows some of my buddies have gotten killed doing this same kind of thing. She knows I am pushing the limits and am riding in areas that are extreme and you can get hurt. So I understand her position. I know her concern is valid. But the desire is so strong; I can't resist.

After I finished that Five Coast Ride in 2009, Patty was so torn up and fearful that I told her I would not do another extreme ride unless we had some agreement. She said, "I don't believe you!" I told Patty a little about the ride I was planning. There are only two Canadian Provinces that I have not been in and this will get me into one of those. She said, "You realize you have had buddies killed doing just the kind of thing you are planning. You have classmates that are in nursing homes and

Tim's Story

you are out here trying to do stuff that a 20 year old might not be able to do." I got to thinking later, "She has a point."

Patty knows how much I want to do this, but she also knows that she couldn't stand it if something happened to me. And there have been some close calls. I told Patty that if I do this ride I will not do it unless I am with someone who is skilled and somebody I think I can get along with without shooting them.

That doesn't help her much and she probably feels like I'm painting her in a corner. I've been married to her for 45 years. When I got home from my previous extreme ride, I was pretty sure the locks were going to be changed. I decided I finally needed to stop being selfish. So at that point I didn't know if I would do Jack's Bay ride or not, but it was always on my mind. I kept thinking of all the things I could see up there. It is something nobody has ever done, and it is an adventure I haven't done.

At the Moonshine Lunch Run, created by fellow MTF member Terry Hammond, I was standing in front of the hotel and a young man walked up to me and said, "You are an inspiration. At your age to be able to do something like this, gives us all hope that we can do something like that between now and the end. I want to do something like you have done."

So when Patty says, "What are you doing, you are 68 years old?" I'm happy about that. It is what is driving me to do more. Maybe at 68 I'm not as strong physically. Maybe I'm not as strong mentally. I keep inventorying this stuff. I'm having a little trouble with balance. I have some trouble with other stuff, my leg, and my knees. I've had a couple of bad wrecks. I had an ankle that got hurt which will hardly hold me up when I'm on a heavy bike. When that ankle starts giving away, I think, "Why do I want to go to Goose Bay again? I can't even hold myself up here in the drive."

Chapter 3

I don't really know what it is inside me. I just have this desire to do this kind of thing. Most people are goofy when they are young. I'm getting goofy in my old age.

A psychologist might say that we are all affected by our early years; but, in Tim's case, most of his core values were initiated and matured at various stages in life. After identifying his core values, I asked Tim if he realized that his success in his business life and his success in his long-distance motorcycling life seemed to be a never ending search to satisfy his core values. This was a heart-wrenching moment. Tim finally responded, "Not until right now." Tim clearly followed the Proven Path identified in The Great Discovery, but did not recognize that the Strong Spirit that motivated him was powered by his core values.

My desire is that, as you read this story, you keep in mind that both Tim and I are just ordinary people. We have accomplished what we accomplished in life, whether we knew it or not, by aligning our dreams with our core values. We did this in our business lives and we also did it in our lives as long-distance riders. Have we done extraordinary things? That is really for you to decide. But as I view my life, I'm astounded as to what I have been able to accomplish. Even writing this book is an extraordinary act to me.

The ride Tim and I completed was extraordinary, but Tim and I are just ordinary people. Many of our friends and others in the long-distance and adventure motorcycle riding communities have also done extraordinary things – maybe they are extraordinary, but I imagine if they told you their story, you would find they are ordinary people too.

Let this story inspire you to:
Dream, Believe, and Achieve the Extraordinary.

4

Passion in the Wind
What is Long-Distance Riding?

I have *friends who consider themselves long-distance motorcycle riders, but have a very narrow definition when applying that term to others. In the motorcycling community, this narrow interpretation of "long-distance" often leads to arrogance and divisiveness – "I'm better than you" and "I don't care about some dumb certification." Some of the narrow definitions have been developed simply because the person using them is only familiar with one aspect of long-distance riding. I hope this chapter will provide some background and broaden the definition of "long-distance" when associated with motorcycling.*

The Iron Butt Association (IBA) certifies "long-distance" rides. To become a member of the IBA you must complete their entry-level ride called the SaddleSore 1000 (1,000 miles in 24 hours). Does this mean that after you have completed your first SaddleSore 1000 you should be considered a long-distance rider? Of course! The majority of motorcycle riders would not attempt such a feat and would think, as I did when I first heard about the IBA, that such a ride is crazy. Is the term "long-distance rider" reserved for only those riders who have received a certification from the IBA? Of course not!

Horizons Unlimited is an internet group which is dedicated to motorcyclists who travel around the world. The Adventure Rider motorcycle forum has stories from many riders who

Chapter 4

have done extreme rides requiring long-distances. Many of these riders have never heard of the IBA and some who have, discount the need for certification. These riders, even though not certified by the IBA, have earned the title of long-distance rider.

While in Prudhoe Bay, Alaska on our **35 Bay by Bay Adventure**, Tim and I met two Brits who had traveled from Ushuaia, Argentina to Prudhoe Bay. Along the way, we also met many other motorcycle riders who were on extended rides, including one Aussie who had been on the road for over eight months. These riders were not familiar with the IBA, but surely should be considered long-distance riders.

Being a long-distance rider is a state of mind. It is dreaming of a trip that others would think is crazy, and then having the ability to plan and execute the ride. Anybody that does such a ride deserves the title of long-distance rider, certification or not. This is not to diminish the value of an IBA certificate and the role the IBA has played in long-distance riding. I believe the IBA has done more to promote safe long-distance riding than any other organization.

I started the Motorcycle Tourer's Forum in 2001. My goal was to provide a place where riders on any brand of motorcycle could meet to share their dreams and experiences. As the MTF evolved, our objective became to simply encourage riders to challenge themselves to ride more. For some, that meant to just start riding.

The MTF has what they call "Flower Sniffers" who may ride several hundred miles or more to meet for lunch or a weekend ride. Their preference is to ride 250-300 miles a day and "smell the roses" along the way. They are not long-distance riders by IBA standards but are long-distance riders when compared to the majority of motorcycle riders.

What is Long-Distance Riding?

Most of the riders on Horizons Unlimited are very skilled in field repairs and might wonder how anybody who cannot maintain and repair their own motorcycle could possibly call themselves a long-distance rider. I remember the first time I had a chain-driven bike. I didn't know anything about chains and my friend Bob Moore was riding with me in Alaska. My chain and sprockets were worn out and I had no idea how to make the repair.

Before this trip, I made a special effort to understand my motorcycle, plan for failures, and learn how to do most repairs on the road. To me this was a huge step in maturing as a long-distance motorcycle rider. When we had failures on this trip, I felt like a complete long-distance rider by being able to make the repairs. IBA certification should not be a prerequisite for being called a long-distance rider and neither should there be a requirement to be a mechanic.

My challenge to you, as you read this story, is to not get hung up on the definition of "long-distance rider." My hope is to simply encourage you to increase your skill level, and challenge yourself to ride more and farther than you ever thought possible. If you are new to motorcycling, a ride to the beach might be a long-distance trip for you. If you have crisscrossed the country on your touring bike, you probably have a different idea of the term "long-distance." If you consider yourself a long-distance rider, that is all that matters. If you don't even care about the term, that is okay too!

Just: "Dream, believe, and achieve the extraordinary."

5

Passion in the Wind
Developing an Epic Ride

After my *crash in Texas, I quit riding, got rid of my motorcycles, and gave away all of my gear. I did not ride again for about 18 months. As I was turning 60, I got to thinking about how most of my friends had to stop doing serious rides in their late 60's and early 70's. I decided that I was missing riding too much, so I bought a motorcycle. And then another.*

As Brenda said, motorcycle riding is an important part of my life and long-distance motorcycle riding gives me the challenges and self-satisfaction of achievement that is part of my core values.

Tim Yow had completed what the Iron Butt Association certified as the Circumnavigation of North America Insanity in 2009 (Mexico is part of North America so, technically, this is only the circumnavigation of the U.S. and Canada). Tim's ride was about 17,000 miles starting in Key West, Florida, and going to San Diego, California, Prudhoe Bay, Alaska, Goose Bay, Labrador, and back to Key West. Although Tim had asked me if I wanted to go along, I had plans to spend the summer in China working on a special project, so Tim did the ride by himself.

After the ride was certified, Mike Kneebone, President of the Iron Butt Association, mentioned to Tim that he planned to

Chapter 5

add Inuvik, Northwest Territories to the ride and call it the Circumnavigation of North America Insanity Gold. Tim began thinking about repeating the ride at the Gold level.

Around this time our mutual friend Jack Gustafson of Glennallen, Alaska, told Tim about an 18 Bay Ride that he was thinking of proposing to the Iron Butt Association. Tim got it in his mind that he would combine the Gold level of his Circumnavigation of North America Insanity ride with the 18 Bay Ride, and then invited our close friend Terry Hammond, me, and two other friends to participate. I told Tim I wasn't sure I could commit to such a ride since I had only been riding again for a short time after an 18 month layoff following an accident in December 2008. I also recently had a pacemaker implanted to help deal with some of my health issues.

Terry Hammond was a hugely popular figure in the motorcycling community, having established the Moonshine Lunch Run. In November 2010, he died of a heart attack at age 53. It was a shock to everybody, but Terry's death hit Tim and me especially hard. Every day of our ride, Tim wore a Moonshine sweatshirt with Terry's picture on the back and left his passenger pegs down, a sign that there was an invisible passenger riding.

I started to think about how many of my friends had to stop serious long-distance riding in their late 60's and early 70's. I also thought that, at age 68, this might be Tim's last big ride and, given my health issues, mine as well.

Tim had promised his wife Patty that he would not do the ride by himself. The other two riders didn't seem to be fully committed to the ride, so I started to give the ride further consideration. My primary reservation was that I had not done any long-distance rides since the pacemaker and, with the layoff after the accident, I was not sure I would be capable.

Developing an Epic Ride

In March 2011, I went to the Iron Butt Association meeting in Jacksonville and decided that I would participate in the Gator 1000 ride which was 1,000 miles in 24 hours inside the state of Florida. I felt good after the ride and decided to commit to Tim's ride.

Ride Research

On several occasions, I requested information from Tim on the ride. I didn't know this at the time, but Tim is a "get on and ride" kind of rider who does very little advanced planning. He knew that the IBA would allow 60 days for such a ride and figured he would just handle any problems on the road and would still have time to complete it. Essentially, he just kept telling me he was repeating his earlier ride with Inuvik added, and combining it with Jack's 18 Bay Ride.

I am an engineer and, therefore, a stickler about planning. I don't have to follow the plan (at least that is what I say), but I must have a baseline. Realizing that I was not going to get any detailed information from Tim, I started researching the ride and developing details on my own.

The first thing that I learned was that when Mike Kneebone created the Gold version of Tim's 2009 ride, Circumnavigation of North America Insanity Gold, he not only added Inuvik, but also added Brownsville, Texas. Brownsville is the southernmost point on the Mexico/U.S. border. It seemed that by adding it, Mike was trying to force a true circumnavigation, encouraging riders to take the border road back to I-10.

I also found a ride called the Ultimate Canadian Insanity which required riders to touch the extreme points in Canada: Little Gold Creek, Yukon (West); Inuvik, Northwest Territories (North); Point Pelee, Ontario (South); and Cape Spear, Newfoundland (East). It seemed that if we were going to do a true "Ultimate" circumnavigation of North America, the extreme Canadian points should be considered in such a ride.

Chapter 5

Jack's original 18 bays were:

1. Southernmost Point of U.S.A (Key West, Florida)
2. Mobile Bay (Mobile, Alabama)
3. Galveston Bay (Galveston, Texas)
4. Coronado Bay (Coronado Island, California – San Diego)
5. Coos Bay (Oregon)
6. Neah Bay (Washington)
7. Kachemak Bay (Homer, Alaska)
8. Prudhoe Bay (Alaska)
9. Destruction Bay (Yukon)
10. Yellowknife (Northwest Territories)
11. Thunder Bay (Ontario)
12. James Bay (Fort Rupert)
13. Goose Bay – Happy Valley (Labrador)
14. Chignecto Bay (Alma, New Brunswick)
15. Cape Cod Bay (Provincetown, Massachusetts)
16. Delaware Bay (North Cape May, New Jersey)
17. Chesapeake Bay (Cheriton, Virginia)
18. Biscayne Bay (Homestead, Florida)

Combining the extreme points of the United States and Canada seemed consistent with the spirit of the 18 Bay Ride – forcing riders to the coast – since all mandatory locations would require riders to go to the extreme perimeter of both countries. These criteria were used to develop what Tim and I initially called "35 Bays – Ultimate Circumnavigation of North America." Note that the bays grew from 18 to 35. This was done to force riders off the interstate, providing a circumnavigation closer to the coastline.

Developing an Epic Ride

The IBA will not typically approve a ride until someone has actually ridden it to determine how it should be documented. This meant that one of our goals during the ride was to ensure that documentation was available at each of the mandatory stops and to add any additional stops necessary to force riders along a specific route.

An Aggressive Schedule

When I developed the plan for the ride we were about to undertake, I planned a pretty aggressive schedule, particularly for the first three days:

Day 1: Southernmost Point (Key West, Florida) to Addison Bay (Marco Island, Florida) to Tampa Bay (Tampa, Florida) to Apalachicola Bay (Apalachicola, Florida) to Mobile Bay (Mobile, Alabama). My Garmin MapSource mapping software showed this as 948 miles in 16 hours, 44 minutes plus stops.

Day 2: Mobile Bay (Mobile, Alabama) to Galveston Bay (Galveston, Texas) to Brownsville, Texas to Kingsville, Texas. MapSource showed this as 980 miles in 15 hours, 29 minutes plus stops.

Day 3: Kingsville, Texas to Casa Grande, Arizona. MapSource showed this as 1,062 miles in 16 hours, 26 minutes plus stops.

Tim had done SaddleSores (1,000 mile days) the first two days of his 2009 ride. I had already seen all of the area we would be covering in these first three days on previous rides and just wanted to crank out the miles and get into "Iron Butt mode" (the mindset of enduring long days of riding). I sent the plans to Tim to make sure that such an aggressive first three days would be okay. He said yes, so I went about planning the rest of the route.

Chapter 5

The MapSource software indicated the overall route was 23,141 miles requiring 20 days, 9 hours, and 30 minutes of riding time. (This does not include time for stops and sleeping). We set our final ride plan for 37 days. Allowing for two maintenance days with zero miles, this meant we would need to average about 661 miles each day. I developed detailed plans for each of the 37 days on what was no doubt an aggressive schedule; however, we both were comfortable that we could complete the ride as scheduled, barring unexpected maintenance issues.

As mentioned above, our original plan was to call this trip the 35 Bay Ultimate Circumnavigation of North America. As it turned out, we dropped some bays and added others but still ended up with 35 bays. Since we did not include Mexico, the North America descriptor was not technically accurate. We decided to propose this ride to the Iron Butt Association as the **35 Bay by Bay Adventure with a time limit of 60 days and a 35 Bay by Bay Adventure Gold with a time limit of 47 days.**

A Comparative Ride

The Iron Butt Association has a ride called the Trans-Americas Challenge which entails riding from Prudhoe Bay, Alaska to Ushuaia (Yoos – Why –a), Argentina or vice versa. When I first saw this ride I thought it was something that nobody else was likely to repeat. There is no time line for this ride because Alaska and Argentina have opposite seasons and the trip usually requires a long wait at one end or the other. The Trans-Americas Challenge ride is about 15,000 miles and has numerous border crossings.

As of this writing, four riders are certified by the Iron Butt Association as completing the Trans-Americas Challenge. One of those riders, Tom Sayer, actually rode both directions. Dick Fish completed the ride in 21 days, 2 hours, 8 minutes. Most would consider the Trans-Americas Challenge an extraordinary ride, but Dick Fish's ride is simply amazing. Other riders are

Developing an Epic Ride

known to have completed the ride, pending certification, and yet there are many other riders who have done this ride only for the feat and are not concerned about the certification – for example the two British riders we met in Prudhoe Bay. It is on my dream list but, because of the opposing seasons, will have to wait until I retire.

With the turmoil in Mexico, many riders are concerned about their safety while riding in this area. We believe that our ride, the **35 Bay by Bay Adventure,** will be attractive to riders who would like to do the Trans Americas Challenge but do not want to deal with the reported "safety issues" in Mexico.

The **35 Bay by Bay Adventure** that we developed is approximately 23,000 miles plus 11 ferry rides. It is not as challenging from the perspective of opposing seasons, language differences (except Quebec), and border crossings. However, there are at this time over 2,700 miles of gravel roads providing sufficient challenge for most riders. There may be fewer gravel roads in the future as many of these roads are being paved.

Breaking the Big Ride into Components

Iron Butt Association rides fall into three categories:

1. Timed Rides based upon 1,000 or more mile days (the majority of the rides fall into this category)
2. Distance Rides that require extreme distances and are provided generous time restrictions (such as the Trans-Americas Challenge)
3. Unrestricted Rides (Such as the National Parks Tour)

When doing this ride we began to think of how others who might not have the time or money to do the entire ride could enjoy doing portions of it. In addition to the **35 Bay by Bay Adventure** which clearly falls into category 2, we will also propose that the IBA certify components of the ride as described below.

Chapter 5

The IBA uses the modifiers "Challenge," "Insanity," "Gold," and "Insanity Gold" to progressively indicate more rigorous levels of their rides.

The focus of the **Bay by Bay** ride series is to encourage riders to ride long-distances with a relaxation of the typical Iron Butt Association pace so they will have some time to take in the beautiful coastline views and slow down in the remote parts of Canada. So as not to infringe on the IBA's existing "modifiers," we have added three modifiers:

- **Tour** indicates a ride completed with a 300 mile per day average.
- **Power Tour** indicates a ride completed with a 500 mile per day average.
- **Adventure Tour** is used when road conditions are very demanding and the ride deserves specific criteria for that particular ride.

Shorter rides with relaxed time restraints do not currently fall into any of the three IBA categories and may not be consistent with the Iron Butt Association brand. The IBA will have to decide if the series of **Bay by Bay** component rides are consistent with their brand. If not, some other organization might be interested in certifying such a series. Regardless, later chapters are organized based upon the idea of component rides.

All rides which are a component of the 35 Bay by Bay Adventure will require riders to visit the intermediate extreme points and bays between the start and stop. The component rides are as follows:

1. **29 Bay by Bay Tour and Power Tour**
   This ride excludes mandatory points from the **35 Bay by Bay Adventure** which would require travel on gravel roads. This route is all paved and the rider can start at any point. Recommended time for **29 Bay**

Developing an Epic Ride

by Bay Tour is 60 days and for the 29 Bay by Bay Power Tour is 37 days.

2. **15 Bay by Bay Tour and Power Tour**
   This ride consists of the points within the U.S. and the route between Neah Bay, Washington and Eastport, Maine. This route is all paved. Recommended time for **15 Bay by Bay Tour is 35 days and for the 15 Bay by Bay Power Tour is 15 days.**

3. **Southern Bay by Bay Tour and Power Tour**
   Key West, Florida to Coronado Island, California (or vice versa). This route is all paved. Recommended time for **Southern Bay by Bay Tour is 11 days and for the Southern Bay by Bay Power Tour is 6 days.**

4. **Western Bay by Bay Tour and Power Tour**
   Coronado Island, California to Neah Bay, Washington (or vice versa). This route is all paved. Recommended time for **Western Bay by Bay Tour is 5 days and for the Western Bay by Bay Power Tour is 3 days.**

5. **Western Bay by Bay Plus Tour and Power Tour**
   Coronado Island, California to Homer, Alaska (or vice versa). This route is all paved. Recommended time for **Western Bay by Bay Plus Tour is 14 days and for the Western Bay by Bay Plus Power Tour is 8 days.**

6. **Western Bay by Bay Adventure**
   Coronado Island, California to Prudhoe Bay, Alaska (or vice versa). This route includes gravel roads. Recommended time for **Western Bay by Bay Adventure is 11 days.**

7. **Northern Bay by Bay Tour and Power Tour**
   Homer, Alaska to North Sydney, Nova Scotia (or vice versa). This route is all paved. Recommended time for **Northern Bay by Bay Tour is 20 days and for the Northern Bay by Bay Power Tour is 12 days.**

8. **Northern Bay by Bay Plus Tour and Power Tour**
   Homer, Alaska to St. John's, Newfoundland (or vice versa). This route is all paved. Recommended time

Chapter 5

for **Northern Bay by Bay Plus Tour is 23 days and for the Northern Bay by Bay Plus Power Tour is 13 days.**

9. **Northern Bay by Bay Adventure and Adventure Gold**
   Prudhoe Bay, Alaska to St. John's, Newfoundland (or vice versa). This ride includes Prudhoe Bay, Alaska; Inuvik and Yellowknife, Northwest Territories; James Bay, Quebec; Goose Bay, Labrador. This route includes gravel roads. Recommended time for **Northern Bay by Bay Adventure is 35 days and for the Northern Bay by Bay Adventure Gold is 21 days.**

10. **Eastern Bay by Bay Tour and Power Tour**
    Eastport, Maine to Key West, Florida (or vice versa). This route is all paved. Recommended time for **Eastern Bay by Bay Tour is 7 days and for the Eastern Bay by Bay Power Tour is 4 days.**

11. **Eastern Bay by Bay Plus Tour and Power Tour**
    North Sydney, Nova Scotia to Key West, Florida (or vice versa). This route is all paved. Recommended time for **Eastern Bay by Bay Plus Tour is 11 days and for the Eastern Bay by Bay Plus Power Tour is 6 days.**

12. **Eastern Bay by Bay Gold Tour and Gold Power Tour**
    St. John's, Newfoundland to Key West, Florida (or vice versa). This route is all paved. Recommended time for **Eastern Bay by Bay Gold Tour is 13 days and for the Eastern Bay by Bay Gold Power Tour is 8 days.**

Whether the components of the 35 Bay by Bay Adventure are certified by the IBA, some other organization, or not at all, I hope you take them on as a personal challenge.

Developing an Epic Ride

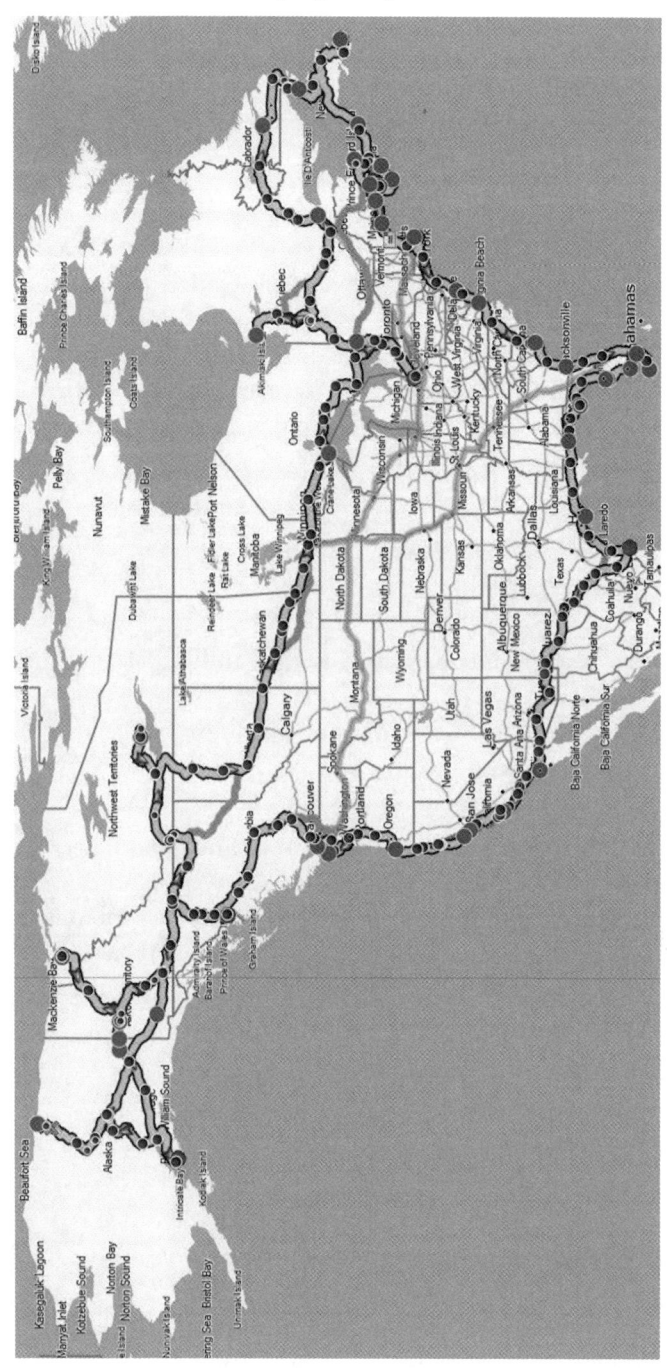

Dream, Believe, and Achieve the Extraordinary

6

Passion in the Wind
The Equipment and Preparation

More than *a few motorcyclists are gearheads - the ones who know every detail about every motorcycle. I'm not one of them. This chapter covers the equipment we used and our preparations leading up to the **35 Bay by Bay Adventure.** For those of you who are not into sub-frame upgrades and GPS devices, the sub-titles will allow you to skip those sections.*

Bike and Accessories

Alan's KLR 650 packed for the trip
Photo by Alan Leduc

Chapter 6

Both Tim and I selected older style Kawasaki KLR 650s for this trip. Kawasaki changed the design on this motorcycle in 2008 and we both preferred the older style which is a very basic motorcycle – it even has glass fuses. Tim chose a 2007 and I chose a 2006. Tim had ridden his motorcycle on his 2009 trip and I had purchased my motorcycle used, and had the top end of the engine rebuilt at 17,000 miles, so both were well broken in.

We both added many accessories to our bikes to make them more suitable for long-distance riding, including tank panniers, tank bag, and rear side cases. Stock from the factory, the KLR needs several mechanical modifications including what is known as the doohickey and sub-frame upgrade. Both bikes had skid plates, radiator guards, and light guards to protect them on the gravel roads we would experience on this trip. For visibility, both bikes had LED brake lights and I had added LED headlights to replace the stock headlight and LED auxiliary lights. Tim had a custom Mayer seat and I had an aftermarket flat Corbin seat.

Stock, this motorcycle sells new for around $5,900. If my bike and all of the accessories I put on it were purchased new, it would have cost nearly $12,000 plus the labor required to install the accessories. This gives you some idea of the heavy modifications made to the bikes in preparation for this trip. Fortunately, since I bought the bike used and did my own work, I only had a little over $7,000 invested.

Could we have chosen some other type of bike? Absolutely! A dual-sport (on road/off road) bike of some sort is recommended. However, riders have ridden to Prudhoe Bay, one of the most difficult roads on this ride, with about every kind of bike made. Riding a road bike on this type of ride is beyond my skill level, but I have friends who could. One thing to keep in mind if you elect to take your nice shiny bike, it will not look the same when you get done and you likely will never be able to get it clean again.

The Equipment and Preparation
Spare Parts

Tim and I also carried an extensive array of spare parts. We knew that we would be in areas where it would be difficult to get parts. I was carrying two extra front and rear sprockets and two chains; a full set of throttle and clutch cables; two sets of front and rear brake pads; a shifter; front and rear tire tubes; a complete set of valve shims; five oil filters; two pair of fork seals and dust covers; a service manual; maintenance videos; spark plug; engine gaskets; two quarts of oil. I was also carrying a variety of wire; clamps; wire connectors; a first aid kit; a complete set of tools. Tim had several spare parts, as well. If we had a problem on the road or in some remote city, having parts would save us a significant amount of time and could even save us from having to abort the ride. We knew we could probably find a mechanic if we needed help. However, finding parts specific to our bikes could be very difficult.

Along the trip, people would often ask if we were carrying spare parts and then when we said, "Yes," would say, "Since you're riding the same type of bike, then you can share." Intuitively this makes sense. However, it is advisable that each rider carries their own spare parts and tools, particularly common ones. This way if the riders get separated, each will be prepared. Sharing the same style of bike does have its advantages in that the shared mechanical knowledge of the riders combined is likely greater than any single rider. Also, larger, less likely to be needed, spare parts can be divided between the two bikes.

Satellite Tracker

Both bikes were equipped with Spot satellite trackers which allowed family and friends to track us. This is an extremely beneficial accessory for a trip like this. We knew we were going to be in remote places where there was no internet or cell service. The Spot tracker marked our position automatically every 10 minutes. If we stopped for gas or for the evening, we could push an OK button indicating to our followers that we

Chapter 6

were okay and had stopped. The OK button is very important. If we stopped but only had tracking, our families might be worried because we haven't moved for some time. By pushing "OK," they still won't know why we have stopped, but will know that there is no need to worry.

The tracker also has a HELP button which we had both set up to send an email to a special friend telling them that we were okay but needed help – and to send a tow truck. We had given our friends our emergency roadside information and other information that they might need. In hindsight, if we were in a different time zone than our friends and pushed the HELP button, they are not going to be much help if they are asleep. Spot offers an emergency roadside service, for a fee, that sends the help message directly to the emergency roadside service dispatchers and this is likely a better option.

The tracker also has an SOS button that, when pushed, sends an alert directly to a Spot dispatcher who will call emergency services. Tim and I both felt we should not do a ride like this without a satellite tracker.

I told Brenda, "If you see the HELP icon, don't worry, that just means that I am having some kind of mechanical trouble and have arranged for a tow truck. If you see the SOS icon, it is okay to worry, but don't panic. It could be that I pushed the button for someone that we came across on the ride – it might not even be me or Tim! But, even if it is me, the message is going directly to emergency services and I'm sure they will be contacting you before you can contact them. I'm carrying my emergency information in my riding jacket so they should be able to find you pretty quickly."

We hoped we would never have to press SOS, and we knew our family would probably still panic; however, it is better than any other option.

The Equipment and Preparation

When you have a riding partner it is unlikely that both of you would be in an accident in which nobody could see you. However, this could happen if riding alone. Let's say you are lying in a ditch unconscious and can't push the Spot SOS button. If the tracking device shows you in the same spot for an extended period of time, your family can report your last known location allowing emergency services to find you.

My friend and fellow rider, Jason Jonas, developed a program called Spotwalla which interfaces with the Spot satellite tracker and other devices. Spotwalla has some key features, not available on the Spot shared pages, which provide extra security and privacy. For example, you may not want people to know where you are stopping for the night; you may want to password protect your location so that only authorized friends and family can access it; or, like me, you might not allow the public to see HELP and SOS icons so as to avoid speculation and redundant activity.

GPS and Communication

Tim likes the Garmin 2610 GPS. This is an older GPS used by a lot of motorcycle rally riders. Tim had bad luck on his previous ride and wanted to be prepared in the event of failure so he carried three of them. The deficiency of this GPS is that you can no longer update the maps.

I had a Garmin 2820 with updated maps and a 2610 for backup. Having different GPSs with different versions of maps created some issues. On more than one occasion Tim's GPS would be sending him to the right and mine would be sending me to the left. We would have to stop and figure out what was going on and decide which route to take. Sometimes this meant chasing down the other rider. If you are going to have a riding partner, strongly consider using the same model GPS and have the maps updated to the same version.

Chapter 6

One thing that several riders we met on the road asked about was bike-to-bike communications. It might have been convenient and would have saved a few chases, but we elected to not have bike-to-bike communication. This was never really a major issue, although we did have one 66 mile detour and a few other temporary separations. If you elect to have no bike-to-bike communication you should establish a planned location to get back together each time you stop for gas. A few times Tim and I got separated and it might have been by luck that we found each other.

A substantial portion of this trip is ridden in Canada. I contacted my cellular provider and purchased a comprehensive U.S./Canada telephone and data plan. They had to move my line from my shared plan to a single plan and it cost me nearly $200 per month. However, I was pleased at the amount of cell coverage available. Of course, I didn't have coverage in remote areas, but I did have coverage in most towns and cities.

Preparation

I felt it was necessary to learn as much about my motorcycle as possible in case repairs were needed alongside the road or in a remote area. I decided to essentially tear my bike down to the frame. While doing so I made two major modifications. I replaced the stock shock with a "high-end" aftermarket shock and put cartridge emulators in the front forks. I also completely rewired the bike so I would know exactly how all of the accessories were connected and to provide backup sockets so that in the event something quit, I could just move it to another circuit and go on. Part of the wiring project, of course, was to replace the glass fuses with blade-style ATO fuses. The KLR has weak stock brakes so I upgraded to a larger wave rotor and Galpher pads as recommended by my friend Jack Gustafson, who has ridden his KLR many miles in extreme conditions.

The Equipment and Preparation

Our trip started in the middle of May in Key West, Florida and we planned to be in Fairbanks, Alaska 12 days later. Tim had commented in a post on the Motorcycle Tourer's Forum that "we might experience some cold weather." I posted back, "be sure to bring your electric clothing." He said, "I never leave home without it."

There are several manufacturers of electrically-heated clothing that plugs into the motorcycle, including jackets, gloves, pants, and socks. I normally only wear a heated jacket and gloves unless I am expecting to ride in temperatures below 20 degrees Fahrenheit for extended periods of time. I also pack some chemical heat pads as a backup for my gloves and for my shoes in case of really cold temperatures.

Tim packed his electric vest with arm chaps but did not bring his electric gloves. After riding for an extended time in the 30's, Tim's hands were freezing. When I asked him why he wasn't wearing his electric gloves, he replied, "I didn't think I would need them so I didn't bring them." We were going to Alaska and the Northwest Territories; what was he thinking?

More than once I reminded Tim with a smile that, "I would never leave home without my electric gear." Tim always retorted, "I'm never going to live that down am I?" "Nope, not as long as I'm around." Razzing your friends is just a way of life in the long-distance motorcycling community. My friends have several stories about me, which I am reminded of on a regular basis.

Tim and I, like most experienced long-distance riders, believe in ATGATT ("all the gear all the time"). You will rarely see us without full riding gear. We both had full face flip helmets which allowed us to flip them up to talk, drink, or eat. Tim had a Joe Rocket jacket and pants and I had a Kevlar Motoport jacket and pants. Tim's jacket and pants had been waterproof at one point but were leaking and the Motoport has no

Chapter 6

water protection at all so we both had rain layers. For added protection, we both had sturdy riding boots and leather gloves.

Tim never mentioned it, so I don't know whether he had emergency papers on him or not, but I did have his emergency contact information. Having been in accidents before, I have "EMERGENCY" embroidered on one of my jacket pockets and a typed list of emergency information including doctor, emergency contacts, insurance information, medication, credit card information and legal contacts. I also had a living will. All of this was in a waterproof pack stored in the "Emergency" pocket.

Our friend Jack Gustafson, who had the original idea for the 18 Bay Ride, was planning a Memorial Day weekend ride to Prudhoe Bay and was encouraging Tim and me to try to do the Haul Road 1000 as part of our ride. Only two people are certified as doing the Haul Road 1000 (although we know of others who have done it) – Jack Gustafson and another friend of ours, Jack Shoalmire. The Haul Road 1000 is approximately 1,000 miles in 24 hours starting and ending in North Pole, Alaska and traveling to and from Prudhoe Bay on the Haul Road which is also known as the Dalton Highway or, more recently, as the Ice Road Truckers Road.

Both Tim and I have been on this road twice before. The conditions are constantly changing and you never quite know what to expect. It is important that you slow down if you see any color or textural change or come upon a hill or curve that restricts your vision. You might just go over the top of a hill to find the road changing from pavement to gravel.

Tim and I were not sure we would be up to doing the Haul Road 1000 but wanted to time our ride so that we would at least be able to ride with Jack up the Haul Road to Prudhoe Bay. So we calculated backwards from the day we were to meet Jack, added an extra day, and set the start of our ride as Monday, May 16, 2011.

The Equipment and Preparation

We had a planned maintenance stop in Fairbanks, Alaska to change from street tires to knobby tires, change the chain and sprockets, and do any other maintenance necessary before starting to ride on gravel. Key West to Fairbanks is about 8,200 miles, all on pavement. We both were using Metzeler Tourances for street tires. These tires typically have an 8,000-9,000 mile life. Rather than chew up our tires just getting to the start line, we decided to trailer the bikes to Key West. Our friend Tom Coppedge let Tim store his truck and trailer at his home in Marathon, Florida. This meant we would not have to change tires until we got to Fairbanks.

The proper equipment is the equipment that suits you and the conditions which you are going to encounter on your individual challenge. There is no perfect machine that fits everybody. Whatever you choose, prepare it to sustain the worst conditions you can imagine and prepare yourself for the worst situation you can imagine.

7

Passion in the Wind
Getting to the Start

On Friday, *May 13, 2011, I had lunch with Brenda and started the 170 mile ride to Tim's house. I had only gone a few miles down Interstate 70 when I noticed traffic was backing up. Fortunately, I was at an exit so I decided to turn off and take the back roads. All of a sudden four low flying jets went zooming across in front of me. I immediately stopped, wondering what in the world was going on. Then I recalled the Mt. Comfort Air Show was that week and this was the Blue Angels. What a send off!*

When I arrived at Tim's I noticed my motorcycle sounded louder than normal. I found that the exhaust was loose and held to the engine by only one bolt. I didn't want to take time to work on it then, figuring I would have time to work on it when we got to Marathon, so I just loaded the bike on the trailer. In the process, I got the forefinger of my right hand caught between the fender and fairing. I hadn't even left yet and had already lost some major skin!

Tim's wife Patty was nice to me, so I assume she didn't blame me for dragging Tim around the continent and had come to grips with the fact that Tim and I would actually be leaving on this adventure the next day.

We left Tim's around breakfast time the next morning. We weren't on the road very long when Tim said, "If we do a

Chapter 7

BunBurner Gold (1,500 miles in 24 hours) we can make it to Tom's in one day." I really didn't want to drive all night and be worn out upon arrival in Key West, but I knew that we were likely going to be driving straight through.

About 150 miles after leaving, Tim realized that he had left his riding boots. Crap! Even with months to plan, you sometimes do something stupid due to the excitement of the moment. It was pouring rain and if we turned around and went back, it would delay us several hours. We immediately started calling on our friends from the MTF. Since it was a weekend we knew that Patty could not ship Tim's boots until Monday and the earliest they could arrive was late Tuesday morning. Our friend Barb Smith lives in Houston and was planning to meet us on the road. So we emailed her from the smart phone and made arrangements for Patty to ship Tim's boots to her. The irony of this solution is that both Tim and I wear full riding gear all of the time and this solution would require Tim to ride in tennis shoes for some part of the ride. We needed to look for a better solution.

I called friends Bob Moore and Kevin Lechner to see if they knew anybody along our route that carried motorcycle boots. Bob provided a list of boot shops but none had motorcycle boots. Kevin recommended that we call Bob Wooldridge at BMW of Atlanta. We called and, sure enough, they had Sidi riding boots.

To complicate the issue, Tim was not sure of the size of his Sidi boots as they are in European sizes and his American size was between the two European sizes. It also looked like we would be arriving in Atlanta very close to closing time. So we called upon other friends, Dan and Janie Ross, who live about 15 minutes from BMW of Atlanta. Dan agreed to go to the shop and wait in case we were not going to make it in time. If we were going to be late, we were going to call the store and buy both sizes of boots on Tim's credit card and have them give the boots to Dan. Dan would then return the size that didn't fit. It

Getting to the Start

was a lot of scrambling and involved a lot of our friends, but it looked like we were going to have a pair of riding boots for Tim. A single forgetful moment has us working on a solution that was so convoluted that it is funny.

As we approached Chattanooga, we came to a complete standstill due to road construction. It took us over an hour to get through Chattanooga and now we were sure we would not make it to Atlanta before the BMW shop closed. I called Bob Wooldridge and to our amazement he said, "We'll wait for you." We called Dan just in case. But, sure enough, when we rolled in, Bob had held the store open for us even though he needed to go to the hospital to see an employee. Dan and Janie were still there too, although it ended up we had wasted their time. Tim was able to get replacement boots and, as many motorcyclists have experienced, we were reminded of the generosity of the motorcycling community.

We wanted to have dinner with Dan and Janie, but already had plans to meet Kevin Lechner in Warner Robins. Quinton and Wanda Grubbs came with Kevin and we had some good barbeque at Sonny's, just south of Warner Robins. It means a lot when friends make a special effort to help and meet you on the road like this.

We arrived at Tom's in the early morning hours on Sunday. Tom was already at work. As soon as we exited the truck, his dogs started barking as did the dogs next door. Soon, Tom's wife Trudi came out and asked, "Are you trying to wake up the whole neighborhood? I usually try to sleep in on Sunday." Trudi put the dogs away. By that time we parked the truck, Tom had returned to meet us.

We unloaded the bikes and Tim decided that we should go to Key West and get our starting receipt and witness papers signed. A certified Iron Butt ride requires witnesses, and the time stamp on the initial gas receipt starts the clock on the ride. Typically, a rider gets the witness signatures, any pictures, or

Chapter 7

souvenirs they want at the start, and then obtains the initial gas receipt right before starting the trip.

Tim's feeling was that, since this ride allowed 60 days to complete and it was unlikely that we would take anywhere near that time, we should get the receipt now and save the hour or so ride to Key West and back the next morning. This is contrary to what most riders would consider Iron Butt protocol, since we would exchange about twenty hours of clock time for two hours of riding time.

Even though we had driven all night without sleep, we mounted up and headed to Key West. This was the first indication that Tim and I might have a conflict in riding style. I would have preferred to wait until the next morning to go to Key West, saving clock time on our pending ride.

This was a huge financial commitment for me, likely costing about 25% of my annual take home pay, and every day on the road added to the expense. Tim is a successful business man and the financial expense was not a real issue for him.

Tim and I have been close friends for a long time, but we had never ridden together. Although we had plenty of time to do the ride, my attitude was that this was an Iron Butt Ride and I would do it as fast as my capabilities would allow and try to keep to the planned schedule. This would also keep my expenses down. Tim, on the other hand, figured we had 60 days to complete the ride and it would take however long it took. Neither philosophy is right or wrong; but, we should have discovered our differences before now.

When we got to Key West, Tim immediately pulled into a gas station to get a receipt. Again, my Iron Butt mentality kicked in. We were planning to go to the buoy at the southernmost point and take pictures. It seemed that we should go there first, get our pictures, and then get our receipt. Tim said, "What does it matter, we have 60 days?" so I pulled up to the pump

Getting to the Start

and got gas which started the clock on my ride at May 15, 2011, 10:21 a.m. EDT.

We had decided that we were also going to try to complete the Iron Butt Association's USA South-West Challenge (Key West, Florida to Homer, Alaska in 14 days) as part of our ride. With a starting time of May 15, 2011, 10:21 a.m. EDT, we would have to arrive in Homer no later than May 29, 10:21 a.m. EDT. We would not be taking a direct route. Our **35 Bay by Bay Adventure** route required us to ride along the southern coast to San Diego before heading north, turning a 5,448 mile ride into a 7,629 mile ride. However, our planned schedule said that we should arrive in Homer on Day 10 so it appeared as though we had plenty of time for the USA South-West Challenge.

Fortunately, a Sheriff pulled into the gas station just as we were getting ready to head to the buoy at the southernmost point. We both had him sign our witness forms. On extreme rides you need two witnesses, one of which must either be a policeman, fireman, judge, notary, or someone on the Iron Butt Association witness list. Tom Coppedge served as one witness and the Sheriff as the other. The witness looks at your odometer and certifies that it is as you have indicated on the form and checks your ID to make sure you are who you say you are.

Upon returning to Tom's house, Tim went in for some much needed rest and I began trying to figure out what was wrong with the exhaust on my bike. The exhaust is held onto the cylinder head by two studs and two acorn nuts. I discovered both studs were in place but one of the acorn nuts was missing and the other was loose. I was disappointed since I had recently paid $1200 to have a bore kit installed. It seems that the mechanic did not properly torque the acorn nuts. I did not see any kind of gasket between the exhaust and the head. This seemed unusual to me, but when I compared it to Tim's bike, it looked the same. I just tightened the one acorn nut that was

Chapter 7

loose and went to the hardware store and got two nuts and put a double nut on the other stud. It still seemed a bit loud compared to Tim's bike, but it seemed about the same as what I was used to hearing. I normally wear earplugs so I wasn't really sure.

Several days later, we met some Canadian riders in Kelso, Washington and one of the riders mentioned how loud my bike sounded. I told him the story about the exhaust coming loose and he asked if I replaced the "donut washer." I had not really thought about a washer fitting inside the exhaust; I figured it would be a flange washer that fit around the studs. I arranged to have a new donut washer waiting for me at the shop in Fairbanks where we planned to do maintenance. Given that one of the acorn nuts was still in place, it is highly unlikely that the gasket was reinstalled at all when the bore kit was installed. This was just the first of several instances of dealing with problems caused by poor quality of workmanship or product.

I got a few hours of sleep. Then Tim, Tom, Trudi, and I went out for dinner and back to Tom's for some more sleep and an early morning start. Since we already had our receipt from Key West, we would head straight north from Marathon.

Tomorrow we will begin the process of achieving our dream!

8 Passion in the Wind
Southern Bay by Bay

Even though *we had some long days, the **Southern Bay by Bay** leg provided a glimpse of Florida cattle country; some great coastal views of Florida's panhandle; a ferry ride at Port Bolivar; Texas Canyon's unique rock formations; Glamis Dunes; the San Diego mountain pass; an unforgettable ride over the bridge to Coronado Island with the view of San Diego Bay; and encounters with two friends from the MTF. Believe it or not, this is one of the boring parts of the ride.*

The **Southern Bay by Bay** was the first leg of our ride, starting in Key West, Florida and ending on Coronado Island (San Diego), California with the following mandatory stops:

- Southernmost Point of U.S (Receipt from Key West, Florida)
- Addison Bay (Receipt from Marco Island, Florida)
- Tampa Bay (Toll Receipt from Sunshine Skyway Bridge; if the toll receipt does not indicate the bridge name you must get gas immediately after and submit both the gas receipt and the toll receipt)
- Apalachicola Bay (Receipt from Apalachicola, Florida)
- Mobile Bay (Receipt from Mobile, Alabama)
- Galveston Bay (Receipt from Galveston, Texas)

Chapter 8

- Southernmost Point on U.S./Mexico Border (Receipt from Brownsville, Texas)
- San Diego Bay (Receipt from Coronado, California)

MapSource (our mapping software) shows this route as 3,343 miles requiring 2 days, 5 hours, 54 minutes riding time. We planned to complete this portion of the ride in four days. This would allow 23 hours for sleep (about eight hours per night) and 4.5 hours each day for gas stops and food.

Day 1
Key West to Marathon, Florida
52 Miles

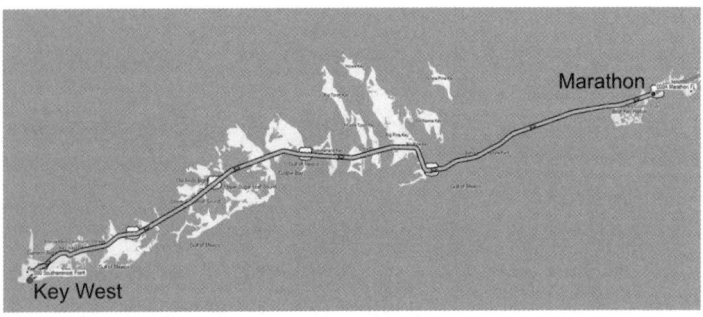

Our clock started ticking as soon as we got our gas receipt in Key West (Sunday, May 15, 2011 10:21 EDT). Because of our decision to avoid an early morning back-tracking ride to Key West, we in essence lost a day on our first leg before we even started. The short 52 miles back to Tom Coppedge's home from Key West would prove to be our shortest riding day of the whole trip!

Day 2
Marathon, Florida to Mobile, Alabama
916 Miles

Our original plan for the first day was to ride from Key West to Addison Bay (Marco Island) to Tampa Bay (Sunshine Skyway Bridge) to Apalachicola Bay to Mobile Bay. This was going to

Southern Bay by Bay

be a long day requiring 968 miles and 17 hours, 11 minutes of riding time. Our short trip on Day 1 from Key West to Tom's place reduced this day to an estimated 916 miles with 16 hours, 3 minutes of riding time.

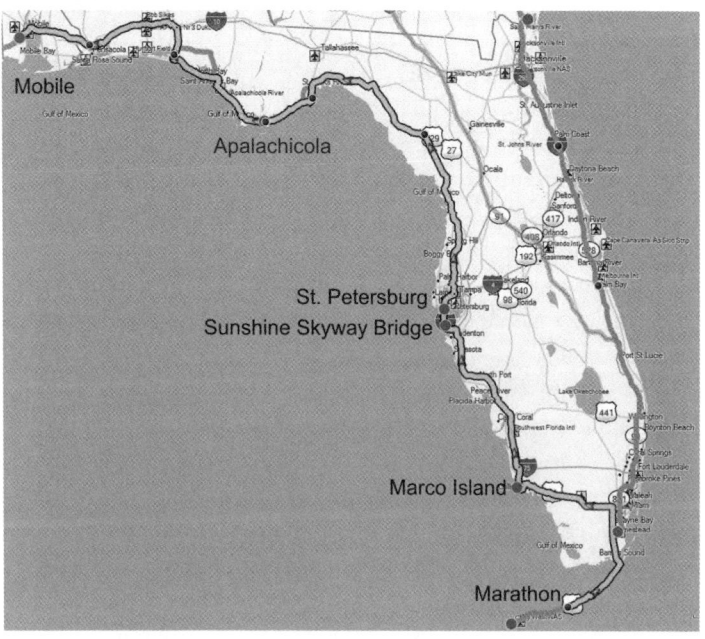

The traffic on the road between Key West and Homestead can be quite heavy during the day through early evening and there are very few passing lanes; travel is only as fast as the slowest vehicle. Once reaching Homestead, we would have to travel on secondary roads to Marco Island and then up the western coast of Florida. We would have 167 miles of interstate around Tampa, but would soon head back to coastal secondary roads until reaching I-10 about 137 miles from Mobile. Only about 30% of the ride from Key West to Mobile would be on interstate.

This is not a typical 1,000 mile Iron Butt ride which consists primarily of cruising down the interstate. Traveling the

Chapter 8

coastline on much less predictable secondary roads made the challenge for this day much more difficult.

Heading North. We left early enough that traffic from Marathon to Homestead was very light. From Homestead, we traveled west through the edge of Everglades National Park and Big Cypress National Preserve. I was really looking forward to Marco Island as I had heard about it many times from my family and friends, but had never visited. As we crossed the bridge to the island, there was a lot of road construction. We didn't want to spend a lot of time hunting for a "great picture location" of the bay because we knew we had a long day ahead of us. So we took a picture from the bridge and headed to the nearest gas station. My first trip to Marco Island was unremarkable.

MapSource shows Marathon to Marco Island as 184 miles at 3 hours, 40 minutes riding time (50 mph average). Add the 51 miles from Key West to Marathon and we were 235 miles toward our Planned Day 1. My odometer showed 244 miles indicating the 9 miles or so we spent roaming around Key West and Marathon on the first day. Spot indicates that we left Marathon around 4:30 a.m. We arrived in Marco Island at 8:10 a.m., right at the predicted 3 hours, 40 minutes.

I took less gas than Tim. The KLR 650 has a 6.1 gallon fuel tank, although the most I have ever put in the tank is 5.7 gallons. I had an auxiliary gas tank plumbed in line that gave me an extra two gallons, for a total capacity of 8.1 gallons. I only used 4.2 gallons of gas, which calculated to a whopping 58 mpg. Of course our speeds were restricted which helped; nevertheless, I was feeling good about getting this kind of gas mileage.

When I did the IBA's **48 States - 3 Countries Mexico to Alaska** ride (Mexico to Alaska via 48 States in under 10 days – you can't get to Alaska without going through Canada, which is the third country), I wanted to copy Ron Ayers' route as he had documented it in his book ***Against the Clock***. Unfortunately, I was unable to find many of the details I needed to duplicate the ride exactly. For this reason, I will include detailed information about our stops as I document this ride, in the event that someone wants to flatter our accomplishment and do the ride as we did it.

From Marco Island we picked up I-75 near Naples and took it to I-275 North just south of Tampa. Our next mandatory stop was the Sunshine Skyway Bridge in Tampa. Tim and I both had a Sunpass, but we needed a receipt, so I pulled into one of the lanes offering receipts. I thought Tim was right behind me; so I paid his $1 toll and got two receipts, saying, "I'm paying for the guy behind me." I pulled forward and Tim was nowhere to be found. I looked ahead and saw a motorcycle heading down the road and thought, "Dang, I thought he was behind me!" He must have been in another lane and beat me out. I couldn't understand why Tim would go racing off like that. I started chasing the motorcycle but he was just too far in front of me.

I had told Tim that I wanted to stop at the rest area right past the tollbooth to get a good picture of the bridge, so I figured he would be waiting on me there. Nope! I took a few photos and then decided to go down the road where there was another rest area on the other side. I pulled in and there was Tim.

"What happened to you?" I asked.

Tim said, "You were way out in front of me so I just came to the rest area hoping you were here."

Tim had tried to use his Sunpass at the cash-only tollbooth and the attendant told him he had to go to the Sunpass lane. So Tim backed up and went through the Sunpass lane. However, he didn't get a receipt, so he stopped and walked back to the receipt booth to get one. Obviously the motorcycle that I saw wasn't Tim. Tim didn't see the first rest area and went to the

Chapter 8

second one, so he missed me waiting on him. Without head-to-head communication we had already almost lost each other.

Gas Woes. We had gone down the road just a few miles when my bike started sputtering. "Hmmmmm, what is going on?" I reached back to turn the knob which opened my auxiliary fuel line but it was already opened. "What!!!!" I pulled to the side of the interstate with vehicles buzzing by and Tim pulled in behind me. I got off the bike and checked the auxiliary gas tank and it was empty. When I filled up in Marco Island, I thought I had the auxiliary tank shut off and didn't bother filling it. That great gas mileage I thought I was getting was because I had actually used an additional 2 gallons of gas, meaning I only got 39 mpg instead of the 58 mpg as I originally thought.

Tim had extra gas cans but had yet to fill them, so I used my siphon hose to transfer some gas from Tim's tank. Thinking Tim was getting about the same mileage as I was getting, we only siphoned a small amount for fear he might run out of gas too, and started immediately looking for gas. We found a station within a few miles but it had taken us nearly an hour to go the 10 miles from the Sunshine Skyway Bridge to the gas station. We were now about 45 minutes behind our schedule. We hoped this was the only stupid mistake of the trip, but of course that would not be the case.

We had not checked the toll receipt at the tollbooth when we crossed the mandatory stop at Sunshine Skyway Bridge. We looked at the receipt when we stopped at St. Petersburg. Oops! We had gotten a receipt. It had a time and date stamp. However, it only said, "Florida's Turnpike Toll Receipt." There was no indication that the receipt was for the bridge. This creates a problem in terms of documentation. The validators could likely do some mileage and time calculations from the receipts obtained immediately before and after the bridge, but this would place additional burden on them. We decided that we would require riders to get a gas receipt immediately after the bridge if their toll receipt did not indicate the name of the bridge. In our case, this was St. Petersburg.

A Welcome Roadside Meet-up. Our next mandatory stop was Apalachicola Bay. Rather than heading up I-75 out of St. Petersburg, like the typical Iron Butt ride, we headed to the coastline requiring use of secondary roads. We wanted to keep to the spirit of holding to the perimeter and stopping at bays.

We took the Sunshine Parkway toward the western coast of Florida to US 19. This is a beautiful part of Florida that many people never see. I had been through this area before but this was the first time for Tim. Most people, when they think of Florida, think of the beaches. But, surprisingly, this is cattle country. In fact Florida's cattle industry is one of the fifteen largest in the country. We passed many beautiful, grassy ranches, and several horse farms as well.

Just south of Fanning Springs, I noticed a rider alongside the road. I waved and then recognized by the way the rider waved back it was someone watching for "Us." We pulled to the side of the road and it was Ray King. Ray had been following us via our satellite trackers on Spotwalla, and talking on the phone with another friend, Richard Buber, to figure out our position.

Ray had waited alongside the road for over half an hour just to show his support. After a few minutes of chatting, we went down the road to Fanning Springs to get gas at the "Tackle Box" on U.S. 19 and chat a bit more. Ray understood Tim and I were on a mission and that we needed to go on, so we soon parted ways.

It is hard to explain to the average person why friends would go to such extremes just to share a few minutes with another rider who is doing a big ride. It is also hard to explain how much it means to the rider that is doing the ride. We had spent no more than 10 minutes with Ray and we were so excited that he made the effort and couldn't believe he had waited alongside the road

Chapter 8

for a half an hour. Ray was going to get some lunch and head back home, likely feeling the same elation.

North Becomes West. We had another 165 miles to Apalachicola. We took U.S. 19 northwest, intersecting with U.S. 98 near Perry. We then took U.S. 98 west and headed south around Crawfordville over Ochlockonee Bay (not a mandatory stop) and then along the coast of the Gulf of Mexico on our way to Apalachicola.

By taking secondary roads, we had been much closer to the coast than if we had taken the "closest interstate." However, for the most part we had not been close enough to see the water. This section changed that. Tim would recall that he had never been to this part of Florida and how much he enjoyed the coastal views.

Apalachicola is where you can find some of the best oysters in the world. I don't think they were in season, but we didn't have time to stop and check. This is a quaint port that has been updated with a variety of bed and breakfasts and unique shops. We got gas a little past 5 p.m. and still had good light, which allowed us to get a beautiful view of the bay from Lafayette Park. We lost another 15 minutes on this section, but also had eaten and spent about that much time with our friend Ray. We were now about an hour behind schedule.

We continued to our next mandatory stop: Mobile Bay, Alabama. Our planned route had us heading north to I-10 at Panama City. We could have taken this route or one of the many other possible routes to I-10, but that was not consistent with the theme of our ride, which was to "circumnavigate" and stay as close to the water as practical. We elected to continue along Highway 98 to Mexico Beach, Florida (not to be confused with Mexico the country) where there are beautiful beaches. I had only been this way once before and it was as beautiful as I remembered. Tim had never been along this part of the coast and was enjoying the view as well.

Southern Bay by Bay

The downside to our selected route is that we had to go through Panama City. Most people know Panama City from the Spring Break Gone Wild shows on television. There were no spring breakers, but the traffic was terrible with poorly timed stop lights. It seemed like it took forever to get through town.

Having suffered through Panama City, we headed north on U.S. 331 over Choctawatchee Bay (not a mandatory stop) toward I-10. This extension along the coast added about 20 miles to the day from what was originally planned. In hindsight, from looking at the map, we should have continued along U.S. 98 to Gulf Breeze in order to truly satisfy the spirit of the ride.

We could have included Ochlockonee and Choctawatchee Bays as mandatory stops since we went through them. However, when developing a ride such as this, you are trying to balance forcing an exact route against the frustration of the rider who must document the additional waypoints and the workload placed on the validators who must check the documentation.

We didn't have enough gas to reach Mobile, so we did a quick on and off at U.S. 29 in Pensacola to fill up. We only had 62 miles to Mobile where we would stop for the night. On a ride with Kevin Lechner a few years before, Kevin had recommended that, rather than hassling to split receipts, we simply take turns leading the ride and whoever was leading would select and pay for the hotel. Tim and I decided we would use this method to pay for hotels. Since I was leading, I stopped at an Econolodge on Tillmans Corner Parkway, getting off with a $57.00 tab.

One of the most common questions that we were asked was, "Do you camp?" It seemed like an obvious question given the number of bags we were carrying; however, our idea of camping is staying at Motel 6. *We stayed in a lot of Motel 6's, so I guess, by our definition; we did a lot of camping.*

Chapter 8

MapSource estimates the final route for this day to be 16 hours, 3 minutes of riding time and 914 miles (57 mph average). It took us about 18 hours, 30 minutes, including stops, which worked out to about 48 mph average with stops. It definitely was a long day.

When I'm doing a ride and then stop for the night, I don't turn the television on in the room. I simply shower and hit the bed or, if I'm really tired, just hit the bed. I'm usually the only one that has to smell me during the day. Tim likes to read and spend a little time winding down. My attitude when I'm on an Iron Butt Ride is that I should only be riding, eating, or sleeping. Tim would slow me down a bit on this ride, which was a good thing.

A Complicating Issue. Despite the beautiful scenery and the excitement of finally making some miles on our epic ride, much of the day's riding was pure misery for me. I was having trouble with my eyes; they were matting shut and were highly sensitive to light. I was constantly blinking and rubbing my eyes. Tim was following me and commented that I was swerving all over the place. Admittedly, there were several times when I crossed the centerline or nearly rode off the edge of the road. Almost every mile was a struggle and I'm sure Tim was wondering what he had gotten himself into by inviting me along.

I had an issue a few months earlier returning from Florida, when I literally went blind. Thankfully, that didn't happen this time! But, when I would wipe my eyes, it seemed to throw off my orientation. Wearing my sunglasses seemed to help. The next day my eyes were not as bad but I still had some problems.

At the end of our trip, on our return drive home, I again had the same symptoms. It got to the point that almost any light would nearly make me blind. I then knew the problem was not the sun or the wind, as we were in Tim's truck with tinted windows and protected from the wind. I noticed that I was

Southern Bay by Bay

also having trouble breathing which meant that something was triggering my allergies. I then remembered that Tom and Trudi had cats. I hadn't been around cats for years but it is obvious in hindsight that I had a severe allergic reaction by being exposed to the cats at both the beginning and end of the ride and that was what was causing issues. Regardless of the cause, I set a bad example. I had no business riding under those conditions.

Day 3
Mobile, Alabama to Kingsville, Texas
728 Miles

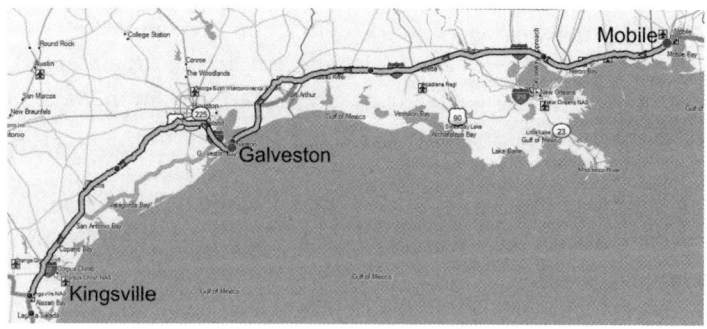

We set the alarm for 6:00 a.m. We planned Day 3 as a 942 mile day, burning-and-churning interstates from Mobile to Galveston Bay to Brownsville, Texas and then back to Kingsville, Texas to spend the night. MapSource indicated 15 hours, 19 minutes riding time. Both Tim and I have done many Coast-to-Coast rides along I-10 so this day was not going to provide anything that we were interested in seeing. We were fortunate the weather was cooperative. We didn't have any rain and had moderate temperatures.

We had quick on-and-off stops at Mandeville and Jennings, Louisiana. Jennings was 282 miles from Mobile. MapSource had predicted a 4 hour, 19 minute riding time. Our gas receipt for Jennings was at 10:21 so we were right on track with our plan, averaging 65 mph. Keep in mind that the KLR 650 has a top-end speed of about 85 mph, so 65 mph is very good.

Chapter 8

The Wayward Bags. When I hit the entrance to the bridge at Lake Charles. Louisiana, I heard and felt a "Thump!" The bike was not difficult to control so it didn't seem like a tire issue. I slowed down, trying to figure out what had happened. Anybody that has been on this bridge in the middle of the day will tell you this is not a place you want to slow down. Traffic was close on my tail. As I was looking in my mirror, I noticed a truck beside me, its driver pointing to the rear of my bike. I could still hear and feel that something was wrong on the rear; but what was it? I finally realized that the Sealine bag I had strapped to my right sidecase had come loose. I needed to get to the emergency lane but there wasn't one on the bridge and after the bridge it was on the right side and I was in the left lane. I knew that with a bag dangling and hitting my tire, I did not want to react too quickly but the drivers around me were getting impatient.

The guy who had pointed to my bag had slowed as well and, when he saw my turn signal, motioned for me to move to the right lane in front of him. He actually moved to the center of both lanes and blocked traffic for me while I changed lanes. Then he moved back to the right lane and blocked traffic for me until I got over to the emergency lane. I wish I could have told him personally how appreciative I was, but a wave of thanks had to do.

I had strapped down the Sealine bag with ratchet tie down straps. I had them tight but, as things shifted inside the bag, the strap had loosened. Fortunately, I had run the strap through the handle of the bag. It just dangled instead of bouncing down the road, in which case, I might not have discovered it was missing until I was long gone.

While the bag was dangling, it had dragged on the pavement, taking a toll on the bag and one of only two pair of pants I had packed. Fortunately, I had brought a spare bag and moved everything over to it and then re-strapped it to the sidecase, being more cautious this time.

Southern Bay by Bay

The Bolivar Ferry and Another Friend. In 2005, during a ride called the RAT (Ride-Around-Texas) ride, I had learned about the ferry from Port Bolivar to Galveston, Texas. Galveston was a mandatory stop on our **35 Bay by Bay Adventure** so it seemed that it would be better to use the ferry than to go in and out of Galveston from Houston. The ferry fit the water and coastline theme for this ride.

We got to the ferry at Port Bolivar and noticed a sign that prohibited portable fuel canisters. Tim was carrying two canisters and had filled them after I ran out of gas in Tampa. Tim asked the attendant if his cans were a problem and of course the answer was yes. We got out of line and discussed our options. I had the Sealine bag that I had dragged across the Lake Charles Bridge, so I suggested that we empty the cans and put them in the bag. Tim got off his bike and removed one of the cans and started toward the ditch. He was obviously frustrated that he had to waste gas.

I said, "What are you doing? Just empty the gas in your tank and make note of it when we get gas in Galveston so your documentation will be clear."

Tim put the gas in his tank and the cans in the bag. We got back in line. The attendant likely saw what we were doing since we were only a short distance away, but he did not say anything to us as we went through.

Barb Smith, a Houstonian and fellow member of the Motorcycle Tourer's Forum (she is actually Vice-President of the MTF), had planned to meet us in Kingsville, Texas when we stopped for the night. She had instead sent an email early in the day, saying she would meet us on the Port Bolivar side of the ferry. While we promised folks we would check my smart phone periodically for email, we didn't.

I was pleasantly surprised after boarding to see Barb and her friend. Not having heard from us and knowing that there is a

Chapter 8

delay before the satellite tracker posts appear at the website, she was concerned that she would be crossing on the ferry in one direction while Tim and I crossed in the other direction and we'd never see each other. Fortunately things worked out and we were able to share the moment.

Again, it is hard to explain the relationship among the members of the MTF. We may only see each other once or twice a year. However, we have a special bond. It was very special that Barb would make an effort to catch us on the road. Barb said, "You two look remarkably good for a couple of guys who have been riding hard these last 2 days."

After getting off the ferry in Galveston, we got our required gas receipt at the Shell station close by. We were 452 miles into our planned 942 mile day. It was 2:35 in the afternoon and we still had about 490 miles to ride. We headed north out of Galveston to take the Sam Houston Tollway to U.S. 59.

A Relationship Chat. We stopped for gas in Ganado, Texas shortly after 5 p.m. Ganado is just over 240 miles from Kingsville. Our plan was to ride through Kingsville to Brownsville and then return to Kingsville for the night, leaving about 370 miles before stopping for the day.

While I was pumping gas, Tim came over to me and said, "I don't understand why we are going to Brownsville, Texas." He was obviously frustrated, and not everything Tim was saying made sense to me. This frustrated me as well, and the moment was very tense between us.

I had been dealing with depression and working on thinking through issues rather than reacting to them as I had done in personal relationships most of my life. I told Tim we would talk after I went to the restroom. I called Brenda to vent my frustration and she calmed me down. When I returned, I told Tim, "Let's go inside and talk."

Southern Bay by Bay

I moved my bike away from the gas pump, pulled the computer from my sidecase, and went in to sit at a table in the restaurant. Tim came in and I pulled up the information about our ride.

"What is your concern?" I asked.

"I don't understand why we have to go to Brownsville, Texas," Tim replied and then began strongly expressing his concern about the dangers along the U.S./Mexican border. Then he said, "And I don't know why we are riding these long days. We still have nearly 400 miles before we stop for the night and it is after 5 p.m."

I dealt with the second question first. You might recall from an earlier chapter that I had trouble getting details about this ride and finally decided to develop the ride in accordance with what I believed was the "Spirit" of the ride expressed by Tim and Jack Gustafson who conceived the 18 Bay Ride. I am anal about planning and felt that I had to have a plan. But respecting that this was Tim's ride, I sent the details to Tim as the ride developed to make sure they met his approval.

I inquired repeatedly about the first three days of the ride, knowing they were very aggressive. Tim had agreed to aggressive days on multiple occasions, and even now acknowledged the email exchanges, but it didn't relieve his obvious frustration.

I tried to explain to him that Mike Kneebone (IBA President) had added not just Inuvik, but also Brownsville, Texas to the Gold version of his 2009 ride.

I felt as if Tim was accusing me of arbitrarily adding stuff to "his" ride. I had tried to retain my frustration, but probably didn't, as I explained how it appeared that Mike added Brownville, the southern-most point along the U.S. Mexico border, in order to force riders to take the route running along

Chapter 8

the border instead of simply burning across Texas far from the border on I-10.

It seemed that Tim's real concern was all of the "hype" he had heard about the border towns and the fact that we were going to get to Brownsville after dark. I have been in this area many times and had no concerns about entering Brownsville, but had planned to ride back to Kingsville to avoid spending the night right on the border.

Finally, I said to Tim, "Maybe I misunderstood what ride you wanted to do. You originally asked me if I wanted to ride with you on your 2009 ride but with Inuvik added, and I had said no. Then you mentioned Jack's 18 Bay Ride and I reconsidered. It is obvious you didn't understand that Mike added Brownsville as well as Inuvik for the Gold version of your 2009 ride. Since Mike added Brownsville, I added the other extreme points of the U.S. and Canada to be consistent. I also added some 'Bays' in order to force the ride off the Interstate and close to the coast."

"What ride do you want to do? All this is water under the bridge. We are sitting here on the third day. You tell me what ride you want to do and I'll decide if I want to do it." Tim replied that he wanted to do the ride as planned, but didn't think he could physically do these long days.

I had calculated the start of the ride so that we could ride to Prudhoe Bay with Jack Gustafson. However, I had built in some short days where we might be able to make up some time and we had a day with zero miles for maintenance that might allow some makeup miles. I proposed to Tim that we stop for the night in Kingsville and then ride to Brownsville and back the next day. This would leave us about 230 miles (about 4 hours) to make up, which should not be a problem. We stopped for the night in Kingsville around 9:00 p.m. We had ridden 728 miles (about 590 on Interstate) in about 15 hours, averaging about 48 mph, including a ferry ride and relationship chats.

The most important thing is that we both agreed to continue with the planned route, despite our differences. I needed to do some mellowing and the next few days were pretty quiet.

I mentioned early on that even though Tim and I had known each other for several years, we had never ridden together. We had both been busy and couldn't seem to find the time to meet one-on-one; it is obvious that email communication did not work. If you are going to plan a ride with a partner, you need to make sure you are on the same page *before* you start the trip.

Note: Tim and I talked about this event a couple of weeks later and his recollection of the tone of the conversation is different than mine. The essence of the story is that we had different riding philosophies regarding this trip and didn't discover it until the third day of the trip. Neither philosophy is right or wrong. Tim's philosophy of minimal planning worked fine for him on his 2009 ride and my philosophy of anal planning has worked for me during my long-distance riding career. More importantly regardless of our differences, we continued and completed the ride together.

Day 4
Kingsville to Fort Stockton, Texas
673 Miles

We had stopped about 9:00 p.m. the night before and actually had eaten dinner. We did not get gas when we stopped the night before, so our first stop this morning was only about 15 miles down the road from Kingsville in Riviera. Our receipt for Riviera was 7:43 a.m., so we had gotten a good night's rest.

When a city is stipulated as a location that must be documented, there is typically no specific requirement for the documentation except that a receipt must have the name of the

Chapter 8

city, state, date, and time. A suburb with a different name on the receipt is not acceptable.

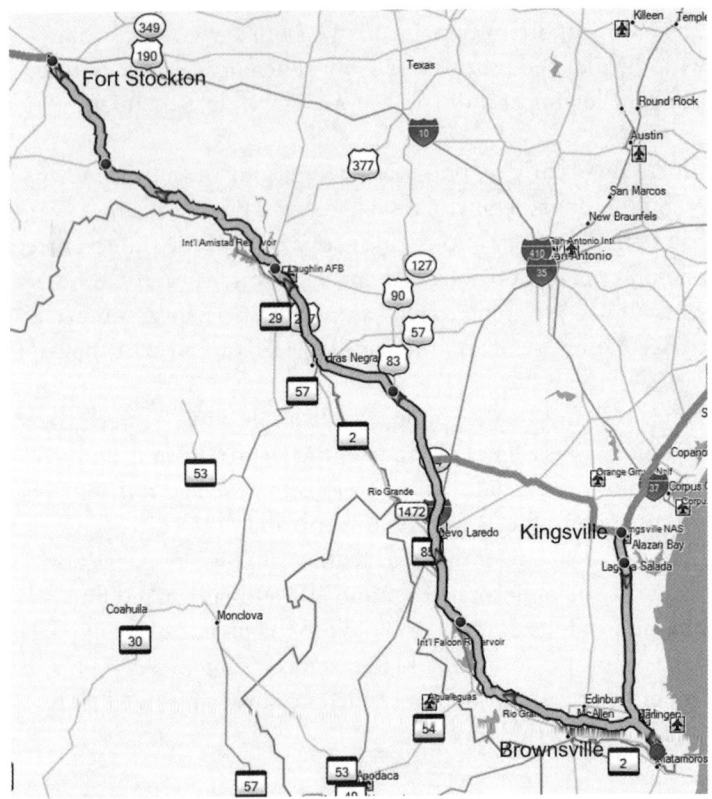

Brownsville has a population of 175,000. This is a "perimeter" ride, but this did not mean that we had to stop at the closest location to the U.S./Mexico border. We just needed to go in deep enough to get a receipt that said "Brownsville." We stopped at the first station that we thought was in the city of Brownsville. The receipt met the criteria, even though we were about seven miles from the border.

Riding Styles. Typically, when riders are riding with a partner or in a group, they ride in what is called a "2 second stagger" – one rider rides on one side of the lane and the next rider rides on the opposite side of the lane, 2 seconds behind. When

Southern Bay by Bay

stopping at a traffic light, it is common to close the formation and have two bikes side by side. Because I rear-ended a friend, I am very cautious about maintaining safety escape routes, although I still don't always practice it 100%. Tim was very good about maintaining space except that when coming to a stop, he would often come side by side before I would come to a complete stop. Tim would also often take off at the same time as I did instead of allowing me to take the lead and then following me.

Our original plan was that I would lead one day and Tim would lead the next. But after our fuss the day before, I was concerned about how Tim would react to a discussion regarding these sensitivities on my part, so it became easier to simply allow Tim to lead, which he did for most of the balance of the trip.

Skirting the Texas Border. Starting at Brownsville, we would spend most of Day 4 traveling along the U.S./Mexico border. We could have gone north away from the border to I-10, since the next required location is San Diego Bay (Coronado Island), California. Either choice is acceptable; however, we chose to stay within the theme of the ride by staying close to the perimeter.

Our original plan called for a 1,062 mile day starting in Kingsville, going to Brownsville, and back to Kingsville to Zapata before ending in Casa Grande (Phoenix area), Arizona. By stopping in Kingsville the previous night, we saved some backtracking and could go directly from Brownsville to Zapata meaning we were really only the equivalent of 169 miles short yesterday, about three hours.

From Brownsville we traveled the border through Zapata and Carrizo Springs to Del Rio. I have been through Del Rio before, but forgot about the scenic views of International Amistad Reservoir. This reservoir is just north of Del Rio on U.S. 90 on the way to Sanderson.

Chapter 8

Patty, Tim's wife, is always kidding him that when she watches Spotwalla (the web page for the satellite tracker), she looks to see if there are any buzzards overhead. Somewhere between Del Rio and Sanderson two turkey buzzards were feasting on road kill. As Tim approached, one decided it needed one more bite. Wrong decision! The buzzard lifted; Tim ducked, but it was too late. Tim clipped the buzzard with the top of his windshield. I'm not sure how, but it continued to fly. When we got to Sanderson we discovered that the buzzard had puked on Tim's windshield and helmet.

Enough Heat Already. We arrived in Fort Stockton at about 9:00 p.m. and Tim was ready to stop. We had ridden about 673 miles and were still about 618 miles from our planned stop. Unlike the three hours we lost yesterday, this was a substantial loss. We were now about 10 hours behind schedule.

We had only ridden about thirteen and a half hours. You might shake your head at it only being thirteen hours. However, as experienced long-distance riders, we typically ride 16 or more hours per day and when we are behind schedule will push until we feel we can no longer proceed safely. We had once again averaged about 50 mph with stops, which was not bad since these were all secondary roads.

I was still pouting about yesterday's events and didn't say anything to Tim. But I knew that by stopping this soon we could seriously jeopardize our opportunity to ride with Jack Gustafson to Prudhoe Bay.

Previous day's temperatures had been moderate. However, this day was different. Most of the day was 103 degrees, meaning that we were drinking a lot of water just to stay hydrated. The 103 degrees made the thirteen and a half hours seem like much longer. While my mind was frustrated about stopping early, my body was in tune with Tim's and I was relieved that we were stopping.

Southern Bay by Bay

Day 5
Fort Stockton, Texas to Yuma, Arizona
799 Miles

We had planned Day 5 to be a lighter day of only 683 miles, ending in Morro Bay, California. The idea was to give us some recovery time and to allow enough time to take in the lower Pacific Coast Highway at a casual pace.

After the heat of yesterday, it had cooled overnight, so there was a good chance we could make up some of our lost miles. We had a 10 hour break, having stopped at about 9:00 p.m. and hitting the road about 7:00 a.m., giving us a good rest. Our first receipt for the day was at 7:53 a.m. in Balmorhea, Texas, about 50 miles from Fort Stockton.

Crossing the Southwest Desert and Bike Issues. Starting from Fort Stockton and heading toward San Diego Bay, the next mandatory stop meant that there would be a lot of burning and churning today. Both Tim and I were very familiar with this part of the ride, as I-10 to I-8 is the route for the IBA's 50CC (Coast to Coast in 50 hours) ride from Jacksonville, Florida to San Diego, California. We were used to cranking out miles on this section and thought we could make up some of the 618 miles we were behind schedule.

We had gas stops at Fort Hancock, Texas; Deming and Lordsburg, New Mexico; and Benson, Arizona covering 467 miles. Western interstate speeds are 75, so we were riding at

Chapter 8

higher speeds which really affected our gas mileage causing us to stop for fuel about every 120 miles.

While Tim was having no problem maintaining the speed limit, my bike started to run poorly and I was having trouble maintaining speed against the head winds. I continued to have problems with my bike off and on, eventually leading to a carburetor removal and cleanout in Inuvik.

After returning home and calculating gas mileage, I learned that I was only getting about 30 mpg, while Tim was getting 50 mpg. This mileage was pretty consistent both before and after the carburetor clean out. Why is unknown:

- It could be the 22 cent mod (whatever that is) to the carburetor by the previous owner.
- It could be related to the way I had my auxiliary gas tank connected.
- It could be that some jetting should have been done to the carburetor after the top end of the engine was bored out.
- It could simply be a bad carburetor.

Whatever the reason, it cost me a lot for gas and caused a lot of inconvenience for both Tim and me.

Tim was losing me in his rear view mirrors because of my carburetor problem. When you are leading, it is very difficult to keep an eye on the rider in the rear. When I'm in the rear, I tend to ride my own ride and may lag back such a distance that this task for the lead rider is more difficult.

Eric Trow writes a section in Rider magazine titled, "Riding Well." In the July 2011 issue: "When riders stop thinking for themselves when riding in a group they are placing too much trust in their fellow riders." It is very easy when you are in a group, even if it is a group of two, to get in the mode

Southern Bay by Bay

of simply following the lead rider and not properly scanning the environment. This situation likely contributed to my crash in San Antonio a few years earlier, where I found myself daydreaming and crashing into the rear of my friend. By lagging back, I can ride my own ride.

At one point, Tim was so far ahead of me that I was out of sight. My bike was running so poorly that there was no way I was ever going to catch him. Still muddling in the conflict from the second day, all I could think about was, "Tim didn't want to push and now he is pushing so hard I can't keep up." In reality, Tim was riding like I would prefer to be doing, if my bike had been running properly, and he simply had not thought to look back for awhile. I just had a warped perspective at present.

I was at the 120 mile interval we were using for gas stops. In a bad frame of mind, I pulled over to get gas. Not worrying about the separation from Tim, I got gas and proceeded down the interstate at my own pace.

Tim had gone to the next exit and when I wasn't there, got gas and turned around, going the opposite direction on the interstate. He saw me on the other side. I'm not sure if he cut across the median or an emergency crossing, but he soon caught up with me. He then led me to the stop where he had gotten gas. I had already gotten gas but he didn't know that.

I'm sure Tim was frustrated with me for not keeping up and for stopping early, and I was frustrated with him for going off and leaving me, although in reality my thoughts were senseless. We had another quiet moment.

When trying to walk my bike backwards, I stepped in a hole and dropped my bike which did not improve my attitude.

Some Diversions En-route to Yuma. On the approach to Benson, Arizona, there are unique rock formations called Texas

Chapter 8

Canyon. They look like a giant manmade gravel pile made of giant boulders.

Our next stop was Gila Bend, Arizona. The stop is a typical Arizona tourist trap, but has some unique gifts. I have stopped here many times and always enjoy looking at the gifts and taking a few minutes to relax. At this point we had ridden 685 miles for the day and it was not yet 5:00 p.m. Tim and I talked about whether or not to go all the way to Coronado Island to avoid the early morning traffic in San Diego. We decided to go to the next stop and decide.

We arrived in Yuma, Arizona, just after 7:00 p.m., having put in 799 miles for the day. Tim said he was ready to stop. Although I wanted to push on and reduce the mileage deficit we had incurred with respect to our plan, I was trying to mellow out and so kept my thoughts to myself.

We had made up about 100 miles of the deficit but were still 518 miles behind our plan.

Day 6
Yuma, Arizona to Coronado Island, California
176 Miles to Complete Southern Day by Bay

San Diego Bay (Coronado Island) is only 176 miles from Yuma, Arizona. We were on the road at about 6:45 a.m. Since we did not have enough range to make it without a gas stop, we decided to stop in El Centro, arriving about an hour later.

Southern Bay by Bay

I love the ride from Gila Bend to San Diego! Maybe the love is because San Diego seems to be the oasis after a long boring ride along I-10 and I-8 when doing the 50CC (Jacksonville to San Diego) ride. However, this section has some unique aspects. Not long after leaving Yuma are the Glamis Dunes, large sand dunes that are highly unusual and beautiful for a Midwesterner like me. The mountain range east of San Diego provides twisty roads with significant grade changes and winds that are typically very strong and seem to come at you from all sides.

Tim was not comfortable with the older maps in his GPS so I was leading us through San Diego to Coronado. I did not have my GPS wired to my earplugs so I had no audio directions. Fortunately, traffic was light, but trying to watch traffic, the road signs, and the GPS was challenging and I missed the turn-off to the Coronado Bridge. I had gone about an eighth of a mile on the wrong side of the split. Tim stopped at the dividing point and watched as I walked the bike backwards up a slight uphill grade back to the turn-off. We arrived in Coronado just before 10:00 a.m.

Southern Bay by Bay Tour Completed

We started the **Southern Bay by Bay** leg of the ride in Key West, Florida – May 15, 2011 at 10:23 EDT and completed it when we arrived at Coronado, California – May 20, 2011 at 09:49 PDT (12:49 EDT). It had taken us 5 days, 2 hours, 26 minutes to complete the 3,345 mile leg, which is a 655 mile per day pace. Of the 3,345 miles on this leg just over half (1,724 miles) were interstate miles.

Using the proposed criteria of a 300 mile per day pace for the modifier "Tour" and 500 mile per day pace for the modifier "Power Tour," the **Southern Bay by Bay Tour** would have a completion time of 11 days, 3 hours, 36 minutes. If offered as a certified ride, a completion time of **11 days** is recommended.

Chapter 8

The **Southern Bay by Bay Power Tour** would have a completion time requirement of 6 days 16 hours, 33 minutes. A completion time of **6 days** is recommended.

Our completion time was well under the proposed requirement for the **Southern Bay by Bay Power Tour.**

9

Passion in the Wind
Western Bay by Bay

*The **Western Bay by Bay** ride starts by crossing the Coronado Bridge with its great view overlooking San Diego Bay and then traveling through the concrete jungles of Southern California to the historic Golden Gate Bridge. We would experience ocean side lunches and beautiful ocean vistas, including a beach full of elephant seals. The twisty roads led us up and down the mountains from the coast inland and back. We found ourselves riding among giant sequoias and only yards from elk resting in a preserve. Our final location was a place of serenity in Neah Bay, followed by fresh chowder.*

The **Western Bay by Bay** starts in Coronado Island, California and ends in Neah Bay, Washington and has the following mandatory stops:

- San Diego Bay (Receipt from Coronado, California)
- Morro Bay (Receipt from Morro Bay, California)
- San Francisco Bay (Receipt from Sausalito, California)
- Bodega Bay (Receipt from Bodega Bay, California)
- Coos Bay (Receipt from Coos Bay, Oregon)
- Neah Bay (Receipt from Neah Bay, Washington)

Chapter 9

MapSource shows this route as 1,602 miles requiring 1 Day, 3 hours, 30 minutes of riding time using only the mandatory stops as routing criteria.

There are many bays along the California coast including the popular Monterey Bay. The bays selected as mandatory points for this ride are sufficient to encourage a rider on the **Western Bay by Bay** ride to take a route which will include most of these bays. As with all legs of this trip, choosing mandatory stops was a matter of balancing the need to force an exact route versus the frustration of a rider documenting stops and the workload on the validators who verify the route for certification.

Day 6 Continued
Coronado to San Simeon, California
359 Miles

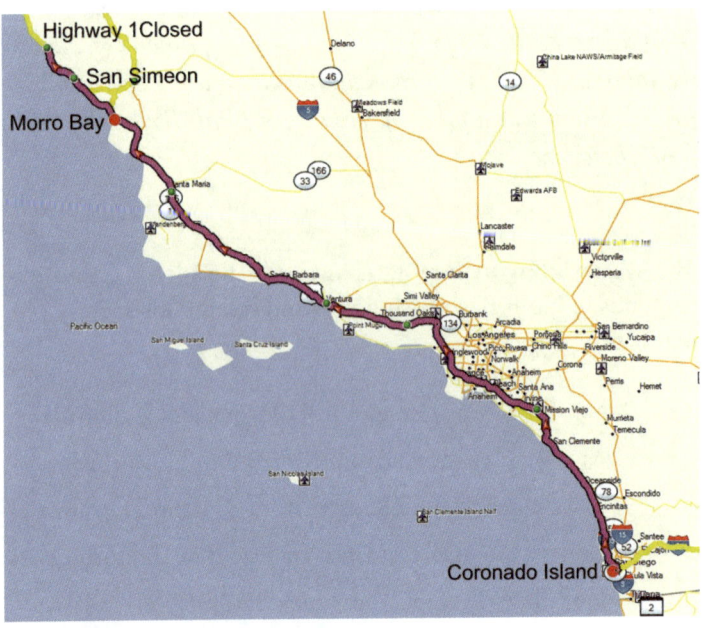

We started Day 6 in Yuma, Arizona at about 6:45 a.m. and took about three hours to ride the 176 miles to Coronado, California, finishing the **Southern Bay by Bay** ride. We now headed north from Coronado 333 miles to Morro Bay, the next mandatory stop.

Going "Californian." Unfortunately, there is no way to get from San Diego to Morro Bay without fighting the traffic through Los Angeles. Thank goodness the temperatures were in the low 70s and traffic did not come to a complete standstill too often. A few bikes were splitting lanes (driving down the dividing line between vehicles, which is legal in California). At one point, when we were stopped in traffic, I jokingly asked Tim if he thought we should split lanes. He wasn't interested! I had tried this once on a Goldwing. I made it about five miles before I lost my nerve and decided that dealing with traffic would be less stressful. Our KLRs were just as wide as the Goldwing and this would not have been an easy task.

We took I-5 from San Diego to I-405 through Los Angeles, picking up US-101 north of the city. We stopped for gas at Calabasas a little after 1:00 p.m. US-101 hits the coast at Ventura, where we decided to reward ourselves for enduring the Los Angeles traffic by having lunch overlooking the Pacific Coast.

We parked on the ground level of a parking structure next to the restaurant we selected. We walked only a few feet through the rails and noticed what appeared to be several homeless people. Fearing that we might not have any of our luggage and electronics when we returned, we decided to look for another restaurant. We found a little restaurant with outside seating called Beach House Tacos not far away in San Buenaventura State Park. We were able to park where we could watch the bikes. The view of the Pacific Ocean beaches with surfers was surreal, given the hard days of riding we had been doing.

We didn't know if we could make the 173 miles to Morro Bay, so we stopped for gas with a quick on and off at Stovell Road in Santa Maria about 4:30 p.m. and arrived in Morro Bay at about 5:40 p.m. We took the time to ride over to the coast and take pictures of the bay. At the entrance to the harbor is a large

Chapter 9

rock standing over 500 feet. Add some fishing boats and it was quite a scenic view.

Our plans called for us to spend the night in Carmel-by-the-Sea, home to Clint Eastwood and Tim's friend Craig Vetter. Craig is well-known in motorcycling circles as the inventor of the Windjammer fairing and other motorcycle accessories. His inventions in the 1960s and 70s helped to popularize motorcycle touring and influenced a generation of motorcyclists and designers. Craig grew up in the same area as Tim and they are good friends.

Pacific Highway Elephant Seals
Photo by Charles Lee / www.beautifulvista.com

Yes, PCH Really Is Closed. A section of the Pacific Coast Highway (PCH) about 19 miles north of San Simeon had collapsed in March and the road was closed. We had heard that the road had been repaired, and Craig assured Tim that the road was open. So when we saw a sign that read, "Road Closed 38 Miles," we pressed on. At the intersection of California 46, another sign said "Road Closed 27 miles." In each case there was nothing preventing us from going ahead, just a warning that the road was closed. We continued to see these signs every several miles but, convinced the road was open, we continued on.

You have probably guessed it by now – the road was really closed. We just had to find out for ourselves.

We did have a side benefit of ignoring the "Road Closed" signs. A few miles north of San Simeon, Tim pulled into a parking lot and said there was something here I needed to see. I looked off the cliff toward the ocean and saw what I thought was a dead animal. Tim laughed and said, "That is an elephant seal. It is alive."

We couldn't make it to Craig's place, so we backtracked 19 miles to a Motel 6 at San Simeon. At least they had a restaurant and we were able to eat dinner. What a treat! We had eaten twice this day.

Energy Bars, Jerky, and Trail Mix. You probably noticed that I have not said much about stopping to eat. This is primarily because we really didn't eat that much. If we ate breakfast, we would typically not eat lunch. If we didn't eat breakfast, we would sometimes eat lunch. If we stopped at night and there was anything open and we were not too tired to eat we might eat dinner. Both Tim and I lost about 20 pounds on this trip. Our staple was energy bars for me and jerky and trail mix for Tim.

A Day Behind Schedule. Including our road closure investigation, we rode 573 miles on Day 6. Our original schedule called for us to spend the night in Morro Bay the previous night. San Simeon is only about 26 miles north of Morro Bay, so we were now 751 miles (nearly a full day) behind our planned schedule. From here, we would have to detour south and east to pick up our route toward San Francisco. It appeared that the chances of riding to Prudhoe Bay with Jack Gustafson were dwindling.

Chapter 9

**Day 7
San Simeon to Garberville, California
476 Miles**

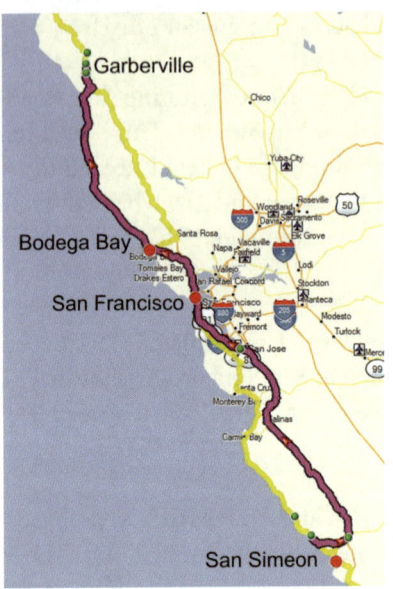

We started this day by detouring south and east on Highway 101 to Paso Robles. This added 29 miles to our route, but more importantly it meant we bypassed Big Sur. That was a highlight I had looked forward to, so a return trip to the PCH will be in my future plans.

We hit the road a little before 7:00 a.m., arriving at Paso Robles about 7:30 a.m. and made our first gas stop in Santa Clara at just after 10:00 a.m.

The Golden Gate View. Our next stop was San Francisco Bay by way of the Golden Gate Bridge. I had never been to San Francisco and was really looking forward to going over the bridge. It appeared that there was a toll at one time, but not now. The website for the bridge says that "9 million people visit the bridge each year," which works out to 24,657 people each day; 1,027 people each hour. I don't know how many people were there during our visit, but it was crowded and we had a hard time finding a parking spot at the overlook. The view of the bridge, Alcatraz, and the bay were every bit as beautiful as I had imagined.

Our expectation was that there would be a visitor's center at the bridge and we would be able to get a receipt to serve as documentation. Unfortunately, the state missed a terrific opportunity. There was a visitor's center, but no shop, meaning no receipt for us. We decided to go north a few miles to Sausalito to get a receipt. It was lunch time, so we had lunch at the Bayside Café. For the **Western Bay by Bay** leg we thought of allowing a receipt from either San Francisco or Sausalito. However, allowing a receipt from San Francisco would make it possible for a rider to get a receipt and not ever go across the bridge. We decided that we would instead make Sausalito the mandatory stop for San Francisco Bay.

A Delightful Discovery. From San Francisco, we wanted to keep to the coast and continue along the Pacific Coast Highway, which we picked up in Bodega Bay, arriving at just before 2:00 p.m. Bodega Bay was not originally on our list of mandatory stops; however, after the beautiful ride getting there, we decided that it would be added!

We did not know it at the time, but this would be the start of one of the most picturesque days of our entire ride. We had to bypass Big Sur and the PCH south of San Francisco, but it is hard to imagine it could be any more beautiful than this section of the highway. As a contributor named "corey G." posted on one of the travel websites, "It is a marvel of engineering. This beautiful road is cleanly carved into the craggy coastal bluffs. It offers all-viewing vistas, zips along the water, and curvy roller coaster rides." It was simply amazing!

The Sonoma Beach Coast State Park website provides an even more graphic description:

Chapter 9

Sonoma Coast State Park is made up of sections that are found along 17 miles of coastline that extends from Bodega Point to Jenner. You can take a lot in by just driving the coast and visiting some of the dozen highway pull offs. Almost every parking area provides easy access to views that include parts of the same set of elements: the Pacific Ocean, prominent rocky sea stacks, the shore, crags, and headlands. The variation that each of the elements can display, the way they can be combined in different ways, and even the light at different times of the day gives you a different sense of Sonoma Coast State Park at each stop.

Pacific Coast Highway
Photo by Tim Yow

We stopped at the first pull off after leaving Bodega Bay. Tim and I had a special moment at this stop. It was just breath taking. For me it was the realization of what drew me to the idea of visiting bays, which helped me to commit to this trip. It was also why, when creating the route, I wanted to make sure to include the Pacific Coast Highway. My "Iron Butt"

Western Bay by Bay

mentality was temporarily gone and Tim's annoyance with my adding mandatory locations to the route was quelled. We sat at this turn-off for several minutes absorbing the view and taking in the Pacific winds and air. This section of the PCH has now replaced the Icefields Parkway in the Canadian Rockies, which goes from Banff to Jasper, as my favorite road. I hope some day soon to return with my family.

A Necessary Decision. We stopped in Piercy, California a little after 7:00 p.m. It had taken us a little over 5 hours to travel the 165 miles from Bodega Bay. Except for the stop at the first turn off, we viewed the remaining vistas strictly from the road. However, the twists and turns and elevation changes had allowed us to only average about 30 mph. Tim and I both commented about how sore our forearms were from counter-steering through the curves.

We stopped at Garberville for the night at about 7:40 p.m. Our room was a suite with separate rooms, which wasn't anything special, but very cool for a mom and pop hotel. Stopping early meant we also had time to eat, so we walked to a nearby Chinese restaurant.

My temporary respite from the Iron Butt mentality that began at the scenic ocean view north of Bodega Bay had now ended. My preference was to push on as we had planned, ending the night at Coos Bay, Oregon. Stopping now left us 284 miles short. This meant that we were now about 1 day, 5 hours behind our original schedule.

It now looked as if there was little chance of making it to Fairbanks in time to ride the Haul Road with Jack Gustafson and his crew. I thought that by building in a safety day when I planned the trip, we would have no problem making Fairbanks in time, unless we had some kind of mechanical failure. We had no mechanical failures; it turned out the only limitation was our inability to adhere to our plan. My good feelings were

Chapter 9

now subdued, knowing I would need to email Jack and tell him we would not be able to meet him.

Day 8
Garberville, California to Kelso, Washington
556 Miles

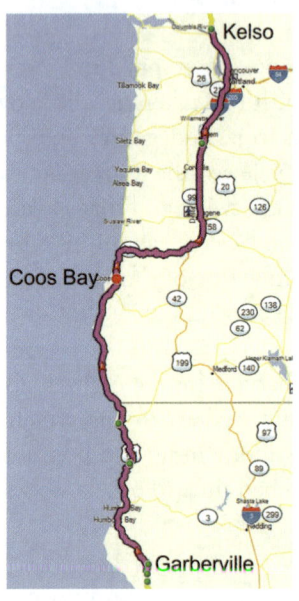

Just over a week into our trip, we had quit setting an alarm. But we were still up and on the road by 7:00 a.m. Shortly after leaving Garberville, we came to the south entrance of the Avenue of the Giants. I've seen many pictures of The Giants, which are redwood trees, but the pictures do not come close to showing the overwhelming magnitude of these trees. Looking at them from the road was one thing, but it wasn't until I got off the bike and stood next to a fallen tree that I got a true sense of its size. The tree had fallen across the road and had been cut in two. I stood at the end of the tree looking up at the other end of the circumference. It was truly "A Giant."

Western Bay by Bay

Although the Avenue of the Giants is not required for the **35 Bay by Bay Adventure**, if a rider who has not been to this area elects to bypass the Avenue of the Giants, they have cheated themselves.

An hour or so later, just outside of a small town named Orick, California, we came upon an elk preserve. The elk were obviously accustomed to vehicles and humans, since they remained in their spots as we pulled in and watched. I'm not sure if they are always in this grassy valley or not, but on this day there was a whole herd of them.

Into Oregon. We made a quick stop for gas in Crescent City, California at 9:45 a.m. and continued on toward Coos Bay, Oregon, arriving a little before 1:00 p.m. Having worked for a structural engineer in the past, I love bridges. You would think that one end of the Coos Bay bridge would be located in Coos Bay. Oddly enough, the bridge spans Coos Bay from one side of the small town of North Bend, Oregon to the other. North Bend is just north of the town of Coos Bay. Maybe this confusion is why they changed the name to Conde B. McCullough Memorial Bridge.

Conde B. McCullough Memorial Bridge

Just north of Coos Bay, we decided to take Oregon 38 inland to I-5 to see if we could make up some time, as our next required stop was the northwestern-most point of the U.S. at Neah Bay, Washington.

Chapter 9

Different Objectives. We made a gas stop in Salem, Oregon just before 5:00. Tim pulled onto the exit ramp in Kelso, Washington and asked if I was ready to stop. I wasn't, but I didn't want to create any tension so I said, "If you want to stop we will stop." Since it was early, Tim wanted something besides a sandwich for dinner, so we ate at Red Lobster.

The short days were driving me nuts. Since my roadside discussion with Tim in Ganado, Texas a few days earlier, I had been trying to strictly adhere to our schedule. But it seemed to me like Tim was only committed to the route and not the timing. I let Tim call the end to our days' travels because I didn't know if there was a physical or mental issue that prevented longer days. But my frustration was mounting as I knew that the way we were going, we would not be able to meet up with Jack in Alaska. In hindsight, I was regretting that we had not gone through the schedule day by day when we had the earlier conflict.

A Chance Encounter and a Decision. We met a group of three riders from Edmonton, Alberta who plan a multi-week ride in the U.S. every year. This year they were riding in Washington and Oregon. One of these riders was the one who commented on my bike being loud and suggested it might be the "donut washer."

We were now about 1 day, 7 hours behind our plan and I needed to go ahead and let Jack know that we were not going to make it. Jack, realizing that we were looking questionable, posted this message on the Motorcycle Tourer's Forum:

> The guy in Fairbanks who is hosting a get-together, with Alan and Tim as the guests of honor, needs to know if they expect to be there Friday night so he can go ahead with planning.
>
> Alan was expecting to make it and then go on up to Deadhorse with us. Depending on how many more

bays they intend to claim on the way north, they may be cutting it pretty close. If they change their routing, and hit Fairbanks as soon as they enter Alaska, they will have a better chance. If you can get some idea from Alan as to their expectations, maybe you could give me a heads up.

Tell those two I said to quit riding like a couple of old grandmas stopping at every antique shop and start putting some miles behind them.

I finally had to tell Jack we simply were not going to make it. It was disappointing, as I had never ridden with Jack even though we had been friends for several years, and I was looking forward to this opportunity. On the other hand, I felt that if Tim's body simply would not allow him to push any harder, then I was okay with that. That doesn't mean I still didn't wish he had taken more time to evaluate our plan and do a full assessment of what was planned and what he was capable of doing. I had let Jack know. While it might still gnaw on me a bit, at least I would no longer feel the stress of trying to make up time.

Day 9
Kelso to Neah Bay, Washington
251 Miles to Complete Western Bay by Bay

We were up at 6:00 a.m. and headed north on I-5. We had about 60 miles of interstate, exiting at Exit 88 (U.S. 12) toward the coast to pick up U.S. 101. This section of 101 provided another beautiful ride full of twisties and coast line views with many changes in elevation. The Washington coastline is much like Northern California and Oregon: rock formations just offshore, waves crashing in, dark sand.

Chapter 9

Finding the End of the Road. We eventually found ourselves riding next to Olympic National Park in search of Neah (Knee ah) Bay which is a mandatory stop. The town of Neah Bay is located on a peninsula and is the most northwestern point in the lower 48 states. It is a Makah tribe reservation, and also the ending point of the Iron Butt Association's Sunrise to Sunset ride.

We tried to find the sign that said "northwestern-most point" and rode all the way to the end of the peninsula where the road ended. We still could not find the sign, nor could we see the ocean. We spotted a border patrol officer eating lunch in her car, so I interrupted and asked about the sign that we assumed would mark the point. "There isn't any sign," she said. "But you can get to the point by walking one-half mile down that trail." We made the walk. The view and the sound of the water coming into the cove was breathtaking and quite beautiful.

Neah Bay
Photo by Tim Yow

The trail is called the Cape Flattery Trail, and is actually a steep downhill, three-quarter mile trail. The climb back seemed like four miles, requiring several rest stops for two fat old men.

We stopped for lunch at Whaler's Moon Delights, a small restaurant on the bay. I had fresh halibut chowder, coffee (my first since leaving on the trip), and a brownie. The owner was a Makah native who held two culinary degrees. She said her family had been in Neah Bay since the 1400s.

The owner told us that the Makah tribe were originally whalers, and retained the right to continue to hunt whale in their treaty. They voluntarily gave up whaling (with some pressure) in the early 1900s. They tried to reinstate what was to be an annual hunt in the traditional fashion in 1999 but were stopped by Greenpeace. She had recorded her immediate family playing traditional Makah music, and played it as we ate, providing a unique experience. We could tell she was very proud of her culture.

Chapter 9

Western Bay by Bay Tour Completed

We started the **Western Bay by Bay** leg of the ride in Coronado, California on May 20, 2011 at 09:49 PDT and completed it when we arrived at Neah Bay on May 23, 2011 at 12:14 PDT. It had taken us 3 days, 2 hours, 25 minutes to complete what for us was a 1,642 mile leg.

Our pace was down to 529 miles per day compared to 655 miles per day for the **Southern Bay by Bay** leg. The MapSource software calculates the **Western Bay by Bay** to be 1,602 miles when based on only the mandatory stops, requiring 1 day, 3 hours, 30 minutes riding time. Our actual mileage was a little higher than this, but certified rides only consider mandatory stops when calculating the shortest distance route.

Of the 1,602 miles for this leg, only 376 miles (23%) were interstate miles. The **Southern Bay by Bay** route was 51% interstate miles, which might explain some of the drop in the daily pace.

Using the proposed criterion of a 300 mile per day pace for the "Tour" option, the **Western Bay by Bay Tour** would have a completion time of 5 days, 8 hours, 9 minutes. If offered as a certified ride, a completion time of **5 days** is recommended.

With a proposed 500 mile per day pace for the "Power Tour" option, the **Western Bay by Bay Power Tour** would have a completion time requirement of 3 days, 4 hours, 53 minutes. A completion time of **3 days** is recommended.

Our completion time qualified us for the **Western Bay by Bay Tour**, but the drop in pace put us over the recommended time for the **Western Bay by Bay Power Tour**.

10 Passion in the Wind
Western Bay by Bay Plus

***There is** something about rolling two wheels into the belly of a ferry and then hiking to the deck to enjoy the fresh air and coast line views. Our second and third ferry rides of the trip led us to the road that travels through Whistler mountains and into Alaska. Arriving at Hyder felt like coming home. I couldn't help but check the pictures on the wall at the Sealaska Inn, which document all of the riders who have completed the 48 Plus ride. I know most of them, and the memories made me feel like they were there with me.*

The "Plus" in the **Western Bay by Bay Plus** ride adds four mandatory stops to the **Western Bay by Bay**:

- Departure Bay (Receipt from Nanaimo, British Columbia)
- Hyder, Alaska (Receipt from Hyder, the southernmost point of Alaska)
- Destruction Bay, Yukon (Receipt from Destruction Bay, Yukon)
- Kachemak Bay (Receipt from Homer, Alaska)

MapSource shows that these four additional mandatory stops add 2,670 miles and 2 days, 5 hours, 51 minutes of riding time to the **Western Bay by Bay** ride which on its own is 1,602 miles, requiring 1 Day, 3 hours, 30 minutes riding time.

Chapter 10

The **Western Bay by Bay Plus** can be done all on paved roads except for construction areas, and adds the challenge of crossing the border into Canada and the joy of traveling to Alaska. The total for the **Western Bay by Bay Plus** is 4,314 miles with an estimated 3 days, 13 hours, 18 minutes of riding time.

The Rest of Day 9
Neah Bay, Washington to West Vancouver (Horseshoe Bay), British Columbia
201 Miles

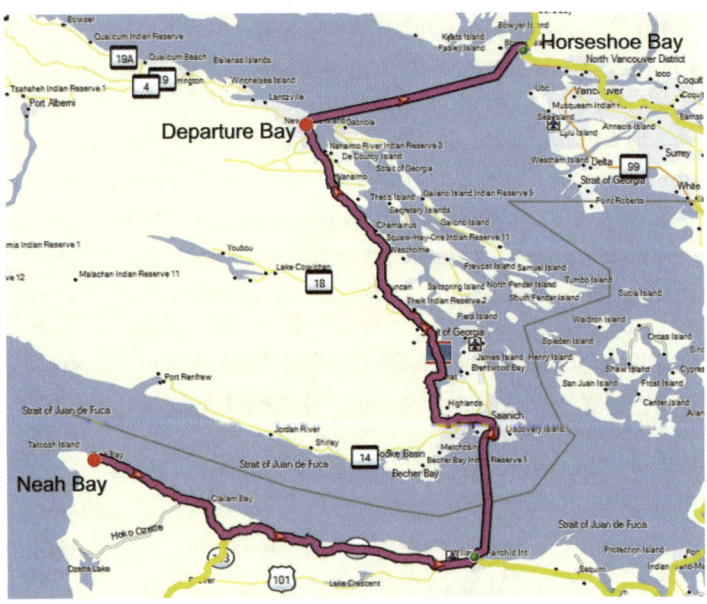

After stopping for lunch in Neah Bay, Washington, our next mandatory stop was Hyder, Alaska by way of Prince George, British Columbia. Our planned route was recommended by Tony Higgins, known as ITSecurity on the Motorcycle Tourer's Forum. Tony's route had us cross into Canada by ferry to Victoria Island and then take another ferry to Horseshoe Bay. Alternately, MapSource recommended that we go further west to the Sumas Huntington Crossing at Washington Route 9 to cross the border. These two routes were essentially the same distance, but MapSource estimated the one through Victoria Island to be 4 hours longer. Tony's experience indicated the Victoria Island crossing actually took less time.

Ferry Decision. Tim had a third option in mind and wanted to take the "truck crossing" at Washington Route 543 just west of the Peace Arch Crossing – the primary border crossing on I-5. Tim knew of this crossing from a previous ride; however, this route is about 20 miles longer than either of the other two choices and would require us to go east, then west, and then back east. I trusted Tony's experience and felt that the ferry rides were consistent with the water theme of our **35 Bay by Bay Adventure**. Tim agreed to go with Tony's advice and take the route to Victoria Island, provided we could get a spot on the ferry.

Our goal was to get to the ferry leaving Departure Bay by 9:30 p.m. The Departure Bay port was 73 miles by road from the port where we entered Victoria. This was going to be tight:

- Ferry departing Port Angles at 5:15 p.m.
- 90 minute ferry ride arriving at 6:45 p.m.
- 73 miles by road to Departure Bay, arriving at 8:30 p.m (according to our MapSource estimate).
- Ferry departing Departure Bay at 9:30 p.m.

We managed to catch the ferry from Washington to Victoria, B.C. and actually had about 45 minutes to spare, but decided not to go back and get gas before boarding the ferry.

We met several motorcyclists on the ferry who live on Victoria Island and were returning home. These motorcyclists had been touring the northwestern U.S. and it seemed they knew every pass. It was great listening to them share. We also met a couple on a R1200GS Adventure. He was asking me about this "Iron Butt stuff," seemingly more out of curiosity than any real interest. He asked why we did such things and asked the typical "Isn't it dangerous" question. It turned out that he and his wife

Chapter 10

had done a three-year sailing adventure to Fiji and back; it is curious how one determines what is dangerous.

Crossing in to Canada. We got through customs with no hassles and started pushing toward Departure Bay, knowing we had a tight schedule. While the ferry actually departed at 9:30 p.m., I thought I remembered the schedule saying 9:00 p.m.

When we were about 15 miles from Departure Bay, Tim pulled up beside me and said, "I'm about out of gas!"

"You're out of gas?" I asked.

"Yes and so are you." Tim replied.

"Have you hit reserve?" I queried.

"No." Tim said.

"You'll be okay," I said. "We only have 15 minutes leeway to catch the second ferry." This was the second time we passed up the opportunity to fill up and it ended up that we actually had 40 minutes leeway and would have had plenty of time to get gas. Since I told Tim we would be okay, I hoped Tim would not have to pay a price for my decision.

We had such a great experience on the ferry, that Tim and I discussed whether to make it a requirement for this ride. We finally decided to add Nanaimo, B.C. (Departure Bay) as a mandatory stop. We did not have any bays in B.C. so this seemed to enhance the theme of the ride.

We arrived in Horseshoe Bay at 11:23 p.m. There is only one hotel in Horseshoe Bay, but fortunately we found a flyer on the ferry and called ahead. We need not have worried, because we might have been the only ones there. It was a premium rate of $130. It was Tim's day to pay, so he got gouged this time. The draperies were not wide enough to close all of the way and the street light shone in through the window. You would think, at a premium price, they could afford properly fitting draperies.

We only traveled 452 miles total for Day 9, which was the lowest mileage day of the trip so far, except for our 52 miles on Day 1. We left Kelso, Washington at 6:00 a.m. and did not get to Horseshoe Bay, British Columbia until 11:30 p.m., averaging only about 25 mph; but we had taken our second (23 miles) and third (35 miles) ferry rides of the trip.

Day 10
West Vancouver (Horseshoe Bay) to
Prince George, British Columbia
441 Miles

We had quit setting the alarm several days previously, instead letting our bodies tell us when to get started. Since we had gotten in very late, we did not get on the road until about 7:30 a.m. Tim led us out of the hotel parking lot, around the block, and then right back to the hotel. This was an inauspicious start!

Chapter 10

The roads in this area are poorly marked and we had simply made a circle. My GPS maps were more current so I told Tim I would get us out of town. I did, but made a wrong turn on the highway and had us going south instead of east. We made a U-turn and backtracked a few miles before selecting the right route on our third attempt.

Gas and Food. We were still dangerously low on gas after twice skipping our fill-up so we could make the ferry. Tim's bike was sputtering when we pulled up to the pumps in Squamish, B.C. He made it, as I promised, but just barely. No price to be paid this time.

We had both been too cheap to buy food on the ferry the night before and the motel did not have a continental breakfast, so we were both searching for food at the gas stop. We each selected a pepperoni stick wrapped in a bread stick. They hit the spot. Tim was still talking about how good they were a week later.

Roller Dogs. Gas station food is a popular topic among long-distance motorcycle riders. Many of my friends despise it. However, my friend Richard Buber aka Oldwing and I always retort, "What is wrong with roller dogs?"

Roller dogs are the gas station hot dogs cooked and kept warm on heated rollers. When I'm doing a long-distance ride, I eat gas station food almost exclusively. Not just hot dogs, but tacos or anything else that might be available. If there is a specialty to the locale, I'm in. My most memorable gas station food was a salted persimmon at a station in western Texas. After that one, I always inquire before I eat something unfamiliar. Let's just say it was not nearly as good as the pepperoni we had this day.

We Got Spotted. From Squamish, we headed through the Coastal Mountains of British Columbia and Whistler, home of the 2010 Winter Olympics. The locals couldn't say enough bad things about this Route 99, talking about how it had been hacked together for the Olympics and about how many people had been killed on it.

The roads were twisties followed by more twisties with some serious up-hill and down-hill grades, but we only encountered one small area of construction and, overall, the road was very good.

There was still snow along the road. We even came upon a spot where there had been an avalanche and the snow was very deep. The mountains, lakes, and rivers provided endless scenic views. We were told there would be a lot of wildlife but we only saw two does.

At around noon, we approached an intersection outside the town of Lillooet, B.C. It looked like an inviting town and the pepperoni stick was wearing off so we decided to have lunch.

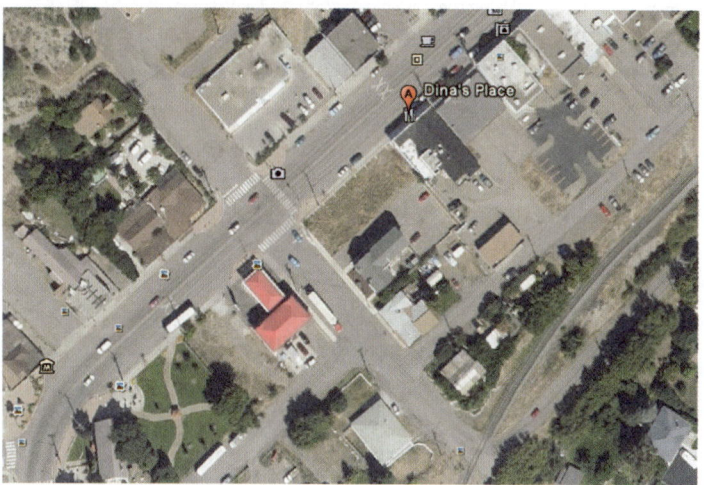

Dina's Place – Google Maps Lillooet, B.C.

While we were eating, Tim got a call from a friend.

Friend: "Where are you at?"

Chapter 10

Tim: "I'm not sure. We stopped at a small town in Canada to get some lunch."

Friend: "It looks like you are in Lillooet."
Tim: "I think that is it."

Friend: "It looks like you are sitting on Main Street in front of Dina's restaurant."

Tim's friend had been following our satellite tracker and by looking at the map in Google Earth, knew our location better than we did.

Another Short Riding Day. We stopped for gas at Clinton, B.C. a little after 2:00 p.m. and about 2 hours after that at Williams Lake, B.C. The roads to Prince George are excellent, but aside from a few lakes, the scenery is pretty boring. We were basically just cranking out miles. This area had really developed since I was here in 2007, particularly Lake Williams and Quesnel.

At about 7:00 p.m. EDT (4:00 p.m. local time) Tim stopped and said, "I have to call in to Sidestand Up. I promised Tom I'd call." Sidestand Up is a motorcycle radio show hosted by long-distance rider Tom Lowdermilk.

Tim called from his bike on the side of the road but Tom must not have recognized his number and they never got connected.

I had in mind that we would spend the night somewhere between Prince George and Hyder, Alaska. However, as we pulled into Prince George, it was approaching 7:00 p.m. Tim mentioned an Economy Inn he had stayed at during his previous trip. So we stopped even though it was still early.

We set a new low (excluding Day 1) for traveled miles two days in a row, covering only 441 miles today. We had stopped for a leisurely lunch and we had ridden less than 12 hours before parking for the night and were now two full days behind our planned schedule.

Tim mentioned something about going to a steak house he had eaten at before. I told him to go ahead, that I just wanted to rest and maybe go to the Dairy Queen across the street later. I really just needed some space.

I was trying to deal with the fact that we would not be riding with Jack and the fact that Tim and I had obviously miscommunicated before the ride with regard to our planned schedule. It was really eating at me; I just was not used to stopping at 7:00 p.m. during an Iron Butt ride and now we had done this several nights in a row.

It seemed too late to deal with it now, so I kept my feelings to myself. Okay, I pouted internally. After we unpacked, Tim said, "I'll just go to the Dairy Queen with you." I wasn't going to get my space after all.

Day 11
Prince George to Iskut, British Columbia
634 Miles

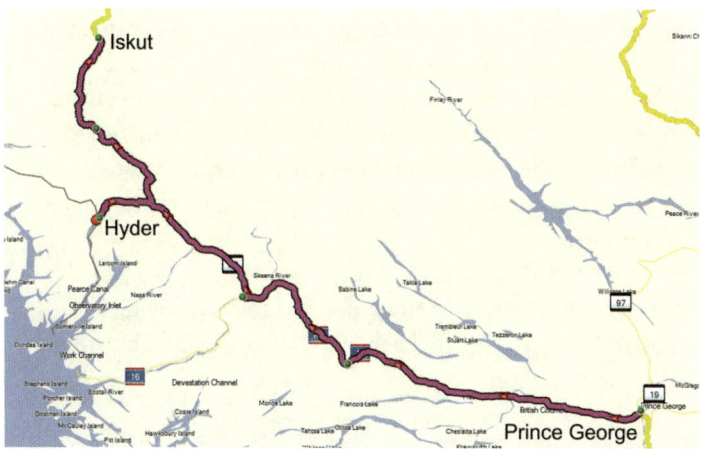

Chapter 10

We were up at 6:00 a.m. and on the road soon after. Tim discovered that the touch screen was not working on his GPS. We needed gas so I led us to the gas station where Tim switched out his GPS.

Tim checked his oil and it was low, but he didn't have any oil to top it off, and the gas station did not sell synthetic oil. I had about three-fourths of a quart left from the two quarts I brought as backup, which was enough to get Tim's KLR to the proper oil level. We found an auto parts store and replenished our oil supply on the way out of town.

We had an interesting routing situation as we left town. Tim made a right turn and my GPS was saying to go straight. I finally chased Tim down and he said that his GPS was taking him that way. We closely checked our routes and, as it turned out, both GPS's were taking us to the same place, just by different routes. This was one of many occurrences where our GPS's provided conflicting information.

Getting to Hyder. Our next mandatory stop was Hyder, Alaska. Hyder was made a "Long-Distance Rider Destination" by Ron Ayers when he used the southernmost point of Alaska as the ending point to his 48 State Plus ride in 1998. Alaska was the "plus" part of that ride. Ron rode the 48 continental states plus Alaska in 7 days, 0 hours, 20 minutes. In celebration of the ride, he created the annual Hyderseek event to encourage riders to duplicate his ride. We added Hyder as a mandatory stop for our ride, because of its southernmost location in Alaska and its prominence in the long-distance motorcycling community.

This was my fourth time to Hyder and I was enjoying the familiar views. We kept a keen eye out for wildlife, but there was none to be seen.

We made gas stops in Houston and Kitwanga, British Columbia. In Kitwanga, a guy mowing the yard at the service station agreed to take our picture in front of the mileage sign.

Kitwanga Gas Stop

Bear Glacier is at the entrance to Hyder. This year the glacier was not extending into the lake as far as it had on my other visits, but it was still a welcome view from the past. We stopped at the Sealaska Inn to get our receipt for the mandatory stop, the Boundary Gift Shop (Caroline's Place) to get some fudge and stickers, and then had lunch at the Glacier Inn. The Glacier Inn is where most people who attend Hyder go to get "Hyderized" – which in laymen's terms means downing a shot of pure Hyder moonshine. We had been to Hyder before, so we skipped the Hyderization.

Brake Trouble. I normally ride with ear plugs, but I wasn't wearing them on the streets of Hyder and I was surprised to hear my brakes squealing. I had noticed earlier that my front brake lever felt mushy, and now I saw that my front rotor was scarred and there were metal filings on the calipers.

My KLR has a special front brake setup. There are a few folks on the MTF who, when they tell me something about my bike,

Chapter 10

I am apt to listen to them. Jack Gustafson is one of those. He has abused his KLR by riding it up the Haul Road many times. Most of the modifications I have done to my KLR are at Jack's recommendation.

One of his recommendations was to add the oversize front brake rotor and Galpher black brake pads, which I did. Now the black Galpher pads were worn all the way down to metal after just 6000 miles. I don't know if this was the fault of the brake pad or a reflection of my hard braking on the trip.

Alan Leduc Brake Repair
Photo by Tim Yow

I ordered Halibut fingers for lunch in the Glacier Inn and went back outside to repair the brakes. Fortunately, my pre-ride mechanical work had prepared me for the task and I had the brake pads changed right about the time they were bringing my lunch.

Wildlife Sightings Enroute to Iskut. From Hyder we took the Cassiar Highway (Highway 37) north toward the Alcan (the Alaskan-Canadian Highway). Each of the previous times I had been to Hyder and on the Cassiar, I saw plenty of wildlife. I remember quite clearly the day I saw my first eagle in low flight over my head on the Cassiar.

Today we saw one deer (it came to the road but turned back), four ducks, and one very large moose cow. But the most plentiful critters were bears. We saw more than fifty black bears. At one point we were seeing a bear every mile or so, grazing alongside the road. Most would run away from the road when they saw we were coming close. But a few would stare as if to say, "What are you doing in my neighborhood?" I believe, given the number of bear that we saw and the number of bear droppings we saw in the road, we answered the age-old rhetorical question, "Does a bear shit in the woods?" It actually seemed that they preferred the road or would shit anywhere.

The first time I went to Alaska in 2004, the Cassiar was all gravel. Now the road is all paved except for one challenging two-mile stretch. While the pavement allowed us to take in the views instead of concentrating on riding a difficult gravel road, I missed the adventure of the gravel I had experienced on my first trip.

Tim had in mind a lodge that he had stayed at on a previous trip. He said it was run by a German lady and the food was excellent. Either it was not yet open for the season or had gone out of business, so we continued north and found lodging at a remote hotel in Iskut, arriving at about 9:30 p.m. The Iskut Motor Inn is a series of trailers connected together. The owner was very friendly and it was reasonably clean. They had a restaurant but it was closed, so we would have to resort to our motorcycle bags for food (energy bars, jerky, and trail mix).

We had covered some good ground today. Our plan was to spend the night in Dease Lake and we were only 50 miles short.

Chapter 10

**Day 12
Iskut, British Columbia to Tok, Alaska
842 Miles**

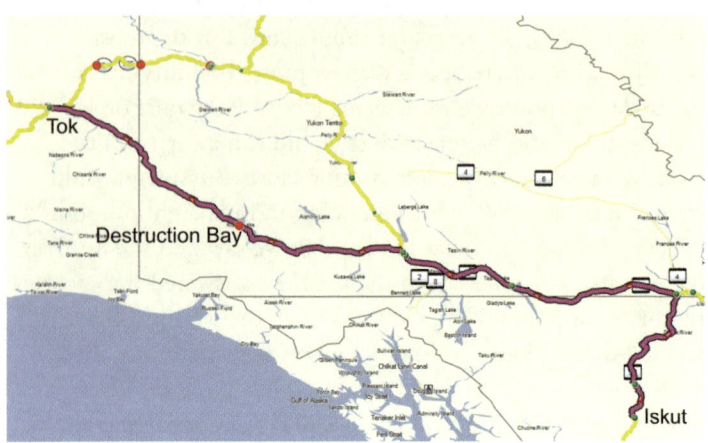

If we were to stay only two days behind schedule, we would need to make the 842 miles to Tok, Alaska today. Given our recent track record, this seemed highly unlikely.

We slept in a bit and didn't get on the road until a little after 8:30 a.m., stopping for gas in Dease Lake, about 50 miles north.

On to Teslin and a Bridge. Our next stop was at Junction 37 – the junction of Highway 37 and the Alcan, just west of Watson Lake, Yukon. I have stopped at this gas station, both up and back, each time I have been to Alaska. They usually have "Alaskan Highway Stickers" and the lady who ran the station was always friendly. This time we had a grumpy old man and no stickers. We met a couple from Newfoundland who were also getting gas and left our bikes parked at the pump as we engaged them in an extended chat. The attendant came out and told us to move our bikes. There were no other customers and, of course, had there been, we would have moved our bikes promptly. So much for the sign in the window that said, "Biker Friendly."

Western Bay by Bay Plus

From Junction 37 we headed west toward Teslin. This is a pretty boring section of road. At least the Alcan was in good shape and we were making good time. Nisutlin Bay Bridge at Teslin, Yukon is the longest water span in Alaska at nearly 2000 feet. This bridge has a metal grate surface and the grates are not aligned. The first time I went over this bridge I was scared silly. Since that time I had learned that the trick is to keep your speed up, and now it seemed like no big deal. We stopped for gas and a late lunch (it was about 3:00 p.m.) just west of the bridge at the Yukon Inn. Location, Location, Location. They are proud of their gas and food and their prices reflect it.

One don't-miss spot is the taxidermy exhibit in the gift shop, a building that sits by itself just east of the restaurant. I discovered this by accident in 2004. I was riding with Bob Moore and he had the nods and needed to take a nap. To kill some time, I went into the gift shop which had just opened. They charged $3.00 to go through the exhibit and I normally wouldn't pay for such a thing, but the owner said I could go through for free. Unbelievable! They have displays depicting wild animals in natural outdoor settings. It is something I'm guessing most people miss, but is a must-see if you are there.

We made a gas stop at Whitehorse at 4:15 p.m. and headed toward Destruction Bay, our next mandatory stop.

Kluane Lake. I have fond memories of Destruction Bay from my first trip to Alaska in 2004. I was riding with Bob Moore and Jon David Powers and when we reached Kluane Lake the sun was bright and was glistening across the lake, making it a beautiful aqua blue. We stopped on the side of the road and spent about 15 minutes taking pictures. A few minutes later we stopped for gas in Destruction Bay and our friend Rob Zielki (aka RocketMan) pulled in on his FJR. We were all headed to Alaska to ride the Haul Road.

Interestingly, on another occasion at Kluane Lake, it was

Chapter 10

overcast and the lake was unspectacular. A tour bus had stopped at one of the pull-offs, hoping to see the lake as it appeared in the travel brochures. As I saw all of the people looking out at the lake, I thought it is too bad they couldn't have seen the lake in its magnificence as I had. I'm sure they were disappointed.

Decision to Press On. It was just after 10:00 p.m. when Tim and I arrived at Destruction Bay. They had a room but we had a dilemma. After telling Jack Gustafson we would not be able to ride up to Prudhoe Bay with him, we had made arrangements to meet him on Friday (tomorrow). He was leaving from Glennallen, Alaska on Friday to go to Fairbanks for the start of his ride and we needed to be near Tok, if we were to meet him. Tok was 236 miles away. We decided to push on, thinking we might find a room somewhere between Destruction Bay and Tok.

Jack had posted on the MTF, "Reports are that the highway between Burwash Landing and the border has really broken up this past winter, and that might slow them down." We hadn't seen Jack's report and to say it was an understatement is not adequate. Burwash Landing is a few miles northwest of Destruction Bay. It is not unusual for the road in this area to have heaves from the permafrost; however, it typically creates a roller coaster effect on the road. This year was much different.

I was riding along and suddenly found myself in a rut that ran diagonally with the road. The rut was about six inches deep and a foot wide. I couldn't seem to get out and it was taking me into the oncoming lane. Fortunately, no traffic was coming toward me. These ruts, combined with heaves, would create some very challenging riding for the next 100 miles or so.

By the time we arrived in Beaver Creek, just east of the Alaskan border, Tim was livid. He ranted about how dangerous that road was and about the irresponsibility of the politicians who allowed it to get that way. There was a hotel and I figured we would stop there for the night, but when Tim commented about how the prices in Beaver Creek were always high, we decided to fill up with gas and go on. Tim took one look at the price of gas and said, "I'm not spending one cent in this town."

It is 226 miles between Destruction Bay and Tok, right at our travel limit. Tim thought there was a place we could get gas between Beaver Creek and Tok, but when we got there they were closed. We were now committed to Tok. One side benefit was that, after the near midnight sunset, the orange skies were beautiful.

We arrived in Tok near midnight. We had ridden about 15-1/2 hours and covered 842 miles. I pulled into the Snowshoe Inn where I had stayed before, and Tim was still cranked up: "Why are we stopping? I'm ready to ride now." I said, "If you want to go on, I'll be glad to go on. We can ride to Glennallen (Jack's home) and meet Jack for breakfast in the morning. But if we go on, we are committed to another two hours at least, and Jack says there is some road construction." We decided to stay put and got a room for the night.

Day 13
Tok to Homer, Alaska
539 Miles

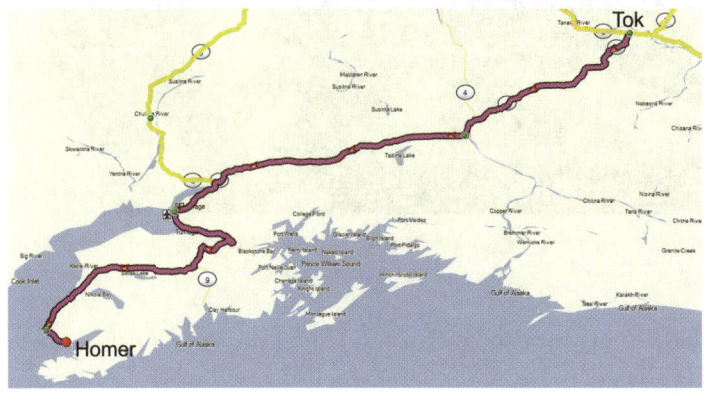

Chapter 10

We sent Jack an email before going to bed and, overnight, he had responded that he would meet us somewhere along the Glenn Highway which connects Tok and Glennallen. We had breakfast at Fast Eddies, a local restaurant. While we were there we met a couple from Vancouver who were driving a motor home. They had torn out a differential on the road from Burwash Landing to Beaver Creek (the terrible road we had ridden last night). They also told us about a fifth wheel trailer with the frame broken in half. We never thought that one of the most difficult roads we would encounter would be paved.

We left Tok a little after 10:00 a.m. We were stopping at a construction zone outside of Glennallen when we spotted Jack.

Tim Yow and Jack Gustafson
Photo by Alan Leduc

He did a U-turn and we followed him back to Glennallen where we stopped alongside the road and had a short chat. It wasn't the kind of ride I wanted with Jack, but at least we were able to meet. It may seem strange that close friends wouldn't take time

Western Bay by Bay Plus

to go to a restaurant and have a nice long chat, but Jack and the two of us were on missions. These kinds of meetings are both common and priceless for long-distance riders.

We left Jack about 2:00 p.m. and continued southwest toward Anchorage, arriving around 5:00 p.m. We were stopped at a red light and when it changed, Tim turned left and I followed. We went one block and Tim turned right, onto a one-way street. At that point I realized that I was just following blindly and that we were also going the wrong way on the one-way street from which we were turning. I said to Tim. "I think we blew that one." "The GPS said to turn that way," Tim replied. I laughed. "I think the GPS was wrong."

We arrived in Homer at 9:45 p.m. The last several miles the temperature was in the 30's, as we were riding next to the ocean with the evening air. Neither of us was wearing heated clothing and both of us were looking forward to a room. I told Tim that our friend Kevin Lechner and I had stayed at the Best Western at the end of our Alaska Insanity Ride (Prudhoe Bay to Homer; 1,000 miles in less than 24 hours). It was expensive but we didn't care; Tim and I were both in the same state of mind this night. Besides, it was Tim's night to pay. For $173.18, we had a nice comfortable and warm bed. The restaurant had closed for the night, but we were able to get some fish and chips in the bar.

We were in our motorcycle gear and caught the attention of one gentleman who had maybe a few too many drinks. He alternated between asking about our ride and complaining about how the Russians were ruining Homer and he was going to have to move away.

We started the **Western Bay by Bay Plus** leg of the ride in Coronado, California on May 20, 2011 at 09:49 PDT and completed it when we arrived at Homer, Alaska on May 27, 2011 at 21:45 AKDT. It had taken us 7 days, 12 hours, 56 minutes to complete what for us was a leg of 4,337 miles. Based strictly on the mandatory stops, MapSource calculated

Dream, Believe, and Achieve the Extraordinary

Chapter 10

the **Western Bay by Bay Plus** to be 4,314 miles with 3 days, 13 hours, 18 minutes riding time. Of the 4,337 miles we traveled for this leg, only 376 miles (8%) were interstate miles.

Using the proposed criterion of a 300 mile per day pace for the "Tour" option and the distance for just the mandatory stops, the **Western Bay by Bay Plus Tour** would have a completion time of 14 days, 9 hours, 7 minutes. If offered as a certified ride, a completion time of **14 days** is recommended.

With a proposed 500 mile per day pace for the "Power Tour" option and the distance for just the mandatory stops, the **Western Bay by Bay Plus Power Tour** would have a completion time requirement of 8 days, 15 hours, 4 minutes. A completion time of **8 days** is recommended.

Our completion time put us just under the proposed requirement for the **Western Bay by Bay Plus Power Tour**.

Completion of the USA South-West Challenge

The Iron Butt Association has a published ride called the USA South-West Challenge, which requires riders to ride from Key West, Florida to Homer, Alaska in less than 14 days. This ride implies that Homer is the westernmost point of the North American highway system; however, it actually is in the town of Anchor Point about 15 miles north of Homer. You must travel through Anchor Point to get to Homer. Homer is the end of the road on the peninsula, and that is likely why it was selected over Anchor Point. MapSource shows this route as 5,447 miles, requiring only a 389 mile-per-day pace.

We started in Key West on May 15, 2011 at 10:23 a.m. EDT. We arrived in Homer on May 28, 2011 at 1:45 a.m. EDT for a completion time of 12 days, 15 hours, 12 minutes. We had completed the USA South-West Challenge under the required time limit, even though we had gone through San Diego as opposed to the direct route. Our route had taken 7,682 miles; 2,235 miles over the direct route.

Even though we had not been putting in the kind of days I had planned in our original schedule, we obviously had been riding at the Iron Butt "Challenge" level. I was still frustrated about missing the opportunity to ride with Jack and was concerned about the impact on my finances – more days means more expenditure for hotels and food – but we were only 2 days behind schedule and, based upon the USA South-West Challenge, had been riding at an Iron Butt level. Our pace since leaving Key West was 608 miles per day.

While I had not confronted Tim directly since our discussion in Texas, I had been silently blaming him for stopping so early. I realized I needed to relax a bit and stop being so frustrated with the short riding days.

11 Passion in the Wind
Western Bay by Bay Adventure

I was looking forward to seeing my Alaska friends. I get the opportunity to visit them far too infrequently. I was also looking forward to the trip to Homer and the ride along the Cook Inlet. I was even looking forward to the challenge of riding the Haul Road to Prudhoe Bay and the one-pound hamburger at the Hot Spot. However, I never imagined that a few days later I would find myself sailing through the air and bouncing down the road near Happy Valley.

The **Western Bay by Bay** series of rides starts or ends at San Diego Bay on Coronado Island. The basic ride (Chapter 9) covers only the mandatory points along the western coast of the U.S. The **Western Bay by Bay Plus** (Chapter 10) adds four additional mandatory stops and requires riders to cross the border into Canada and enjoy the great experience offered by Alaska, ending in Homer. The **Western Bay by Bay Adventure** ride is for those riders who want to add the challenge of unpaved roads by adding just a single mandatory stop – Prudhoe Bay, Alaska.

Most people have heard of the "Ice Road Truckers" road from the television show. This road is formally known as the James W. Dalton Highway, and informally as the Haul Road (it was built for trucks that haul equipment and materials to the oil

Chapter 11

fields at Prudhoe Bay). The Haul Road runs between Fairbanks and Prudhoe Bay.

The road conditions on the Haul Road change very dramatically from day to day and even hour to hour. The state of Alaska has been paving sections of the Haul Road over the years, but much of it is still gravel of some sort.

I asked my friend Jack Gustafson, an Alaskan resident who has ridden the Haul Road many times, how much of the road was now paved and got this reply:

- Pavement: From Fairbanks, AK to the start of the Haul Road (Mile 0) is 78 Miles. There are some frost heaves about halfway that will let you know your suspension is working.
- Gravel: 5 miles of broken pavement to Mile 37.
- Pavement: 13 miles of pavement to Mile 50.
- Gravel: 40 miles of gravel to Mile 90.
- Pavement: 20 miles of old pavement with usual frost heaves to Mile 110 (Beaver Slide).
- Pavement: 25 miles of good pavement to Mile 115, (Arctic Circle) (A lot of people stop here; but the most difficult part of the road is yet to come.
- Pavement: 15 miles of old pavement to Mile 130.
- Pavement: 45 miles of decent pavement to Mile 175 (Coldfoot).
- Pavement: 22 miles of new pavement to Mile 199
- Gravel: 208 miles of gravel and 9 miles of pavement to Mile 415

The distance from Fairbanks to Prudhoe Bay is 493 miles, of which 312 is gravel. Depending on the road conditions, riders may report that this road is over-rated in terms of difficulty or you might read that it is a hellish nightmare. I have ridden the Haul Road up and back three times. I have never ridden it in rainy conditions, so I have avoided one of the conditions which can make it a hellish nightmare. However, this road is different than any other road:

- The road crews use heavy amounts of water with calcium chloride which makes the road very slick and difficult to navigate.
- The road is constantly under construction.
- The road has many textures and surfaces: Pavement, hardpack, loose gravel, pea gravel, base rock, dirt, and occasionally sand.

When riding the Haul Road it is critical that you not over-ride what you can see. The surface can change from pavement to deep pea gravel at the top of a rise. It is also important that you watch for textural or color changes and slow down until you figure out the road conditions. The people who crash on this road are usually the ones who get overzealous. The road is constantly changing, and one should not assume their return trip will be the same as the trip they just made up to Prudhoe Bay.

Day 14
Homer to Trapper Creek, Alaska
337 Miles

We left Homer around 7:30 a.m., stopping 15 miles north at Anchor Point, which is the western-most point of the North American highway system. Some consideration was given to including both Homer and Anchor Point as mandatory stops; however, since they were only 15 miles apart and it is necessary to go through Anchor Point to get to Homer, we decided that only Homer would be used as a mandatory stop. It is worth riding to find the sign noting the northwestern-most point of the highway system by taking the Old Sterling Highway over the Anchor River. The Anchor River is a popular trout fishing area and you will usually see fly fishermen in the river as you cross the bridge.

Chapter 11

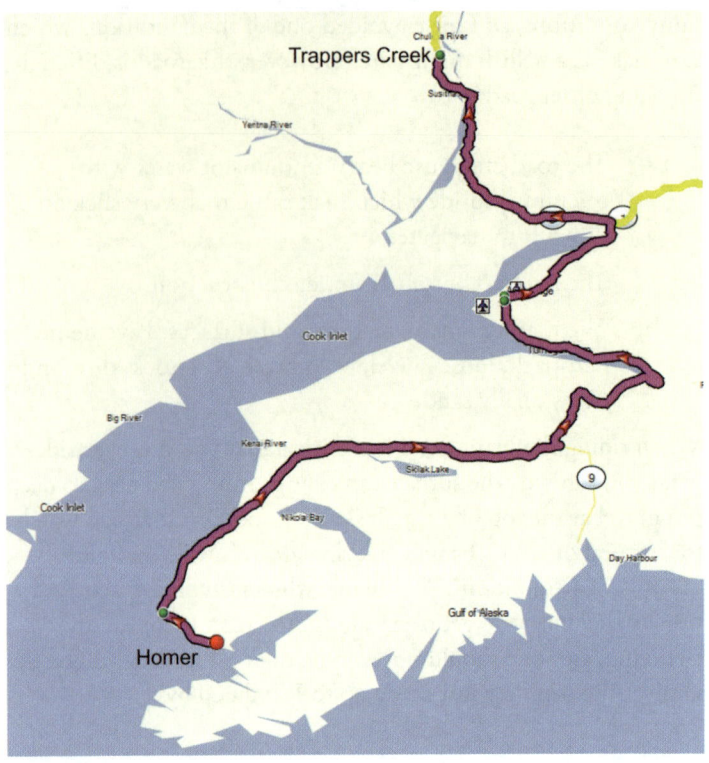

Visiting Alaska Friends. From Anchor Point, we traveled north on the Sterling Highway to the Seward Highway and then west to Anchorage, arriving a little past noon.

The magnetic strip on Tim's credit card had stopped working in California, so he made arrangements to have a new card shipped to our friend Roger Bliss in Wasilla, Alaska. Roger is a charter member of the Motorcycle Tourer's Forum, and his tag line is "When you get to Alaska, the first beer is on me." In 2004 we had 19 members show up to ride the Haul Road. Roger not only bought the beverages but arranged to have a hog roast. The MTF has a tire changer and balancer stored at Roger's place for our members to use whenever they ride to Alaska. Roger owns Wheeldog Trucking and was busy working, so he made arrangements for his close friend Jim Uhl to meet us.

Western Bay by Bay Adventure

Alan Leduc and Jim Uhl with his 1958 Ariel Cyclone
Photo by Tim Yow

Buddy Holly, the legendary singer, purchased one of only two hundred 1958 Ariel Cyclone motorcycles made. Jim Uhl owns one of the nineteen known remaining units and was riding it the day we met him. It was a treat to see such a rare motorcycle.

Roger is a very close friend and I was not about to ride all the way to Alaska without meeting him, so we arranged to meet Roger in the afternoon at the gravel pit from where he was hauling. We only had time to share a soda and a few stories, but it was great to see Roger again.

From Roger's we traveled to Trapper Creek to meet our close friends Joe and Sandra May. Joe, like Roger, is a charter member of the MTF. Joe is also the 1980 winner of the Iditarod sled-dog race. Sandra is an artist and has filled their home with paintings and bronze castings. When you look out their dining room window you have a perfectly framed view of Mount Denali. Joe is one of those people you could sit and listen to all evening, and we did until late into the night. There

Chapter 11

were many bits of wisdom shared that night, but I will share two with you.

> Joe, knowing that we would be traveling to Quebec and Labrador, was sharing stories about his trip where he rode a Honda Shadow Spirit (a cruiser style motorcycle) on these difficult roads. He noted that it seemed to him that traffic was busier in the afternoon so, since it was light most of the day, he set his schedule so that he would ride from 2:00 a.m. until noon. He ended with these words of wisdom, "I don't know if it was a good strategy or not. **We all tend to rationalize our decisions**."

I asked Sandra if she was still making bronze castings and she relayed a story.

> "There was an entrepreneur who was traveling in South America and bought a handmade doll from one of the natives for $4.00. Thinking this was something he could market back home, he asked the native,
>
> "How much would you charge if I purchased fifty of these?"
>
> The native thought for a minute and said $12.00 each."
>
> "$12.00 each? You just sold me this one for $4.00."
>
> "Yes, but if I have to make fifty of them, it is work, not fun."

Sandra, had so many requests for her bronze castings, it was no longer fun.

Joe's son Mark, a veterinarian and dog musher, was spending the night. Joe and Sandra invited us to stay in their guest room and we accepted, unknowingly pushing Mark to the sofa. I got the floor of the guest room and Tim got the bed.

Western Bay by Bay Adventure
Day 15
Trapper Creek, Alaska to Fairbanks, Alaska
256 Miles

We said our goodbyes to Joe and Sandra and filled up with gas at Trapper Creek a little after 8:00 a.m. We then headed toward Fairbanks, where we had arranged to have maintenance performed on the bikes. We made a gas stop at Nenana around 11:30 and arrived at the University of Alaska – Fairbanks (UAKF) about 1:00 p.m.

UAKF allows motorcyclists to stay in the dorms. You have a shared bath and there is no air-conditioning; but, at a rate of $46.00 per double compared to $100.00 or more for other accommodations in the area, you can't go wrong. We did not have a reservation, and the students who ran the welcome desk were not well trained. However, we finally got a room.

Dream, Believe, and Achieve the Extraordinary

Chapter 11

After check-in we left immediately for Adventure Cycleworks, where we had an appointment for maintenance. Owners Dan (father) and Shawn (son) Armstrong were waiting on us. They offer a tremendous service to long-distance riders by taking appointments 24 hours a day / 7 days per week from May to October. We had ridden nearly 8,300 miles on the Metzeler Tourance tires we had started with when we left from Key West. We now changed to Continental KTC 80's, a knobby tire more suited to the gravel roads we were about to encounter.

Because I had the engine bore kit installed shortly before beginning the trip, I had hoped to have the valves checked and I had even brought my shim kit with me. But Dan said, "I'm not about to pull the cams on that bike." They also refused to check the air filter on either of our bikes. When we made our appointment we thought we would be able to get a full service, which we really needed after 8,300 miles on the road. Instead we had to settle for new tires, brake pads, and an oil change.

Both Dan and Shawn worked very hard and their rate was fair, but like many Alaskans, they are a bit independent. Next time, we will know to work out our expectations ahead of time. By the time we got the maintenance done it was getting late, so we decided to go back to the UAKF and order pizza.

Day 16
Fairbanks to Prudhoe Bay, Alaska
505 Miles

We left UAKF at around 6:00 a.m. Tim arranged to drop off his waterproof bags at Adventure Cycle, so we stopped there on our way to get gas near the intersection of Farmers Loop Road and the Steeves Highway.

Western Bay by Bay Adventure

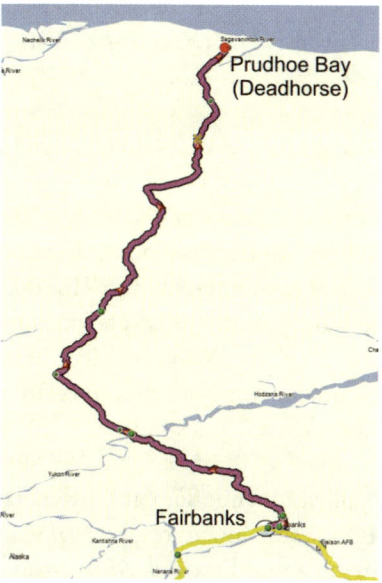

The Haul Road starts about 80 miles north of Fairbanks. This would be the third trip up the Haul Road to Prudhoe Bay for both of us, so we knew what to expect and weren't swayed by horror stories of difficult road conditions.

The 414 miles of the Haul Road only averages about 250 vehicles a day, mostly 18-wheelers hauling equipment and materials. Since about three-fourths of the Haul Road is gravel, most rental companies will not allow you to take their cars to the Arctic Circle or Prudhoe Bay.

At about mile marker 47, the Haul Road starts to descend to the Yukon River where a wood-planked bridge spans about 2,300 feet. On previous trips, I had found the bridge planking in need of repair and tedious to cross. This time the planking was in great condition. The Yukon River Camp at mile marker 56 is the last chance to get gas until Coldfoot at mile marker 175. The camp is a large gravel lot with restaurant and rooms made from connected trailers. The lone gas pump is a hundred yards or more from the restaurant and you must prepay,

Chapter 11

meaning at least two trips to the restaurant. We filled up and picked up some "Dalton Highway" souvenir stickers at about 10:30 a.m.

Ice Road Trucker. Just a few miles down from the Yukon River Camp is the Hot Spot, which serves a one-pound hamburger. We arrived just before they opened so we had to wait a few minutes for our feast. Inside was a poster featuring Ice Road Trucker star Lisa Kelly. I commented to Tim that we should have arranged to have our picture taken with Lisa. Tim then mentioned that George Spears, another Ice Road Trucker, was from Greenup, a small town close to where Tim grew up in Illinois, and that he knew Spear's brother.

An 18-wheeler pulled in while Tim and I were talking and a big strapping fellow came in and ordered some ice cream. He overheard us talking about Lisa and George and said, "I was on that show." We didn't recognize him, but his name was Carey Hall, also known as "Big Daddy." It was fun chatting with him about the show.

Haul Road
Photo by Harry Farthing

Western Bay by Bay Adventure

The southern portion of the Haul Road provides vistas of evergreen forests and typically good quality gravel roads. At points, the gravel road seemed to extend forever.

At mile marker 75 we encountered the "Roller Coaster" known for its steep descent, followed by a sharp ascent. The view when you start down the hill provides the same feeling as sitting on top of the roller coaster when you are about to descend that first drop. The weather was sunny and dry; I can't imagine riding this hill when it is wet and slippery.

Finger Mountain, at mile marker 98, is a weathered rock formation called a tor. This trip, we only viewed Finger Mountain from the road; however, you should definitely stop on your first trip. We soon found ourselves at the Arctic Circle, mile marker 115, and stopped for the obligatory picture.

Alan Leduc and Tim Yow at Arctic Circle
Photograph by Tim Yow

Dealing With Gravel Berms. We arrived at Coldfoot, mile marker 175, a little before 2:00 p.m. The roads had been in good condition. We had encountered a couple of areas where calcium chloride had been used to soak the road and where grading was being done. These areas were slick and required us to cross the graded berms, but we had not encountered any other difficult areas or loose gravel.

Alaska Pipeline
Photo by Harry Farthing

From Coldfoot, we continued through Wiseman, a good choice for lodging for those who only want to do half of the Haul Road at a time. We were soon riding into the Brooks Mountain Range, which offered up yet another type of vista, changing from evergreen forests to mountain views.

The ascent of Atigun Pass, mile marker 242, is about a 2 mile 12 percent grade. We were just hoping that we would not encounter any trucks on this challenging stretch and fortunately we didn't. I looked closely for sheep, something I'd encountered in 2004, but no wildlife was to be seen this year.

Unhappy Valley. We were making good time when we encountered the welcome stretch of pavement at mile marker 334, known as Happy Valley. The transition from pavement back to gravel just after Happy Valley can be treacherous and we know several friends who have crashed there. The paved stretch was not in great shape, so we were only riding about 55-60 mph.

As I came over a rise, I found myself in a full slide, fish-tailing back and forth three or four times. I thought that maybe I had a rear tire blow-out, but it also seemed as if my rear brake was locked. When you lock your rear brake the bike tends to go from side to side, each time swinging farther out. The remedy is to stay on the brake and hit the throttle to try to bring the rear wheel back under you. I tried but this didn't work.

I had scrubbed off speed, down to 10-20 mph, and the next thing I knew, the bike was a full 90 degrees sideways to the road. At this point, there was not much I could do and I remember thinking, "This is going to hurt." I knew I was going to be thrown over the handlebars. Here is Tim's account:

> We had been through a few difficult places but were now sailing along at Happy Valley. I happened to look in my mirrors and my heart jumped as I saw Alan's bike slide sideways one way and then the other way. Then it looked like an explosion as the bike launched in a total flip and Alan was flying through the air with all four limbs extended. I felt sick to my stomach and did a U-turn to hurry back.
>
> I started to press 911 on my Spot satellite tracker, knowing that it was probably going to be necessary. But I decided to wait when I saw Alan instantly jump up. I hurried back to the hill that we had just passed over before the "get off," because we were in a blind spot and traffic would not be able to see Alan and his bike in the middle of the road.
>
> Seeing no one in view, I hurried back to assist Alan, who was attempting to pick up the loaded bike. I thought that the bike was probably done, but amazingly it started right away.

Chapter 11

I went back to the top of the blind spot while he gathered his stuff that had scattered all over the place. I should have stepped off the huge question mark-looking skid mark to measure its length.

Once everything was clear, I rode back down to Alan and the bike. We inventoried Alan first, and then his bike. Alan had bounced a couple of times and reported a sore shoulder, knee, hip, and elbow on the right side. The bike appeared to have little damage.

I believe it was nothing short of a miracle that the accident wasn't worse. I'll never forget that view in my mirrors. I'm forever grateful that my buddy Alan was all right with just a few pains and a couple extra scabs. He jumped back on that bike and followed me into Deadhorse like nothing had happened. When we got to Prudhoe Bay he was only talking of plans for the rest of the trip.

Assessing the Damages to Body and Bike. I found that part of the rear pannier had broken and wedged into the knobby tires, totally locking the rear wheel. I didn't think I had any broken bones, but I could feel blood running down my elbow and possibly my knee. There are no emergency services along the Haul Road and we were only about 80 miles from Prudhoe Bay, so the decision to jump back on the bike and ride behind Tim to Prudhoe Bay was pretty easy.

Tim intended to stop for gas when we arrived at Prudhoe Bay, but I told him I needed to go straight to the hotel. We checked in a little after 8:30 p.m. Upon examination, I found that I had a pretty good bruise on my hip and shoulder and had pulled some stomach muscles, making it difficult to get my gear off. My knee was scuffed but not bleeding; but my elbow was a mess. Evidently, my elbow had landed on a small rock which pushed through the padding in my gear. I had a pretty deep wound. I was able to buy ointment, bandages, and Icy Hot in the hotel store and got patched together.

We were too late for the full buffet offered by the Prudhoe Bay Hotel, but there is never a shortage of food, so we had dinner and then I tried to find a spot to lie on that didn't hurt, hoping for some much needed rest.

Prudhoe Bay Deadhorse Signs
Photo by Harry Farthing

Prudhoe Bay used to be called Deadhorse. The story goes that when the oil fields were being built, a clerk applied for a postal code and it came back as Deadhorse, Alaska. Eventually it was changed to Prudhoe Bay. I think I know how that horse must have felt; when I awoke the next morning, I was stiff and sore. I knew this was not going to be a fun ride, but I was determined to continue. After all, one of my core values is perseverance.

Chapter 11

**Day 17
Prudhoe Bay Alaska Out and Back**

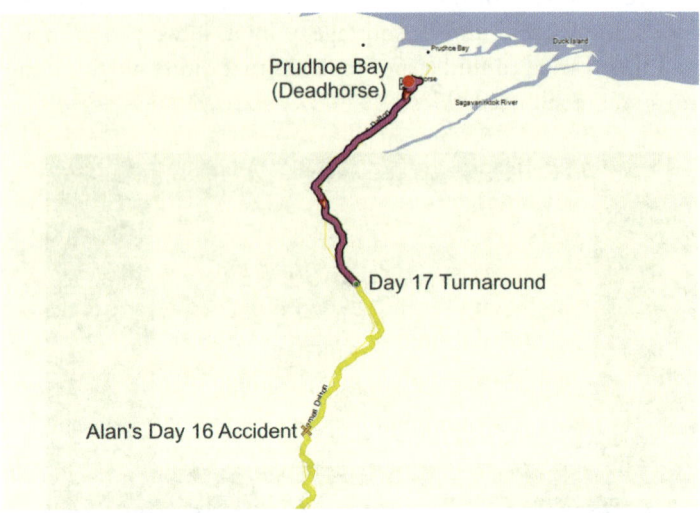

After breakfast, our first task was to get the cross brace for my luggage rack replaced. We went to the NAPA store and they recommended Jerry Coburn, owner of Coburn's Machine Shop. I called Jerry and he agreed to look at it.

Jerry's place is tucked away in a hard-to-find building and when we didn't show up, he came looking for us and led us back to his shop. He and his staff spent a couple of hours fabricating braces and welding up the cross brace for the luggage rack. When done it was better than new.

I asked Jerry how much I owed him and he said, "$175 per hour, times two hours, times three people equals $1,050." It was one of those deals where he couldn't charge me enough so he did it for free. I gave him $100.

Since we were getting a late start, our plan was to stop for the night at Wiseman, which is about halfway to Fairbanks. It was only about 30 degrees, so I plugged in my electric gear, thinking not only would it keep me warm but would also make my aching body feel better.

Uncooperative Weather. We had only gone about 20 miles before it started to snow. The snow and winds continued to get worse, adding to the cold temperatures. We were having difficulty keeping our face shields clear enough to see, which made riding even more difficult. Tim stopped and expressed concern that we might not be able to get over Atigun Pass because of the snow. If we got stuck at the pass, we would not have enough gas to get back to Deadhorse. We were only about 46 miles from Deadhorse, so we decided to return. I was relieved. I was really feeling the pain from the crash the day before and needed some more time for my body to recover.

The 40 miles of the Haul Road closest to Deadhorse has been the most difficult on all my trips, and this trip was no exception. Today we did an "in and out" on the toughest miles in the snow and cold.

Yesterday was my day to pay for the room and I had paid $210 at Prudhoe Bay Hotel. When we returned, Tim stopped at the Aurora Hotel, which is the newest hotel. It was his day to pay and I was too sore to get on and off the bike, so I just waited. When Tim came back he was so excited. Remember, one of Tim's core values is frugality!

Tim said, "I got us a great deal for only $125. It includes internet and all the food we can eat."

Thinking that this was a newer hotel, I couldn't imagine it was that much cheaper than the Prudhoe Bay Hotel. I asked Tim, "Are you sure that's not $125 each?"

"No, $125 total," Tim replied.

"Cool. Let's do it."

Chapter 11

We went inside and Tim filled out the paperwork, at which point the clerk told Tim the room was $250. I wish I could describe Tim's expression! After some discussion, Tim said, "Okay." The clerk gave us the key and told us we were not actually in "the hotel," but in an annex which required us to walk to another building. Not only was it more expensive, but we had been placed in exile! It was a real pain, as every time we went from building to building, we had to put booties over our shoes.

We'll try again tomorrow. Our attempt to get out of Prudhoe Bay had failed. However, we heard reports that Atigun Pass had 8 inches of snow so we had made a good decision to return.

We arrived in Prudhoe Bay on May 30, 2011 (Day 16) at 8:38 p.m. AKDT (9:38 p.m. PDT) after having started the **Western Bay by Bay Adventure** on Coronado Island, California on May 20 (Day 6) at 9:49 a.m. PDT. It had taken us 10 days, 11 hours, 49 minutes and 5,531 miles to cover the 5,388 mile route predicted by MapSource using just the mandatory stops. Using the MapSource prediction and 500 miles per day as a criterion, the allowed time for the **Western Bay by Bay Adventure** would be 10 days, 18 hours, 37 minutes. A time of **11 days** is recommended. We had successfully completed the **Western Bay by Bay Adventure**.

12

Passion in the Wind
Northern Bay by Bay Part I

On both *of my previous trips to Alaska, I had been deprived by forest fires and maintenance issues, of the opportunity to ride the Top of the World Highway from Chicken, Alaska to Dawson City, Yukon. This time I was able to learn firsthand how it got its name – you literally seem to be riding the Top of the World. This would also be my first time to ride the notorious Dempster Highway. What I didn't plan, was how an extra two days in Inuvik would change my focus from a wounded body to a broken bike.*

The **Northern Bay by Bay Adventure** goes from Prudhoe Bay, Alaska to St. John's, Newfoundland with the following mandatory stops:

- Prudhoe Bay (Deadhorse), Alaska
- Inuvik, Northwest Territories (Northernmost point of Canada)
- Little Gold Creek, Yukon (Westernmost point of Canada) documented by receipts in:
  * Chicken, Alaska
  * Dawson City, Yukon
- Yellowknife Bay: Documented by receipt from Yellowknife, Northwest Territories
- Thunder Bay, Ontario

Chapter 12

- Point Pelee, Ontario (Southernmost point of Canada): Documented by receipt from Leamington, Ontario
- North Bay, Ontario
- James Bay, Quebec: Documented by receipt from Chisasibi, Quebec
- Baie-Comeau, Quebec
- Goose Bay, Labrador
- Hawkes Bay, Newfoundland
- St. John's Bay (Cape Spear – Easternmost point of Canada): Documented by receipt in St. John's, Newfoundland

The **Northern Bay by Bay Adventure** has a total of 2,838 miles of gravel roads, including some of the most notorious gravel roads in Alaska and Canada:

- James W. Dalton Highway (Haul Road; Ice Road Truckers Road) from Fairbanks, Alaska to Prudhoe Bay, Alaska: 313 miles of gravel roads each way totaling 626 miles.
- Top of the World Highway from Chicken, Alaska to Dawson City, Yukon: 113 miles of gravel roads.
- Dempster Highway from Dawson City, Yukon to Inuvik, Northwest Territories: 456 miles of gravel roads each way totaling 992 miles.
- Fort Liard Highway from south of Fort Liard to Fort Simpson turnoff: 163 miles of gravel roads.
- James Bay from Matagami to Waswanipi, Quebec: 103 miles of gravel roads.
- Trans-Labrador Highway from Manic-5, Quebec to Red Bay, Labrador: 841 miles of gravel roads.

During our ride, Tim put the amount of gravel in perspective for me: it is approximately 2,400 miles from Jacksonville, Florida to San Diego, California. We rode this distance plus another 400 miles or so on gravel.

Northern Bay by Bay Part I

Riders who want to experience the Northern route without having to deal with the gravel may choose from:

- **Northern Bay by Bay Tour or Power Tour,** which requires the following mandatory stops:
    * Homer, Alaska
    * Thunder Bay, Ontario
    * Point Pelee, Ontario (Southernmost point of Canada): Documented by receipt from Leamington, Ontario
    * North Bay, Ontario
    * North Sydney, Nova Scotia

- **Northern Bay by Bay Plus Tour or Power Tour,** which adds the following mandatory stops to the Northern Bay by Bay Tour or Power Tour.
    * Hawkes Bay, Newfoundland
    * St. John's Bay (Cape Spear – Easternmost point of Canada): Documented by receipt in St. John's, Newfoundland

In addition to the mandatory stops, all of the **Northern Bay by Bay** options require the rider to remain in Canada and Alaska. Using the MapSource mapping software and only mandatory stops, the **Northern Bay by Bay Tour** is estimated by MapSource at 6,156 miles, requiring 4 days, 18 hours, 16 minutes of riding time and, based upon a 300 mile per day criterion, would require 20 days, 12 hours, 28 minutes. The recommended completion time is **20 days**. The **Northern Bay by Bay Power Tour,** based upon a 500 mile per day criterion, would require 12 days, 7 hours, 29 minutes. The recommended completion time is **12 days**.

The **Northern Bay by Bay Plus** which adds Newfoundland is estimated by MapSource at 7,082 miles, including a 110 mile ferry ride from North Sydney, Nova Scotia to Port Aux Basques, Newfoundland. MapSource estimates the ride would

Chapter 12

require 5 days, 18 hours, 26 minutes riding time, including 8 hours, 24 minutes allowance for the ferry ride. As noted earlier, both of these rides may be completed without gravel roads. Based upon the 300 mile and 500 mile per day criteria for Tour and Power Tour respectively for the 6,972 miles of paved road and the 8 hour, 24 minute allowance for the ferry, the rides are estimated to take 23 days, 14 hours, 9 minutes and 13 days, 22 hours, 39 minutes. Recommended times are **23 days** for the Northern Bay by Bay Plus Tour and **13 days** for the **Northern Bay by Bay Plus Power Tour**.

The **Northern Bay by Bay Adventure** is estimated at 10,352 miles, including six ferry rides and 2,838 miles of gravel roads. There is no estimate of time, as the mapping programs have not properly captured Phase III of the Trans-Labrador Highway.

**Day 18
Prudhoe Bay to Fairbanks, Alaska
500 Miles**

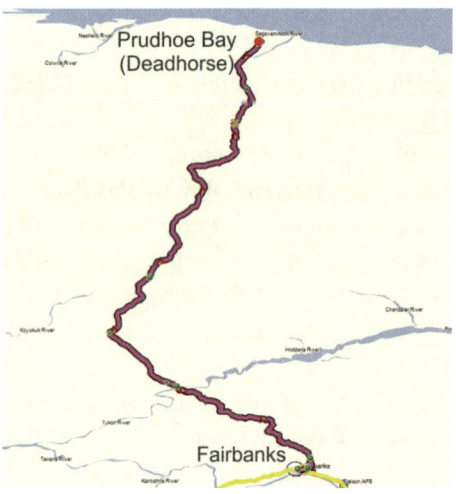

Today we would once again attempt to leave Prudhoe Bay, after yesterday's weather kept us from going to Fairbanks. My

Northern Bay by Bay Part I

body was still sore, but not stiff. The extra day of rest was much needed. It was still very cold, but there were no signs of snow.

I noticed that my voltage meter was only showing 11.2 volts. I had been having problems when running my electric gear, which was necessary in yesterday's snowstorm. Even though the meter would show charging at 13.8 volts, the battery seemed to be draining.

When I hit the starter button, the bike only grunted. Not a good way to start the day! Tim had jumper cables and I rigged up a connection using my electrical clothing connector so I wouldn't have to remove the seat to get to the battery. We got the bike running and headed off to the gas station, filling up at about 7:30 a.m. for our second attempt to leave Prudhoe Bay.

Meeting Other Adventurers. On the way to the station, we saw four other riders at the Arctic Caribou Inn, where I had stayed on my first trip to Prudhoe Bay. We stopped and asked if they were leaving and if they wanted to ride out together. Two were KLR riders from Montana whom we had met at the University of Alaska in Fairbanks a few days earlier. The other two riders were Brits, one on a KTM and the other on a Harley-Davidson 1200 Sportster.

We were ready to leave, but we decided to talk to the two KLR riders about their trip up the Haul Road, and to hear the story of the other two riders. The two KLR riders said they had tried to leave yesterday, but like us, had turned back because of the snow. They were carrying camping gear, but elected to stay in the inn after fighting the snow.

While waiting, we discovered the Harley and KTM riders had ridden from Ushuaia, Argentina. Both had crashed along the way and had an encounter with banditos in Mexico. Interestingly, neither of them had the kind of gear one would expect for riders doing this kind of ride. They were essentially wearing hooded sweatshirts and leather. The Harley rider was not wearing a

Chapter 12

helmet and none could be seen stowed on the motorcycle. The Harley rider had some electrical issues to sort out; the KTM rider was washing out his radiator; and the two KLR riders had a lot of packing to do. We decided to wait and a half hour or so later we all seemed to be ready except one of the riders from Montana, who was struggling to get latex gloves on over his leather gloves. Finally we headed out, Tim in the lead, followed by me, the two Montana riders and then the two Brits. I had not plugged in my electric gear and a few miles out of town motioned the other riders to pass me, so that I could pause to plug in.

Tim is very experienced on gravel and I had pushed my skills to the limit on the ride up. I felt more comfortable in the rear, as I could ride my own ride and not feel obligated to keep up with Tim. About 20 miles out, the Harley rider motioned me around and he and the KTM rider pulled to the side. I assumed the Harley rider was having a bike problem but he motioned me to go on, so I did. Another 20 miles or so later, the KLR riders motioned me around and they pulled over to the side of the road. I think Tim was riding faster than what they were comfortable with, so Tim and I continued on our own and we never saw them again after that. The temperatures were cold, but no snow. We arrived in Coldfoot about 3.30 p.m. With the wait, it had taken us about eight hours to travel the 250 miles.

We made a stop at the Hot Spot for a burger, arriving back in Fairbanks about 9:15 p.m. The roads were in good shape, with only a small amount of calcium chloride and construction, but the cold temperatures and concentration required to ride on the gravel with its different textures had taken its toll, so we headed directly back to the university for the night.

Northern Bay by Bay Part I
Day 19
Fairbanks, Alaska to Dawson City, Yukon
406 Miles

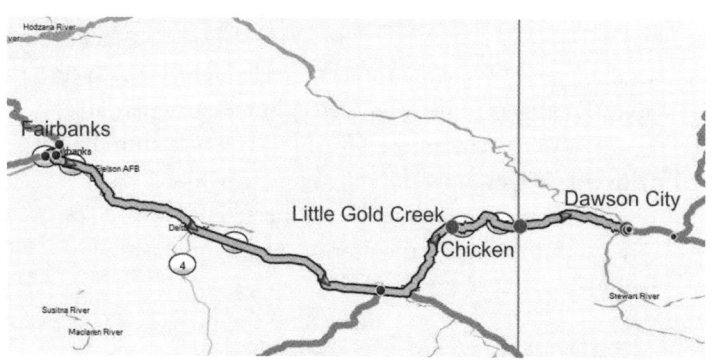

Tim left his waterproof bags at Adventure Cycle earlier, so we picked them up, washed the bikes, and talked Dan into cleaning our air filters. We had an easy ride to Tok where we stopped for gas about 12:30 p.m.

As we were leaving the gas station we saw two other riders, which turned out to be our friends Steve Short and Wiliferd Lair. They traveled to the Copper Canyon area of Mexico with me in 2006, and Steve and I shared a trip to the same area in December 2010. Tim and I knew that the pair were going to Prudhoe Bay, but didn't think we would be able to meet up. Steve had followed our Spot tracker and our timing was perfect! They had already eaten but agreed to join us at Fast Eddies for pie. Steve and Wiliferd are from Missouri, Tim is from Illinois, and I'm from Indiana and here we are, meeting on the road in Alaska for pie. This is the sort of experience that seems to happen frequently with long-distance riders.

On Top of the World. On both of my previous trips to Alaska, I had been unable to take the Top of the World Highway through Chicken, Alaska and Dawson City, Yukon. In 2004, Don Kime, Bob Moore, and I were stopped by forest fires and in 2007 I was stopped due to maintenance issues, so I was

Chapter 12

looking forward to my chance to ride this fabled road.
We arrived in Chicken a little after 4:00 p.m. The Chicken, Alaska website has the following story about how the town got its name:

> In the late 1800's, early miners traveled far in search of gold. Food was sometimes scarce, but a particular area near the south fork of the 40-Mile River was abundant with ptarmigan, now the state bird, which bears a resemblance to a chicken. The miners kept themselves alive with the help of the ptarmigan (if you consider being eaten as "helping").
>
> In 1902, Chicken was to become incorporated, the second town in Alaska to do so. The name "Ptarmigan" was suggested. The only problem was that nobody could agree on the correct spelling. They didn't want their town name to be the source of ridicule and laughter, so they decided on "Chicken."

Chicken is remote and I would have never guessed that it was the second town in Alaska to be incorporated. Today it survives primarily from tourists and locals traveling the Top of the World Highway. I bought a sticker that says, "I Got Laid in Chicken," but otherwise there was no indication that getting laid was an option except if you wanted to rent a room to sleep for the night.

Leaving Chicken, the road turns to gravel for the 113 miles to Dawson City. About 50 miles east of Chicken is a border post. The Canadian side is called Little Gold Creek, Yukon and the U.S. side is called Poker Creek, Alaska. Little Gold Creek is the westernmost point of Canada. The Iron Butt Association requires a time-stamped receipt with the City and State indicated on the receipt. We wanted to use Little Gold Creek as a mandatory stop for our trip but an appropriate receipt was not available at the customs post. We decided that we would use the time on our receipt from Chicken, Alaska and a secondary receipt from Dawson City to show that we had traveled through Little Gold Creek.

The hours of operation for the border crossing are another issue with Little Gold Creek. The sign in Chicken said the border was only open from 8:00 a.m. to 6:00 p.m. We didn't know if this was Alaska time (AKDT) or Yukon time (PDT), which was one hour ahead. We checked around and were assured the border closed at 6:00 p.m. Alaska time. It was nearly 4:30 p.m. and we would have to travel the 50 miles of gravel in less than one and a half hours, which meant we would have to average about 33 miles per hour. The road was in good condition, with only a few spots of loose gravel and no construction zones, and we made it to the border with time to spare.

Top of the World Highway
Photo by Harry Farthing

The ride on the Top of the World Highway was definitely an experience that I will not soon forget and one that I hope to repeat. Ordinarily, when you cross mountains you travel through the valleys between the mountains and then have a steep ascent and descent over a high pass. On the Top of the World Highway, you wind along the top of the mountains, which provides amazing vistas of the mountains and the valleys below.

Chapter 12

Sour What? The only way to get to Dawson City from the west is by ferry. It is a short trip and then a scenic ride bringing you into a town that takes you back to the historic gold rush era. We rode through town and decided to stay at the Downtown Hotel, home of the Sourtoe Cocktail. A much copied quote from the internet explains:

> At the Sourdough Saloon in the Downtown Hotel of Dawson City there is a drink that will make the bravest man cringe. The strange tradition was established in 1973 when a man named Captain Dick Stevenson (AKA Captain River Rat) bought a cabin outside of Dawson City where he found the pickled remains of a human toe. One night he decided to impress his friends and dropped the toe into his drink and downed the drink. It was said that the following mantra was invented then, that still continues to this day: "Do it fast or do it slow, but your lips must touch the toe."

Since we had gotten in early, we went to the Sourdough Bar for dinner. Several patrons were participating in the tradition of the Sourtoe Cocktail. Neither Tim nor I participated, but it was definitely fun to watch the faces of both the participants and observers. I went back to the room and Tim hung out talking to the locals and tourists.

Day 20
Dawson City to Eagle Plains, Yukon
254 Miles

In Dawson City we learned that the ferry which provided access to Inuvik, had just opened the previous day (June 2; our Day 19). We were surprised to be cutting it so close because our friend Don Kime had provided a list of annual ferry openings dating back to 1962 and the latest opening was May 31 in 1962. The average for both the last five years, and for the last 45 years, was May 16. Oh well, at least it is open today.

Northern Bay by Bay Part I

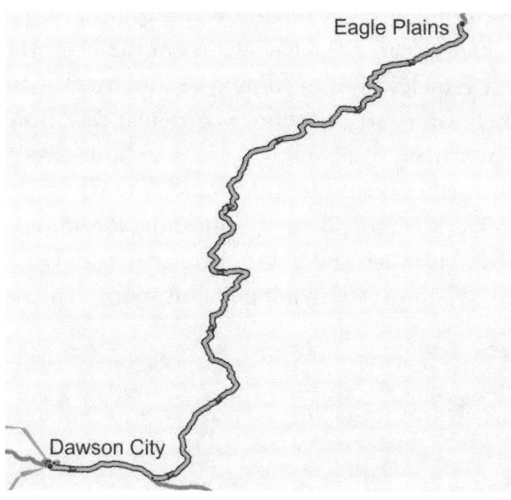

My bike's carburetor was really acting up. I had to constantly engage and disengage the fuel enrichener (choke) and maintain about 4,500 rpms to have any power. While Tim slept in, I got up early to try to track down a mechanic at the NAPA store. I got there as soon as the doors opened, but the guy refused any help. I went back to the hotel and got Tim. The mechanic search delayed our start to 9:30 a.m.

We had about 25 miles of pavement before hitting the 456 miles of gravel on the Dempster Highway. Right before we hit the start of gravel, I spotted a tire store that had a "Mechanic On Duty" sign. I stopped, but the mechanic was a diesel mechanic and claimed not to know anything about carburetors. I had no choice but to deal with one of the most notorious roads of our trip with a bad carburetor. It seemed simple enough to engage and disengage the choke. However, while trying to use more rear than front brake (the opposite of what is used for street riding) and dealing with the various textures and challenges of gravel, this added step proved to be quite challenging. In one tight downhill turn, I seemed to keep picking up speed and it took me several seconds to realize it was because the choke was engaged and the engine was idling very fast.

Chapter 12

The Dempster Highway is very different from the Dalton Highway (Haul Road). The narrowness of the Dalton Highway causes most vehicles to use a common center track – the outside track is for vehicles going a particular direction, but the center track is shared by vehicles in both directions. This usually makes the center track much more attractive to motorcycles as it is more compact, meaning less loose gravel. The Dempster is much wider and there are typically four tracks which are less compacted making it a bit more challenging.

The Dempster Highway
Photo by Harry Farthing

Another big difference is the manner in which calcium chloride is applied. On the Dalton, the construction crews use massive amounts of water turning the road into a muddy, slimy mess, which is very difficult to navigate. On the Dempster, far less water was used. The goo is still slick and slimy but was much easier to navigate.

Northern Bay by Bay Part I

On the Dalton, there are many texture changes: hardpack, loose gravel, calcium chloride, base rock, and if you encounter a color or texture change you better slow down until you are comfortable with the change of conditions. On the Dempster a color change usually just means a different color of rock. We encountered some loose gravel on the Dempster, but it was not nearly as challenging as the Dalton. On another day, conditions might have been different; but our trip up and back was very similar.

No Ferry Today. We arrived at Eagle Plains and filled up with gas. As we were about to leave, the gas station attendant asked where we were going and we replied, "Inuvik."

"Not today," the attendant said. "The ferry is not working."

"They told us in Dawson City that the ferry opened yesterday," we said.

"That was the Mackenzie Ferry. It opened yesterday. But the Peel Ferry hasn't started yet."

"When is it going to open?"

"Maybe tomorrow," the attendant said. "We will be the first to know."

It turns out I had not done sufficient research on the Dempster. When Don Kime sent me the ferry schedule and it looked like we would be arriving a week or two after the normal opening date, I figured all was well. Heck, I didn't even know there were two ferries. Our ride for today was going to end at about 4:00 p.m.

Two More Adventurers. As fate would have it, there were two other adventurers hanging around the hotel: Harry Farthing and Steven Kurowski.

Steven is standing next to his bicycle. Yes, bicycle! Steven had an uncle and a high school classmate who both died of cancer.

Chapter 12

Even though he was overweight and out of shape, Steven decided he would ride his bicycle across Canada in an attempt to raise one million dollars for cancer research. Steven was quoted in the *Dawson Creek Daily News* as saying, "My uncle's battle took him piece by piece. My friend, on the other hand, went to the doctor one day and found out he had terminal cancer and died very quickly." Steven himself found out that he is in a pre-cancer stage of colon cancer. He doesn't have cancer yet, but has to monitor his condition.

Eagle Plains
Alan Leduc, Tim Yow, Harry Farthing, Steven Kurowski

Steven rides several hours a day, only stopping for short power-rests, to have a coffee, eat, and sleep. His trip started in Vancouver, and the first phase of his trip ended in October, 2011 in Quebec where he planned to stay for the winter. At the time this was written, Steven planned to start riding again in the Spring and complete the trip by riding to St. John's Newfoundland, which will take another four months.

Harry is an accomplished mountaineer and former managing partner of Cushman & Wakefield, a global real estate company. Harry climbed to the peaks of Kilimanjaro and Mount Denali,

Northern Bay by Bay Part I

and in 2006, he nearly peaked Mount Everest. Harry had spent six years planning his attempt of the world's highest peak, but at the balcony (8,500 meters), he was dealing with concerns about repeat frostbite in his fingers and feet, and decided he didn't have enough strength left to ensure a safe descent.

> I have given it absolutely everything I have got. After 12 trips through the Khumbu Icefall, around 200 ladder crossings, and four round trips on the mountain to 6,100 meters, 6,400 meters, 7,000 meters and 8,500 meters, I can at least say I have climbed Mount Everest, even if I didn't summit. I am alive, well, and still have ten fingers and toes. The summit was always the bonus.

Like Steven, Harry used his endeavors for charity. He made many of his climbs for his company's charity, Schools Around the World. Harry, a Brit with an American wife and daughter, recently moved to North Carolina and was riding his motorcycle to Alaska where he would once again visit Denali, this time to reminisce and not climb.

Since we were stranded and it was early afternoon, the four of us struck up a conversation in the hotel lounge. Steven's and Harry's reactions were similar to those of the gentleman I talked to on the ferry to Victoria Island. He had sailed a boat to Fiji but thought riding 800 miles a day on a motorcycle seemed dangerous. We all were enamored by each other's challenges.

As our discussion went through dinner we came to realize that while each of our challenges was uniquely different, we approached them the same. Tim and I had a daily goal, but made decisions one tank of gas at a time. Steven had developed an itinerary and simply focused on making it to his next stop. Harry's focus was one portion of the mountain at a time and, as the climb neared the end, one step at a time. We realized that we had more in common than we had differences.

Chapter 12

Day 21
Eagle Plains, Yukon to Inuvik, Northwest Territories
229 Miles

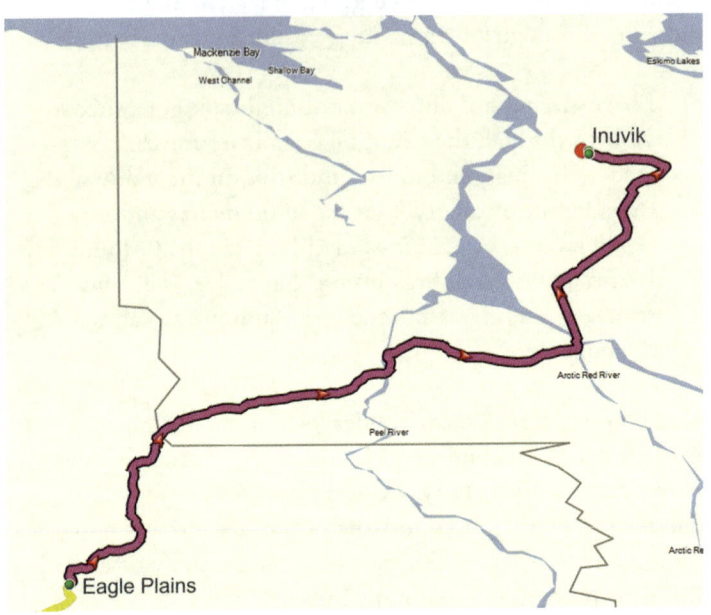

The next morning after breakfast we waited for word about the ferry. We were told the hotel would be first to know, but nobody seemed to know anything. Around 11:30 a.m., there was a flurry of activity and we learned that they had received a report that the Peel Ferry was indeed open.

Harry quickly packed and left a bit ahead of us. As we left the parking lot, I took the lead, thinking Tim was right behind me and would soon take his normal spot in front. I kept looking back for Tim, but he was nowhere to be found. I finally went back and discovered he had taken a road back to a campground instead of following me to the main road. A short time later we caught up with Harry at a pull-off where he was taking pictures. He had stopped to hang his Mount Everest Flags on the sign at the Arctic Circle and asked if we had seen them. In

Northern Bay by Bay Part I

fact, we had missed the turn off and didn't even stop. Harry rode with us the rest of the way to Inuvik.

A Shock-ing Dilemma. The Peel Ferry is a cable ferry. A cable is strung across the river and the ferry is held from the strong downstream currents by the cable. Unlike other ferry crossings I had encountered, the landing was a simple sloping dirt ramp upon which the ferry gate was dropped. Entering and exiting the ferry was challenging, as the entrance was muddy with deep ruts. We made the crossing with no worries and then started for our next boat, the Mackenzie Ferry.

The road between the Peel Ferry and Mackenzie Ferry was the most difficult part of the Dempster Highway. There was deep loose gravel and, since there had been little traffic, the tracks were poorly defined and narrow. The Mackenzie Ferry did not have a cable and drifted significantly downstream and then powered upstream to the landing. It was fascinating to watch the control by the captain.

After the Mackenzie ferry, the rest of the Dempster Highway was in good condition. We arrived in Inuvik at about 7:30 p.m. We had taken roughly 8 hours to travel the 230 miles of gravel from Eagle Plains, averaging slightly less than 30 miles per hour, including the ferry crossings.

We crossed town to fill up with gas. After I paid and was returning to my bike, I noticed oil under the bike. Crap!!! Did I bust my engine case? I leveled the bike and checked the oil through the sight glass and it was okay. I continued to investigate and noticed the oil was dripping further back on the bike. My shock absorber was leaking! As I looked closer, I could see oil was spewing out of the top of the shock. Figuring there was nothing I could do so late at night, we decided to ride back through town and get a room at the hotel. By the time we got to the hotel the shock was completely gone and I was simply riding on a spring.

Chapter 12

The hotel didn't have any double rooms so we all got single rooms, which worked out well since I would be up most of the night emailing my friends for advice and trying to determine my options. One thing I knew for sure was that I was not going to attempt the 500 mile ride back on the Dempster without a shock. I was already dealing with the carburetor issue, and there were some steep grades with tight turns and I didn't think my skills were up to dealing with a bouncing rear end under those conditions.

I had purchased, just for this trip, an aftermarket shock advertised as "a proven, high quality solution for the KLR 650 whether you are a long-distance traveler or a hard core Dual-Sport rider." I had ridden slightly over 10,000 miles and had only used the shock for 18 days before it gave out. While about 1,200 miles had been on gravel, the gravel was not nearly as difficult as what I had experienced on previous rides. For comparison, Tim's bike had a stock shock with 40,000 miles on it. You can imagine how frustrated I was.

I examined my options, none of which seemed very attractive:

- Most of my friends felt that successfully rebuilding the shock was very unlikely.
- Being in Inuvik, anything shipped from the U.S. would have to clear customs and go through Edmonton and Whitehorse. There was a postal strike that was affecting all shipping companies and most seemed to think it would take 8-12 days for an overnight shipment. The manufacturer of the shock said they would ship a shock, but this would leave me stuck in Inuvik for 8-12 days at $150 per night for hotel and would jeopardize our ride.
- Neil Ward, a Canadian, agreed to ship me his shock, which would avoid customs, but with the postal strike there was no reasonable guarantee for delivery.

- I might be able to fly to Glennallen, Alaska and borrow Jack Gustafson's shock or might be able to hire a bush pilot to fly it to me.
- I might be able to rent a car and drive back toward Glennallen and meet Jack part way.
- I posted on several forums hoping to find someone in Inuvik who might be able to help.
- My friend Tom Southwood who lives about 50 miles from my home in Indiana even volunteered to go to my home and get my stock shock and ride it up to me.

Day 22
Inuvik, Northwest Territories
0 Miles

I decided the best option was flying to Glennallen to get Jack's shock or have someone fly it to me, but we could not find a way to make this happen. So I started to check on rental cars. I would need about 3 days and the cost of the rental car was going to be about $1500. It was going to be expensive, but at least it was an option. The people who had the rental car also ran the Arctic Chalet and had rooms available – plus they had tools and a place where I could work on the bike. The owner of Cogent Dynamics, the company who made my custom shock, said I might be able to rebuild the shock, so I decided that I would take a chance and see what I was up against. We moved from our current hotel to the Arctic Chalet. Harry was planning to take an air tour to Tuktoyaktuk so he moved with us.

Help in an Unexpected Place. I had emailed Cogent Dynamics around midnight, asking them to send me pictures and instructions on how to rebuild the shock. Since it was Sunday, I figured I wouldn't get an answer until Monday and decided to go ahead and remove the shock, since I would have to do this anyway.

Chapter 12

Alan's KLR Shock Rebuild
Photo by Harry Farthing

The work space was a pole barn with a gravel floor. The owner, Olav Falsnes, helped me move a piece of steel from the back of the barn to lay on the floor in case I dropped a bolt or nut, and provided a floor jack to raise the bike. I used my ratchet straps to tie down the front end, providing three-point stability, and the bike seemed to be pretty solid. To remove the shock, I had to remove the rear seat and rear wheel, which left the bike looking pretty sickly.

 I had not yet gotten any instructions from Cogent Dynamics, but it was obvious that I had to first remove the spring from the shock. I tried everything I could think of with no success. Olav said that he thought he knew somebody who could help:

Northern Bay by Bay Part I

"The Midnight Mechanic." This guy had been recommended to me at that gas station and had already refused to help me. However, the Midnight Mechanic did a lot of work for Olav and Olav thought that if we went over to his shop he might help. The guy was very independent and was in a bad mood because he was in the middle of a feud with another resident who wanted to borrow and not rent an engine lift.

After some discussion, the Midnight Mechanic agreed to help get the spring off of my shock. He and another guy, who was hanging around, used two pairs of channel lock pliers to remove the spring. The guy who was helping knew about carburetors and agreed to come by Olav's later in the evening to look at my carburetor. When we got back in the car, Olav told me he wasn't thrilled about the guy coming to his place as he had a bad reputation and it was important that I not leave him alone. The carburetor guy came over that night and showed me how to remove the carburetor. After a bit of investigation, we found a piece of debris in the main pickup.

Cogent Dynamics is in North Carolina and I was in Inuvik, North West Territories; therefore, Cogent Dynamics was three hours ahead in time. Cogent Dynamics sent me an email about 9:00 a.m. their time on Sunday morning; it was already noon, Inuvik time. They told me to check the shock's seal head to see if it had come loose. It seemed, by this message, that this must be a known problem. Sure enough, the cap had backed off about 3 threads. Unfortunately, they did not respond with the rebuild instructions and pictures I had requested, so I had to ask again and remain in waiting mode.

I received another email from Cogent Dynamics about 3:00 p.m. their time telling me that the shock was repairable and warning me that "terrible things could happen" if I didn't carefully let the gas out of the shock – it was under 150 psi of pressure in the cylinder. I cautiously removed the plug on the side of the shock that was supposed to hold gas, but there was no gas in the shock. Again, there were no detailed instructions or pictures on how to do the rebuild, so I made a third request.

At 11:00 p.m. Inuvik time, I received an email with some brief instructions regarding procedures for refilling the shock with oil and the pressure requirements for the nitrogen. However, no pictures were supplied.

When I disassembled the shock, I counted threads so I would know where to reset the preload and with this information decided to go ahead and try to rebuild it. Once I tore into the shock, I discovered that it looked like one o-ring had blown out, and that one was cut. I would have to wait until the next day to get a response back regarding the o-ring sizes. It was now 4:00 a.m. and I had wasted the whole day waiting for instructions.

Day 23
Inuvik, Northwest Territories
0 Miles

Not knowing when I might get a response, I went into town and hit all of the automotive, industrial supply, ATV, boat, and hardware stores looking for o-rings that might fit, with no success. I also could not find fork oil, so I would have to use automatic transmission fluid.

Around 1:00 p.m. Inuvik time, I finally got answers to clarify questions I had regarding instructions, but still no pictures. I decided I would go ahead and try the rebuild. I went to town and bought some McPherson strut compressors and other specialty tools that I thought would help, at a cost of $180.00 – nothing in Inuvik is cheap.

Arctic Tour. Harry had convinced us that since we were stuck, we should take the Tuktoyaktuk tour, so both Tim and I made arrangements to go with Harry on the $400 tour. We were supposed to leave at noon, but the weather was bad and the tour had been postponed hour by hour. I spent this time

Northern Bay by Bay Part I

modifying the strut compression tool so it would work with my spring, and making a spanner wrench to make sure I could get the cap tight.

I had a problem in that I could not find suitable replacement o-rings. The seal cap had two o-ring grooves, and I had originally thought that the top one must have blown out. However, Cogent Dynamics advised that they had redesigned the shock with the smaller o-ring toward the bottom and did not use the top o-ring groove any longer. I asked about using both o-rings and they provided some rationale about building up pressure between the o-rings that didn't make sense to either Olav or me, so we decided that we would put in both o-rings. If the bottom o-ring is doing its job, it makes no sense that there would be any pressure between the two and it seemed this would be a good back-up, particularly since the bottom o-ring had to pass over sharp threads and it seemed that this was likely why the o-ring was cut.

Olav's wife Judi was arranging the tour and said that we needed to leave, so I had to wait until we got back to see if the rebuild would work. A father and son joined us for the tour, making a total of five of us.

There are only two ways to get to Tuktoyaktuk: by air and, during the winter, by ice road. We took a small plane, which flew up the delta. We were surprised to see that there were several cabins along the river. The tundra was water soaked with many small shallow ponds from the thaw. As we got closer to the Arctic Ocean, we began to see more snow.

When we arrived at the Tuktoyaktuk airport we were greeted by our tour guide who was a native. Tuktoyaktuk is best described as a village filled with small cabins or shacks. In addition to learning about the native culture, we had some great sightseeing moments.

Chapter 12

Tim Yow, Alan Leduc, and Harry Farthing

The community had an icehouse built some 20 feet below the permafrost. This was used as a year-round freezer and each family had a storage room for food. We were able to climb down into and walk through the icehouse. We were also able to walk right out onto the frozen Arctic Ocean. Due to restrictions, we didn't get to the Arctic Ocean while in Prudhoe Bay so this was a real treat and one particularly enjoyed by Harry. He had brought a flask and enjoyed a toast as he took in the view.

Tuktoyaktuk means caribou and the natives spend most of the winter hunting, returning to the town during the summer where they fish. They are one of the few native tribes that are allowed to hunt whale and they find a use for every part of it.

During the 1950s, the U.S. built radar domes along the coast to monitor air traffic and detect possible Soviet intrusions during the Cold War. The domes, which we were able to view from a distance, are no longer manned, but are monitored by camera and audio. In the 1970s the oil companies expanded, constructing various facilities in the area. But many of these large buildings are now vacant too, as the oil companies found other areas where exploration was cheaper. In 1995, the Molson

Northern Bay by Bay Part I

Brewing Company arranged for several popular rock bands to give a concert in Tuktoyaktuk as a publicity stunt to promote their new ice-brewed beer. The publicity campaign was dubbed The Molson Ice Polar Beach Party, and featured Metallica. Now all that is left is the village and the abandoned buildings.

Tuktoyayktuk Arctic Ocean
Photo by Harry Farthing

Natural features in the area are called pingos, conical shaped mounds formed by the freezing and thawing of lakes in the permafrost. We climbed up one of them to get a good overlook of the city. We also saw the same pingos that are displayed in the promotional materials on our return flight.

It was past dinner time when we returned from the tour. Tim and Harry went to dinner and I went back to work. Olav is an aeronautical engineer and a licensed aircraft mechanic. He had a large box of miscellaneous o-rings which was like searching for a needle in a haystack, but we finally found a large and small one that we thought would work.

Shock Rebuild. With some more grinding, I finally got the McPherson strut compressors to work on my shock's spring and completed the spanner wrench needed to tighten the seal cap. Fortunately, Olav had grinders, a drill press, and miscellaneous pieces of steel for me to use.

Chapter 12

We filled the shock with ATF, using the procedure provided by Cogent Dynamics, then installed the two o-rings on the seal and tightened the cap. We installed the spring and then it was time to pressurize the other end with 150 psi of nitrogen. Olav had a dive tank containing nitrogen and also had a hypodermic needle with a grease fitting. We had to figure out some way to connect the grease fitting to the hose from the nitrogen tank.

Olav found some plastic hose and used wire to safety tie the needle to the hose. I was holding the needle in the shock and Olav was watching the gauge, ready to turn it off as soon as it hit 150 psi. POP! The hose exploded in my hand and I jumped back. Olav then found a nylon reinforced rubber hose and safety-tied it to the hose from the nitrogen tank. POP! I again jumped back as the force of the hose exploding in my hand was downright scary. Olav said to me, "You know, if you had pulled the needle out, we would have some pressure on the shock."

I made Olav smile when I replied, "You are exactly right, Olav. However, I was about two feet off the ground each time and didn't have much leverage."

We found a hydraulic hose and were finally successful in getting the nitrogen into the shock. It was now after midnight for the third night in a row and I decided, rather than install the shock, I would go to bed and check the shock in the morning. I was concerned about a later failure and sent an email to Cogent Dynamics asking them to send two spare o-rings to a location in Edmonton where I was planning a stop.

The Arctic Chalet was not a bad place to be stuck for two days:

- Olav was knowledgeable and helped me think through the process of rebuilding the shock.
- I had a place to work and the tools necessary to do the job.
- The atmosphere was amazing.

Northern Bay by Bay Part I

Judi and Olav have Siberian and Malamute white husky dog sled teams. Our room overlooked the kennel and a lake beyond. There was a canoe, but I didn't have time to go out on the lake. I did help push Harry off and it looked like so much fun. Olav had built his own geothermal system and there were several kilometers of pipe under the lake that was used for heating in the winter.

We were able to feed the dogs and watch as they were taken on runs and summer pulls using the ATV.

Arctic Chalet White Husky Kennel
Photograph by Harry Falling

Day 24
Inuvik, Northwest Territories to Dawson City, Yukon
480 Miles

I got up early and inspected the shock. It appeared to be retaining oil and gas so I started the reinstall procedure.

Tim had some time to think while we were at the Arctic Chalet and had dreamed up a Circle to Circle Iron Butt Association ride –Prudhoe Bay, Alaska to Inuvik, Northwest Territories or vice versa. We had talked to Harry about this ride and kidded him that if he did the documentation and got the witness

Chapter 12

forms, he might be the first one to complete the ride from Inuvik to Prudhoe Bay. Harry's original plan was to stop at Eagle Plains on the way back, but as he was preparing to leave, he was talking about riding all of the way to Dawson City and then maybe doing the Circle to Circle ride. We didn't really believe he would do it, but we got some enjoyment from our enabling of Harry with regard to long-distance riding.

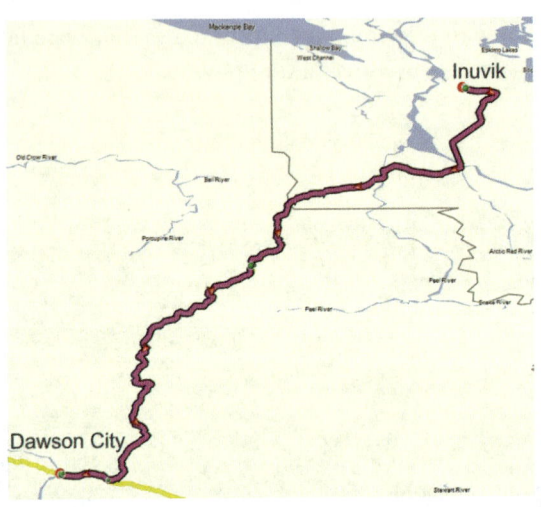

I finished the install about 12:30 p.m. and thought I should check my email before leaving. I had a message from Cogent Dynamics that said, "I can get the o-rings in the mail, but I understand that there may be significant customs charges. What do you want me to do?" I was pissed! My custom shock had failed after 18 days and 10,000 miles. They expected me to stay in Inuvik for a week or two waiting to receive a replacement shock and they wouldn't or couldn't provide detailed instructions to rebuild it. Meanwhile, I had to learn on my own how to rebuild the shock, but they couldn't get two o-rings shipped from North Carolina to Edmonton? I replied with a short message, "Forget it."

Olav had indicated that he was appreciative of the opportunity to help me and actually seemed to enjoy the challenge, so I thought it might be insulting to offer him money. I thought I would send him a gift when I got home. However, when I checked out, Judi said that I had consumed a lot of Olav's time (I actually hadn't) and that I should pay for it. I gave her an additional $300 for Olav and the use of the space. The failed shock had cost $180 for tools, $300 for an extra two nights' stay, and $300 for Olav. I was out about $780 plus the cost of food. But the stress and the bumps from lying on a gravel floor for two days, along with jeopardizing some of the sub-component Iron Butt rides we were trying to accomplish, were priceless.

Fire! We left the Arctic Chalet about 1:00 p.m. We had only traveled about 20 miles when a car going the other way flagged us down. He said there was a forest fire ahead and the road was closed. Tim and I discussed what to do and I recommended that we go ahead. If the road was closed, we could get more information and it might be that they would actually let us go through.

As we approached the fire, it was burning wildly, but the wind was taking the smoke away from the road. We were stopped by a fireman, but he said he would provide an escort through the fire. Even though the fire was burning right next to the road, we didn't feel any danger. Whew, we dodged that bullet! We could have lost yet another day.

We arrived at Eagle Plains at about 7:00 p.m. Tim was ready to call it a day and I wanted to push on. I told Tim that since Harry's bike was not there, it was obvious that we had enabled him and he had ridden all the way to Dawson City. It was just wrong to talk him into doing something we were not willing to do ourselves. We decided to continue on to Dawson City.

Going north on the Dempster Highway, we had encountered a mountainside called Elephant Rock because it looks like the head of an elephant with a trunk. Heading south from Eagle Plains, I saw a mountain and it seemed to clearly have the face of a man on it. The image was so clear it was distracting. I couldn't seem to take my eyes off of it. I could clearly see the

Chapter 12

round shape of a face with hair at the top, an ear, two eyes, a nose, and a mouth. There was no sign marking the formation, so I simply called it Face Mountain.

Face Mountain
Photo by Harry Farthing

It was raining lightly and we saw double rainbows. What was more amazing was the rainbows seemed to be translucent and they formed color over the face of the mountain. It was something I had never seen before and was simply a beautiful site.

I'm sure Tim was frustrated that I had pushed us on, as we didn't get back to the Downtown Hotel until 1:30 a.m. I told Tim he could sleep in and we would leave when he was ready the next morning.

13

Passion in the Wind
Northern Bay by Bay Part II

I was *excited to hear the story about our newly long-distance-enabled friend, shocked when I learned he had crashed, and surprised to learn that the crash had not squelched his spirit. We rode to the top of a dome, and ate a cinnamon roll as big as a hubcap. Variety is the spice of life and we had plenty: the beauty of Muncho Lake; herding buffalo by motorcycle; riding the worst road in Canada; taking a long detour; being treated like celebrities at our maintenance stop; and enjoying some time with our friends.*

The next morning I was glad to see that Harry's bike was still parked on the street. I went to the front desk and called his room but got no answer. I checked the dining room and then went outside to leave a note on his bike before returning to the dining room for breakfast. I didn't want to miss seeing Harry and hearing about his decision to ride straight through from Inuvik to Dawson City.

Harry found me shortly afterward and joined me for breakfast. I told him that I noticed his bike wasn't in Eagle Plains and how I had shamed Tim into riding till the early morning to get to Dawson City late last night.

Harry said, "I really get it now. I set my sights on Dawson City and was determined to make it all the way."

Chapter 13

Then he told me that he had crashed between the Mackenzie and Peel ferries. This section of the road had a narrow tire track and loose gravel. Harry was running street tires on his BMW GS Adventure and had gotten out of a track, causing his front wheel to wash out and resulting in a low side crash. He came off the bike, but was just a little banged up. His bike had slid all the way off the road and several feet down the bank, lodging itself upright in the willows lining the road. Fortunately for Harry, a passing truck and two other riders stopped to help.

One of the riders was Australian, while Harry is British. During the 18th and 19th centuries the British sent many convicts to Australian penal colonies. The connection between the British and Australians is undeniable, and is sometimes the source of some good-natured ethnic humor. The Aussie rider said, "I have to get a picture of an Aussie helping a Brit get his bike out of the ditch. Wait until I post this on Adventure Rider!"

Harry shot back, "What are the odds of me getting saved by an Aussie on a KTM? That picture better not show up until I get home to tell my wife!"

Even in the seriousness of the situation, they were having fun with each other. With the help of the truck driver, they were able to get Harry's bike out of the ditch. The willows which had caught the bike minimized the damage.

I said, "I assume that ends your plans for riding to Prudhoe Bay."

"Likely," Harry said. "But I haven't completely ruled it out."

Tim joined us about the time "Dawson Dick," the former owner of the Downtown Hotel and host of the Dust 2 Dawson motorcycle ride, walked in. Harry was interested in that ride, so Dick joined us for a few minutes to chat.

I couldn't help but feel some joy in Harry's attitude and his still considering Prudhoe Bay after the crash. He was a true adventurer.

Northern Bay by Bay Part II
Circle to Circle Insanity Gold
Prudhoe Bay, Alaska to Inuvik, Northwest Territories
1,370 Miles

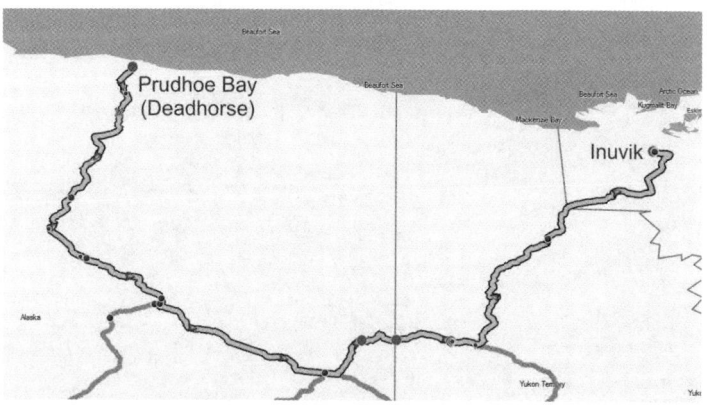

Tim and I had left Prudhoe Bay at 7:29 a.m. AKDT (11:29 a.m. EDT) on Wednesday, June 1, 2011, arriving in Inuvik at 7:33 p.m. PDT (10:33 p.m. EDT) on Saturday, June 4, 2011. It had taken us 3 days, 11 hours, 4 minutes (83 hours, 4 minutes) to complete the ride.

Of the 1,370 miles for this ride, there was about 530 miles of pavement and 840 miles of gravel. Using our established criteria of 300 miles per day for gravel and 1,000 miles per day for pavement, the Circle to Circle Insanity ride would have a required completion time of 79 hours, 55 minutes and has a recommended time of 80 hours. Our stop in Eagle Plains waiting on the ferry had prevented us from meeting the criteria for this ride.

The **Circle to Circle Insanity Gold,** using the criteria of 500 miles per day for gravel and 1,000 miles per day for pavement, would result in a required completion time of 53 hours, 12 minutes and has a recommended time of **55 hours.**

Chapter 13

Day 25
Dawson City to Watson Lake, Yukon
597 Miles

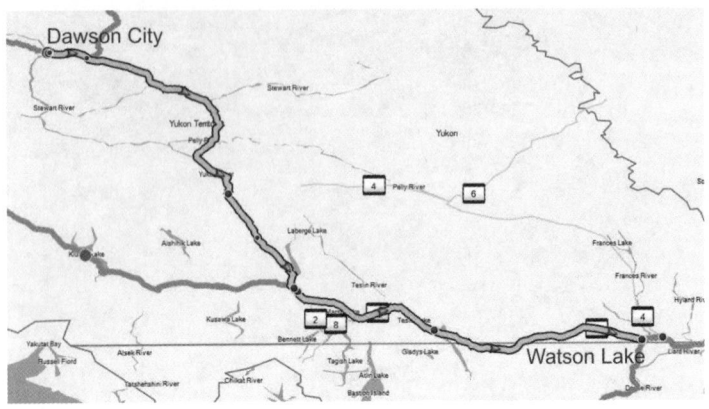

Heading to the Dome. We said our goodbyes and best wishes to Harry, packed up, and headed to the gas station. It was nearly 11:00 a.m., but Tim had gotten some much needed rest and we had a great time chatting with our friend of only a few days.

Tim had suggested we ride the Dome Road, which is just outside Dawson City. It is a five mile long road to the top of the 2900-foot Midnight Dome where people have gathered for decades to view the midnight sun. The top of the Dome overlooks Dawson City and provides a panoramic view of the confluence of the Yukon and Klondike rivers.

There is a hiking trail up to the dome and we met a couple that appeared to be in their 50's who had hiked the trail all the way to the top. It was quite steep and their exhaustion showed how rigorous the trail must have been. We exchanged cameras and took pictures documenting our respective experiences.

Northern Bay by Bay Part II

**Dawson City Midnight Dome
Alan Leduc and Tim Yow**

Giant Cinnamon Rolls. From the Dome we headed south and east along the Klondike Highway about 330 miles where we would intersect the Trans-Canadian Highway – Highway 1. We stopped for gas at Carmacks a little after 4:00 p.m. and about 45 miles later stopped at Braeburn Lodge home of the giant cinnamon rolls.

Steve Watson, the proprietor, was sitting at a table, about half asleep and half watching television, when we walked in. There was nobody else in the lodge. We went to the counter and picked up a roll and Steve just sat there. We finally asked if we could get some coffee and he got up and prepared our coffee and collected our money and then went back to his table. We tried to strike up a conversation, but Steve just was not interested. When Tim and I left, we both commented about Steve's grumpy disposition. At least the cinnamon roll was worth the stop.

Chapter 13

Steve Watson – Braeburn Lodge
Photo by KARO Enterprises

Tim saw a couple of porcupines on the Dempster Highway. Since I'm usually trailing behind, he often scares away the wildlife and I miss them. However, today I saw my first porcupine as it wandered across the road in front of me. What an ugly dude. He waddled along and didn't seem to care that I was there.

We made a quick stop in Whitehorse at about 6:30 p.m. for gas and then proceeded to the Teslin Yukon Inn. While I was paying for my gas, I noticed a lady waving at me. It was a woman I had chatted with back in Dawson City. She was traveling with her mother, and I had told her about the giant cinnamon rolls at Braeburn Lodge. I went over to the table where they were eating dinner and she thanked me for the tip on the cinnamon rolls. I told her that if she had not yet been to the taxidermy museum across the parking lot, she should be sure to go.

Northern Bay by Bay Part II

Taxidermy Museum – Teslin, Yukon

It was about 9:00 p.m. when we got to Teslin. Tim and I had not stopped at the museum on Day 12 when we were traveling through going in the other direction, so we took a few minutes to visit. Tim was glad we did. The taxidermy museum is a series of displays with the animals in their natural settings. The wolves chasing after the moose is one of my favorites.

We once again had the opportunity to cross the 2000 foot long grated Nisutlin Bay Bridge, this time with knobby tires. I had learned that speed was my friend and just cranked it up, crossing the misaligned grates with only a mild feeling of angst.

We stopped for the night about fifteen minutes to midnight at the Beaver Lodge just west of the junction with the Cassiar Highway, and about 12 miles west of Watson Lake. We got the last two sleeping rooms – a trailer with small rooms slightly bigger than a bed. There was so little room it was difficult to sit on the edge of the bed and remove my riding pants because my feet hit the wall. It was my night to pay and I paid $80 each

Chapter 13

for the two rooms. I thought I had negotiated two spaghetti dinners to be included in the price of the rooms. At such a late hour, Tim and I were relieved that we were going to get some real food, as all we had eaten this day was the giant cinnamon roll. The spaghetti was great, but when I went to pay for our two sodas, they charged me $35. Surprise! The spaghetti dinner wasn't part of the room rate.

Day 26
Watson Lake, Yukon to Fort Liard, Northwest Territories
429 Miles

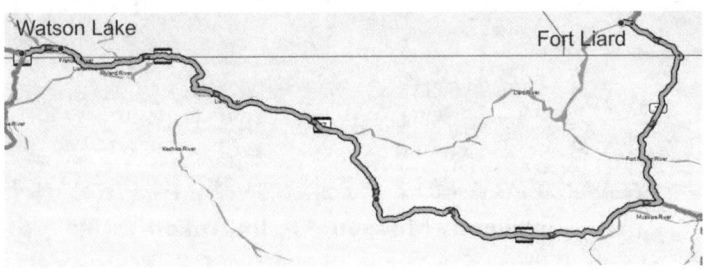

The next morning we got up and marched across the gravel lot to the washroom. We left at 7:30 a.m., stopping at Watson Lake, the home of the Sign Post Forest. We got a pretty early start, given that we hadn't gotten to bed until about 1:00 a.m.

Canada Critters. The ride from Watson Lake to Muncho Lake is among the best along the Alcan – lots of water, mountains, and curvy roads. There are also lots of animals. We saw several horses grazing along the side of the road and the customary bison in this area. Two black bear wandered across the road in front of me, giving me a startle.

My Sealine bags had come loose twice so far on this trip. This time it was Tim's turn. Fortunately I was behind him and was able to get him stopped. Tim's rear tire had already ripped his license plate loose after hitting a bump. When the bag came loose, it had pushed a stiffener for the license plate into the tire so I removed it, and we continued on our way.

Northern Bay by Bay Part II

Sign Post Forest – Watson Lake
Photo by Benjamin Tupper

I had forgotten the beauty of Muncho Lake. The color of the lake on this day was a magnificently bright aqua. We decided to eat lunch and I walked down to the lake to take in the magnificence of the view. We both had schnitzel and, even though it was very expensive, it was well worth it. When I walked down to the lake I noticed some rustic cabins and inquired about them at the front desk. To my amazement, they were only $110 for two people. Given the price of lunch and gas, I expected it to be much more. If I were coming up the Alcan, I would strongly consider this as a stop; after all, we paid $80 each for sleeping rooms the night before.

We were reminded of the danger posed by wildlife; not long after leaving Muncho Lake, we saw a dead cow moose lying along the side of the road. Lying next to the moose was a car mirror which made me wonder how the driver fared in the collision.

Stone sheep are often in the road near Stone Mountain. On a trip through this area in 2004, I mistakenly referred to them as mountain goats and was set straight by a local. On that trip, the sheep were blocking the road and we had to stop, as they

Chapter 13

just didn't seem to be afraid of us. This time, they scrambled across the road as we approached. Tim went on, but I stopped to see if I could spot them as they came up from the ditch. Wow! There were about eight of them. I enjoyed the moment as they climbed straight up the rock.

Not long after, Tim came around a blind curve to discover several more sheep scrambling across the road in front of him. I came around the curve to find Tim locking up his brakes with several sheep right near his wheels. I locked up my brakes and when I stopped, I was sitting on the crown of the road. Since my shock rebuild, I couldn't touch the ground unless the road was level. The slope of the road caused me to drop the bike, landing on the same elbow I injured in the crash on the way to Prudhoe Bay. Ouch!

When we got to the bridge on the Liard Highway, a bucket truck and a water truck were washing down the bridge. We had elected to avoid a 30 km detour to Fort Nelson for gas and now found ourselves with an hour wait on a mosquito-infested road. Much of this road is beautiful pavement, with the last 20 miles or so being loose gravel.

It was about 7:30 p.m. when we arrived at Fort Liard and the only restaurant closed at 8:00. Tim was worried about a hotel. I thought he went out to the bike, but instead, he went to get a room without ordering any food. Not knowing this, I called the hotel from the restaurant and reserved a room, telling them that we were going to eat and would be there right afterward. What we had here was a "failure to communicate." I could have saved Tim the trip if I'd known what he was doing. I ordered a burger and fries and, at 7:45 p.m., ordered the same for Tim since he wasn't back yet.

As we were eating, a Yellowknife TV crew wanted to interview us about our trip. They were doing a story about how terrible the road was between Fort Liard and Fort Simpson. We would not ride that portion of the Fort Liard Highway until tomorrow, but they did about a fifteen minute interview with us anyway.

At the hotel, we only had one bed and a roll away. I decided to sleep on the couch instead of the roll away. Fort Liard is a tiny town and looks like it would be a good place to be from – past tense.

Day 27
Fort Liard to Yellowknife, Northwest Territories
500 Miles

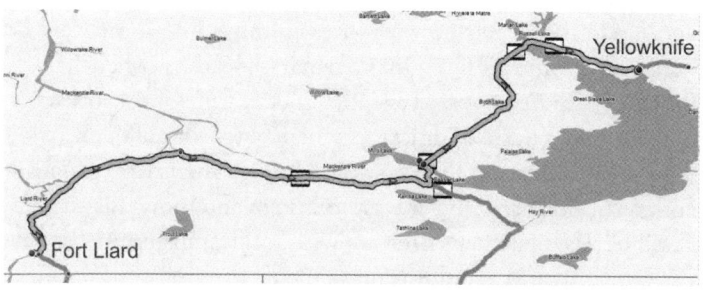

The road leaving Fort Liard was gravel. The locals told us that we would hit pavement at the turnoff to Fort Simpson, which meant only 135 miles of gravel. The TV crew had deemed this stretch of road as being the worst road in Canada. We had already ridden the Haul Road and the Dempster Highway and couldn't imagine it was as bad as they described. We were wrong and the TV crew was right! In places, the base was firm, but in others it was loose sand with gravel on top. You could not distinguish between the two conditions. In some areas the entire road was washed out with deep sandy ruts.

A Herd of Buffalo. As we were fighting to maneuver along the sandy road, we came upon a herd of about 25 buffalo, including bulls, cows, and calves. I knew we needed to be cautious when mothers with calves were near. In this case we had no way to

Chapter 13

be anything but cautious because the herd was lounging in the middle of the road and there was no way to go around.

We stopped and Tim said, "What does the book say to do about a herd of buffalo in the road?" We both laughed at the ridiculousness of the situation. After awhile, we started our bikes and Tim nudged up the right side of the road. I followed, lagging a bit behind. The lead bull saw or heard Tim and got up and started running, with the entire herd behind him. They were running right down the middle of the road at full steam (about 15 mph) with Tim and me in tail. There was no way for Tim to pass as the tail of the herd kept wandering back and forth, making it unsafe for any kind of attempt.

I remember once stopping in Canada at Head-Smashed-In Buffalo Jump near Fort Macleod, Alberta. One of the locals told me that a buffalo jump was where natives would run buffalo off a cliff and then harvest them for their winter food. Following this herd gave me more insight into how this was possible. They just kept running with reckless disregard.

Finally, the lead bull turned his head, saw Tim, and then turned immediately into the large cutaway area along the road. I had read that buffalo have an excellent sense of smell and great distance vision, but that they had almost no peripheral vision. Tim and I can attest to the almost non-existent peripheral vision.

The herd followed the bull and Tim was able to get past. I was lagging and didn't want to follow Tim until I knew he was clear. As soon as Tim passed, the buffalo herd came back onto the road in front of me and I had to repeat Tim's procedure. It was an amazing experience. We chased the herd down the road a mile or so.

We made it to the Fort Simpson turnoff and, as the locals said, we hit pavement. However, no gas was available at the intersection. It was 40 miles in and 40 miles out to get to

Northern Bay by Bay Part II

Fort Simpson. This would add at least an hour to our day and maybe two. We knew that it was almost 300 miles from Fort Liard to Fort Providence where we were sure there was gas, but this was at the limit of our gas range. Tim and I discussed it and decided to go ahead, thinking that there would likely be gas somewhere along the way.

As we turned north toward Yellowknife, we encountered more buffalo lounging in the cutaway along the side of the road, but no gas. About 20 miles from the Mackenzie Ferry crossing I ran out of gas and had to borrow some gas from Tim. We crossed on the ferry and I noticed a Shell station but Tim continued on, turning west toward town. I knew I was really close on gas but didn't want to lose Tim so I followed.

Right after turning the corner I ran out of gas again. There was a campsite across the street and I saw some campers cooking dinner. I walked over and asked if I could buy a gallon of gas. They obliged and I gave them $20.00, the most I had to pay for a gallon for gas!

Tim returned as I was putting the gas in my tank. I asked him why he didn't stop at the Shell station. He said, "There wasn't any station back there." He would find out differently, since we stopped there on our return out of Yellowknife.

Shortly after getting gas I noticed something flopping around my front tire. I pulled to the side of the road to discover that my speedometer cable had pulled out of the instrument panel. I thought that was strange, but simply removed the cable knowing that I had zeroed my GPS at the start of the trip and could use that for documentation purposes. I would find out a couple of days later when having maintenance done by a dealer that the reason the cable failed was that my front axle was loose and it had allowed the speedometer gear to spin out of its retainer. I should have been checking my bike a lot more closely!

Chapter 13

I had the crash on the way to Prudhoe Bay and had the whole back end torn apart in Inuvik to repair the shock, but had not done any work to the front end of the bike since Day 15 in Fairbanks. It seems that if the front axle was that loose I would have noticed it. Riding mostly on gravel may have camouflaged the issue. The cotter pin that fits through the axle and serves as a safety to hold the axle bolt was not installed. My recklessness in not properly inspecting the bike or perhaps the carelessness of the guys who did the work on my bike in Fairbanks could have been tragic.

We arrived in Yellowknife to discover a modern airport and a five-story hotel. We opted for a cheaper hotel and got checked in around 8:00 p.m. On the way to the hotel we spotted the Vietnamese Noodle House and decided that we would go there for dinner. The restaurant closed at 8:00 but let us in for what was an excellent meal.

Day 28
Yellowknife, NWT to Peace River, Alberta
628 Miles

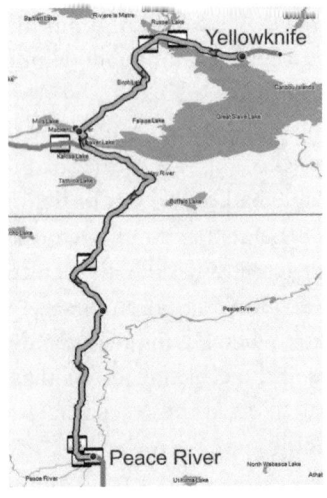

Northern Bay by Bay Part II

Both Tim and I were tired after fighting the sandy gravel on Fort Liard Highway, so we slept in and didn't get started until about 8:30 a.m. I led until we got back to the main highway leading out of town and then Tim took over. We came to a "Y" in the road and Tim turned right when I was thinking we should have turned left. Tim is always at full speed in the mornings. As I'm checking my GPS to make sure I'm not wrong, Tim is racing away. We should be going west and we are going east!

I tried to catch up to Tim but his bike was a little faster than mine and, while the road was paved, it was hilly and curvy. I could get close, but couldn't pass him. I was blowing my horn, flashing my lights, all to no avail. Once again, we encountered a situation where it might have been nice to have a two-way communication system.

I hit a stretch where I thought I had a chance to catch Tim. I was riding about 70 mph when I crested a rise and found a downward sloping, off-camber, right hand turn leading onto a wooden floored bridge. Wooden bridge floors can be very slick, so I was trying to scrub off speed while managing the downward slope and difficult curve. As I hit the bridge, I was still going about 55 mph and I noticed that on the other side of the bridge the road had turned to gravel. I thought, "Wow! I'm in trouble!"

I immediately stood on the pegs, just hoping to get through the curve without crashing. In the meantime, Tim had slowed because of the gravel and I was literally right beside him – my front wheel even with his rear wheel. He was in the right track and I was in the left. I was still fighting desperately to keep the bike under control and was too scared to blow the horn.

Tim must not have realized I was right beside him. Just as he cleared my front tire he changed tracks from the right track to the left track which I was in. He slowed as he switched tracks

Chapter 13

so I had to hit the brakes making my situation worse. I pulled to the side of the road and Tim went on, evidently not aware of what had just transpired and still not knowing that we were going the wrong direction.

From the map, it looked like the road would end and that Tim would have to come back, so I decided to wait beside the road. The mosquitoes were so bad I couldn't stand it, so after a while I continued on at a very slow pace.

After a half hour or so I saw Tim coming back. We both stopped and looked at each other.

I asked, "Tim, what does your GPS say?"

Tim replied, "It says I was going the wrong direction."

"Exactly," I replied.

We would not have enough gas to make it to Fort Providence so we had to return to Yellowknife and fill up again. Our little detour had lasted for a total of 66 miles.

We made our second attempt to leave Yellowknife at about 10:45 a.m. This time we headed the right direction and arrived in Fort Providence a little after 2:00 p.m., stopping at the Shell station we missed on the way up. In celebration of all of the buffalo we had seen, we decided to have a buffalo burger.

Our original plan was to stop at High Level, Alberta, which is 1,016 miles (1,600 kilometers) from Yorkton, Saskatchewan where we planned a maintenance stop. Our plan was to do a SaddleSore 1600 (the metric equivalent of a SaddleSore 1000, 1,000 miles in 24 hours) since neither of us had ever done one and this portion of the Trans-Canadian Highway is pretty boring. Tim decided if he was going to do it, he wanted to do it as a SaddleSore 1000 and wanted to do it on my bike so he could add to his record. We got to High Level about 8:00 p.m.

Northern Bay by Bay Part II

I didn't want to switch bikes, so we decided to continue having a shorter than 1,000 mile day the next day and forgetting about the SaddleSore.

We arrived in Peace River about 11:30 p.m. It was Tim's day to pay and we ended up stopping at three hotels before he made his selection. I was not thrilled about the hotel search; however, as we crossed the bridge each direction, the Peace River was glowing in the city lights and was beautiful. We finally stopped at a Nova Inn which was the brand of inn we stayed in the first night in Inuvik and found to be very nice.

Day 29
Peace River, Alberta to Lanigan, Saskatchewan
707 Miles

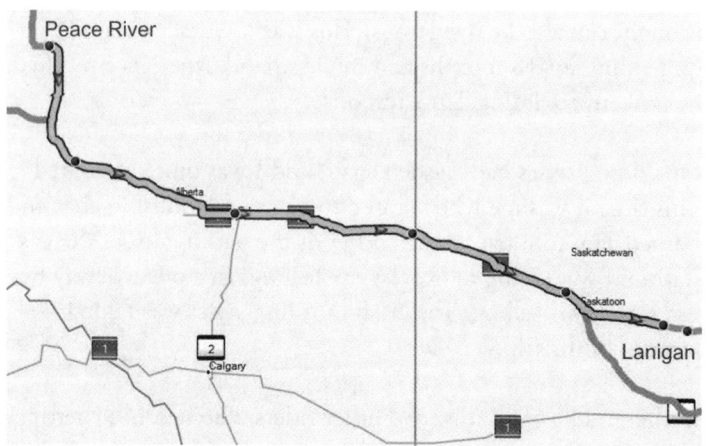

We got in late the night before and with a long day ahead of us, decided that we would take time for the continental breakfast at the hotel. We left at about 8:30 a.m. and made our first gas stop at Fox Creek a little after 11:00 a.m. We continued on to Edmonton, arriving about 2:45 p.m. Edmonton is in Leduc County and the city of Leduc is just south of Edmonton. I usually stop at the Leduc visitor's center and buy souvenirs. But we had too many miles in front of us to be distracted by a stop for souvenirs today.

Dream, Believe, and Achieve the Extraordinary

Chapter 13

We stopped for gas at Walmart in Lloydminster, Alberta at about 5:30 p.m. We only averaged about 58 mph on this leg and the Canadian speed limit on most of this road is 60 mph (100 kph). While there were a few small towns, most of this leg was wide open and I typically would have been riding 65 mph or more. Tim was dropping to 55 mph on wide open stretches. I asked him why we pushed on gravel but lollygagged on pavement and his response was always, "I'm thinking."

Many riders clear their heads while riding. However, as I learned when I crashed into my friend Bob Moore, obsessive thinking can become a distraction and lead to inattentiveness. We have all been behind someone talking on a cell phone, allowing their speed to vary because they are distracted from the task of driving. Daydreaming or dropping deep into thought can also be dangerous. This was the exact reason I had quit riding for 18 months and my firsthand experience resulted in concern regarding Tim's response.

Our riding styles had clashed again and I was quite frustrated. This time it was me who wanted to have a relationship chat and I asked Tim to move to the corner of the parking lot of the gas station. I was trying to express my feelings in a positive way but I'm sure I was yelling. The clash in riding styles was taking the fun out of the trip.

In the middle of all this, two other riders who had been getting gas rode over to the corner of the parking lot where Tim and I were talking. They were Paul Lawson and his father Mike. They had both completed the 48 Plus IBA ride (48 States plus Alaska in less than 10 days) which ended in Hyder, Alaska, at the Hyderseek 2011 event. Hyder is the southernmost point in Alaska (we had stopped there earlier in the trip) and, ever since Ron Ayers first completed the ride, it has been an annual gathering point for others completing the ride. I completed the ride in 2005.

Northern Bay by Bay Part II

Alan Leduc, Paul Lawson, and Tim Yow
Photo by Mike Lawson

Ron stopped sponsoring the Hyderseek event and Paul had assumed the responsibility of coordinating the event for 2011. Paul was on a Yamaha FJR and his dad was on a GL1800 Honda Goldwing. We chatted about their ride and our ride, took some pictures, and then they departed.

Meeting the two other riders had taken the steam out of Tim's and my relationship chat, so I told Tim, "Just do me a favor and crank it up a bit."

Our next stop was Langham, Saskatchewan, arriving at about 8:30 p.m., averaging a little over 70 mph. Maybe Tim had overreacted a bit about my comments, but I was not complaining. I would even have been happy to pay his speeding ticket.

A Sudden Weather Change. So far we had been blessed with great weather. We had only encountered light rain on a few occasions, but now were paying the price, as we were in a

Chapter 13

downpour. The road had narrowed to two lanes and it was getting dark. With the dark and the rain it was just about impossible to see. I couldn't even see the white warning line on the side of the road and had wandered onto the rumble strips a few times. Although we needed to be at Yorkton first thing tomorrow for maintenance, I was thinking it might be wise to stop for the night and get up early in the morning.

Suddenly we spotted another motorcycle on the edge of the road. Tim and I had both agreed early on that we wouldn't want a motorcycle to pass us if we were in need; therefore, we were not going to pass a fellow motorcyclist in need. We stopped. It was a young Canadian fellow riding an old Yamaha. He was not familiar with the scarcity of gas stops in these parts and had run out of gas. We gave him some of our spare gas and then led him to the next gas station. He had a helmet, but was poorly dressed for the conditions. He bravely continued on.

We were in Lanigan, Saskatchewan, about 130 miles from our maintenance stop in Yorkton. It was about 11:30 p.m. and Tim and I were both cold and tired, having fought to see through the rain for the last several miles. We found a small mom-and-pop hotel and stopped for the night.

Day 30
Lanigan, Saskatchewan to Headingly, Manitoba
400 Miles

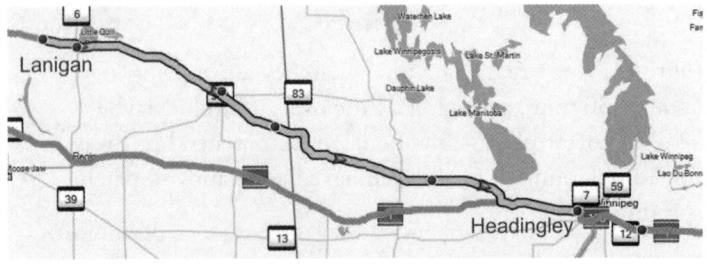

We left the hotel about 6:45 a.m. Even though we had escorted the stranded motorcyclist to the gas station the night before,

Northern Bay by Bay Part II

we had not gotten gas ourselves, so we stopped at Dafore, only 24 miles down the road. I called Schrader Motorsports and told them we were running a bit late for our maintenance appointment, but would get there as soon as we could. We arrived around 9:30 a.m. and they were waiting for us.

The folks at Schrader opened up the service bay and we started removing gear from our bikes. They showed us where the power washer was and encouraged us to wash the bikes off before they started working. They had reserved one mechanic for each bike and had instructed the other mechanics to provide support as needed. Service extraordinaire!

The shop in Fairbanks had told us we would be lucky to get 3,000 miles out of the TKC 80 knobby tires that we had selected for the gravel roads and we had gotten over 5,200 miles. My front tire was in good shape but the back was pretty well worn out. Tim and I were both installing another set of TKC 80's and would need equally good mileage to get us through the last of the gravel in Labrador. We would carry a set of Metzeler Tourance street tires on the back of the bikes in case our tires failed somewhere we could not find tires. These, we hoped, would get us to the end of our trip.

In addition to the tires, we both had the oil changed. I was relieved that my bike was not using any oil, since I had the top end of the engine rebuilt right before leaving on the trip. The mechanic was replacing the broken speedometer cable and this is when I learned that a loose front wheel had caused the speedometer to fail.

My turn signals had quit working. This was very important, as using the turn signals was the primary communication between Tim and me. The flasher was bad and had to be replaced. I also replaced the battery since it had been dead twice on mornings after I had run my electric riding gear. The total cost for the maintenance stop was $1478, which included two sets of tires, one set mounted and one set to take with me.

Chapter 13

Tim and I did not have the same maintenance philosophy. My philosophy on a trip like this is to always have the bike in such repair that I'm relatively sure that I will be able to make it to the next planned maintenance stop. Tim's philosophy is more like "I'll deal with it when it breaks." For example, Tim had been carrying the Metzeler Tourances that were taken off in Fairbanks. These rear tires only have about a 8-9,000 mile life and his had over 8,300 miles when removed. From Yorkton to the end of the trip we had about 9,500 miles to go. It was highly doubtful that the new TKC 80 plus the worn out rear Metzeler Tourance would combine for this kind of mileage. It took a lot of talking to convince Tim that he needed to buy a "new" rear Tourance tire to finish the trip.

Tim also had the impression that sprockets would last 20,000 miles plus – replacement approximately every other chain change. I explained to Tim that, from my experience, given we did not always take time to properly maintain the chain and the amount of gravel riding we had done, the chain and sprockets should both be replaced at a maximum of about 10,000 miles. I reminded Tim that he had started the trip with a new chain and sprocket and that they were worn out by the time we traveled the 8,300 miles to Fairbanks and he had to replace them. I thought we would need to change the chain and sprocket when our knobby tires wore out in about 5-6,000 miles and told Tim he should have a new chain and new sprockets so we could do this maintenance on the road if needed.

Tim's maintenance philosophy comes from his core value of frugalness, which was developed during his early years. Tim has told me several times, that although he did not live through the Great Depression, he had his own depression. He certainly had that same tendency to not waste anything. It is against his core values to waste the extra rubber left on his tires or to change a chain before it is absolutely necessary.

Northern Bay by Bay Part II

We had planned on losing a whole day for maintenance, but we had ridden about 130 miles in the morning and, because of Schrader's great service, were back on the ride by about 3:30 p.m.

Dinner with MTF Flower Sniffers. Our next goal was to be in Thunder Bay to meet the Motorcycle Tourer's Forum "Flower Sniffers" who were touring counter clockwise around Lake Superior and had a dinner stop planned at Thunder Bay. We had not filled up with gas at Yorkton so we stopped at Langenburg about 45 miles down the road. We only needed to ride a little over 700 miles to get to Thunder Bay by 6:00 p.m. the next day, so we decided to stop for dinner.

The Trans-Canadian Highway across Manitoba is usually lined with canola fields that, when in full bloom, provide a beautiful yellow glow over the horizon. I knew that canola was used to produce a vegetable oil; however, Tim had encountered a "local" on one of his earlier trips who told him the name was really an acronym for Canadian Oil Low Acid. On this trip, most of the canola fields were covered in water as Manitoba was having severe flooding.

We stopped for gas in Neepawa at about 7:30 p.m. before stopping for the night at a new Motel 6 in Headingly, a suburb just west of Winnipeg, at a little after 10:00. We had about 530 miles left to Thunder Bay.

Day 31
Headingly, Manitoba to Marathon, Ontario
638 Miles

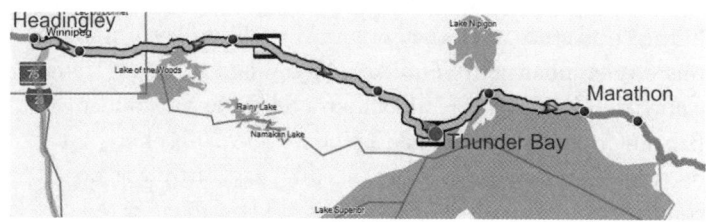

Chapter 13

A Girl and a Dog. We were on the road by about 8:00 a.m. and made our first gas stop in Richer about an hour later. We left the gas station heading north to the intersection with the Trans-Canadian Highway. Tim was in front and I was staggered in back and to his right. I noticed a young woman standing beside the road. She had just gotten out of a car and appeared to be hitchhiking. She was dressed rather oddly for a hitchhiker in that she was wearing a cropped top showing midriff, with a body a little too heavy to be shown, and high heels. She had just set down her bags and was standing between them along with a young large dog. The dog was leashed to the bag on her right.

The highway was divided so we had two lanes available to turn into going east. Tim drove across the first lane to the second in order to not disturb the dog. All of a sudden the dog started chasing Tim, dragging the bag to which it was attached. The girl then started to chase the dog in her high heels. Tim was pulling away and the dog stopped in the middle of the two lanes and the girl bent over to pick up the bag.

I decided that since the girl and the dog were in the middle of the road, I would take the inside lane. As soon as the dog saw me move, it started chasing me, which was just about the time the girl was about to grab the bag. The girl literally almost fell on her face. I looked in my mirror to see the girl chasing after the dog once again. It is not nice to laugh at others' misfortune, but the circumstances brought tears of laughter to my eyes. Tim watched all of this from his mirrors and several times during the trip he would talk about this incident, each time breaking into tears of laughter.

Our second stop for the day was in Vermillion Bay, Ontario. I was very familiar with Vermillion Bay. When I did the Trans-Canadian Gold ride – Halifax, Nova Scotia to Vancouver, British Columbia in less than 75 hours – in 2004, I arrived in Vermillion Bay late at night, needing gas. There was no convenient station on the highway and I had to enter town and ended up wandering the whole town in search of gas. As

Northern Bay by Bay Part II

Tim turned off for gas, I had a sense of déjà vu and Tim and I repeated the experience. At least it was daylight this time.

We made a short stop in Upsala a little before 4:00 p.m., arriving at Naxos Bar and Grill in Thunder Bay at about 5:15. It was great to meet with our friends from the MTF. They were elated to see us and we were glad to see them. We chatted in the parking lot before heading inside for dinner.

**Glory Elliott, Alan Leduc, Dave Hinks,
Gary Gagnon, Bill Schneider
Tim's bike in forefront, Alan's bike to rear**
Photo by Bob Elliott

Tim and I sat at opposite ends of the table so we could share with as many people as possible. It was great to talk to our old friends and meet many new friends whom we will likely have to meet several more times before we remember their names. We all had a common bond.

When we decided to join the dinner, we told Bill Schneider, the MTF Director of Flower Sniffing, to put us at the top of

Chapter 13

the order list, as we needed to keep moving. Bill not only did that but also paid for our meal!

Bill is known for giving folks that join his rides a comedic token. In true Bill fashion he said that he had consulted with Fletcher Clark and Don Norwood to determine what it took to do the kind of ride Tim and I were doing. He said the consensus was "stones." Bill presented both Tim and me with two polished stones as a token of our visit.

We left dinner while everybody else was still eating, and headed down the road, stopping in Nipigon for gas around 9:00 p.m. The views of Lake Superior as the road twisted and turned along the coast were spectacular.

There is a lot of wildlife in this area. We had already spotted a large bull moose. A car was stopped along the road watching the moose, which was at the edge of the woods alongside the road. Tim went on but I turned around and went back, stopping on the other side of the road some distance back. The moose seemed very irritated that the car was encroaching on his territory. I saw the moose start to go back into the woods and then look at the car and take a few steps toward it, staring, and then turn back toward the woods. The moose did this repeatedly. I finally went to catch up with Tim and the moose and the car were still dueling.

Concerned about the wildlife, we stopped in Marathon for the night at about 11:30 p.m. We had more than 4,900 miles before arriving in St. John's, Newfoundland to complete the **Northern Bay by Bay Adventure** ride.

14

Passion in the Wind
Northern Bay by Bay Part III

I was *really looking forward to this day. The route we would be following holds a special place in my motorcycling heart. It was along this route, crossing the top of the mighty Lake Superior, that I began to cement the foundation that would set me on a path to achieving my long-distance riding dreams. One of these dreams continues to be unfulfilled.*

In May 2003, I was beginning my third season of motorcycle riding and began to think I had the potential of being a serious long-distance motorcycle rider. I had put my eye on applying for entry in the Iron Butt Rally – 11,000 miles in 11 days – but I felt that I needed to prove to myself that I would be able to complete such an extreme ride.

The Motorcycle Tourer's Forum was offering a 50CC ride (coast to coast: Jacksonville, Florida to San Diego, California in less than 50 hours) in May 2002, and TeamStrange was offering a new ride called The Great Lakes Challenge a week later. The Great Lakes Challenge started and ended in Eau Claire, Wisconsin, with 2,450 miles around all of the Great Lakes in between. My goal was to do both rides back to back. This meant I would have to do the 50CC ending in San Diego and then ride to Eau Claire in one week to do the Great Lakes Challenge. I felt that if I could complete both of these rides, I would be worthy of applying for the Iron Butt Rally.

Chapter 14

The Iron Butt Rally is only held every other year and commonly has 2000 to 3000 riders who apply for only 100 positions. A lottery is held for those who the committee deems are qualified to participate. Getting into the rally is a combination of showing you have the ability to successfully participate and being lucky enough to be drawn in the lottery. The Iron Butt Association had authorized TeamStrange to offer a spot in the 2003 Iron Butt Rally to one lucky, randomly-selected rider who finished the Great Lake Challenge in less than 50 hours. This offering attracted many riders who wanted to enhance their opportunity to get into "The Big Ride."

When the ride was over, 48 of us had completed The Great Lakes Challenge in less than 50 hours. I did not win the lottery but was honored to be included in this group of riders, many who have since completed the Iron Butt Rally. My close friends Richard Buber, Rick Martin, and Mike Senty were among these riders.

The Great Lakes Challenge was the beginning of my acceptance into the long-distance riding community. Not only had I finished, but I was the first person to finish, completing the ride in 41 hours, 12 minutes, 44 seconds, which was a faster time than Eddie James, one of my heroes and the founder of TeamStrange, who had conceived the ride.

In 2003, I was selected to participate in the Iron Butt Rally. Unfortunately, I crashed at the end of the first day and would likely have died in the desert between Winnemucca and Gerlach, Nevada, if my friend Jason Jonas had not returned to find me and then made arrangements for a medical helicopter to pick me up and take me to the hospital. Circumstances have not allowed me to participate in other Iron Butt Rallies, so at this point, completion is an unfulfilled dream.

Most people who go across the north shore of Lake Superior either take Highway 17 along the coast or Highway 11 which is a smooth loop further north. Eddie routed all of the Great Lakes Challenge riders along a third route, Highway 129. This

Northern Bay by Bay Part III

was the route that Tim and I were going to take as part of the **Northern Bay by Bay** ride.

Day 32
Marathon to Woodstock, Ontario
753 Miles

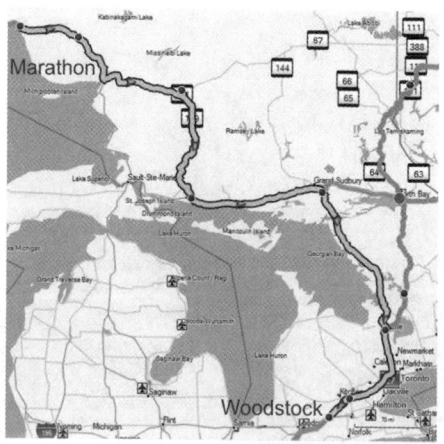

We left the hotel about 7:15 a.m., traveling along Highway 17 and stopping for gas at White River around 9:00.

About an hour later we turned onto Highway 101, entering Wawa. As you enter Wawa the first thing you see is a giant goose. Seeing the goose instantly took me back to 2002 and my Great Lakes Challenge ride. It was such a good feeling.

I told Tim it was important that we stop at Chapleau for gas. This would require about a 12 mile in and out detour, but during my 2002 Great Lakes Challenge experience I nearly ran out of gas on this stretch of the road. Eddie James had a checkpoint at a gas station along Highway 129 where we had to write down the price on the gas pump. He told us that even though this was a gas station, they would not sell us gas. When we arrived at the checkpoint, we found out the reason they wouldn't sell us gas was that the station had burned down. I thought that Eddie had said, while they won't sell you gas,

Chapter 14

there is other gas in the area. I bypassed Chapleau and nearly ran out of gas. Tim and I stopped at Chapleau around noon and I couldn't resist getting a donut at the Miss Muggin's Donut shop that was housed in the gas station.

Wawa Goose

As we turned back onto Highway 129, I reflected on my Great Lakes Challenge experience and my friend Eddie James who was killed in an accident doing what he loved – riding. Eddie's death was a shock. While traveling in the HOV lane in Atlanta, a van had a flat tire and, while there was room to pull to the side of road, the driver of the van decided to stop in the middle of the road in a blind curve. Eddie came around the curve and attempted to take evasive action, but hit the van and was killed. Highway 129 brought back both my light and dark memories of Eddie.

Riding Highway 129 during the Great Lakes Challenge was also the first time I saw a moose. I was riding along the river and looked to my right to see a large bull moose walking right beside me. The moose was standing in a ditch and his head

Northern Bay by Bay Part III

was about even with my head. It startled me and I quickly accelerated to get away, but it is an image that is burned into my mind for life.

I'm not sure that this stretch of Highway 129 is as spectacular in real life as it is in my mind due to the fond memories that I have from the Great Lakes Challenge. Every time I meet Richard Buber and Rick Martin, we are sure to strike up a conversation about our memory of our ride and Eddie James. Whether only spectacular in my mind or for real, it is a great motorcycling road and during our **Bay by Bay** ride it had recently been paved, making it even better. We stopped for gas at about 2:30 p.m. at Iron Bridge and Tim commented about how much he had enjoyed the ride.

From Iron Bridge we traveled along Highway 17 to Sudbury, stopping for gas around 5:30 p.m. From Sudbury to North Bay is about 80 miles. While North Bay is a mandatory stop for the **35 Bay by Bay Adventure**, we first had to travel to Point Pelee, the southernmost point in Canada and another mandatory stop. This meant that we had to travel 856 miles instead of 80 miles to get to North Bay. Worse, we would have to go through Toronto city traffic both on the way to Point Pelee and back to North Bay.

We had made arrangements to meet our friend Don Kime at Point Pelee for lunch. Tim's son lives near Detroit, so he called Timmy and invited him to meet us as well.

We stopped at Barrie about 9:00 p.m. for gas with the goal of getting through Toronto and stopping at Kitchener for the night. Our friends Jim Gordon and Francine Laliberte live in Kitchener and we wanted to try to arrange meeting them for breakfast. Unfortunately for us, the university was having a graduation and all of the hotels were sold out, so we ended up staying down the road, arriving at Woodstock around 11:00 p.m. I didn't attend the Woodstock festival when I was young,

Chapter 14

so I guess I would have to settle for a short night at the Tulip Motel in Woodstock, Ontario.

**Day 33
Woodstock to North Bay, Ontario
564 Miles**

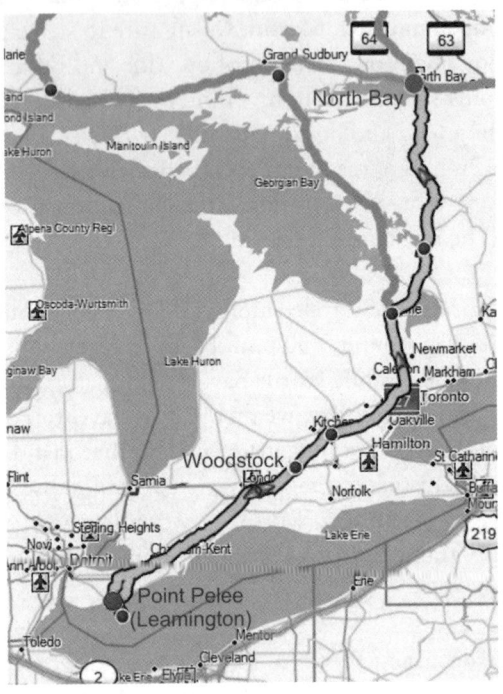

The next morning, our friend and fellow KLR rider Neil Ward was in the parking lot as we left our room. He noticed from our satellite tracker that we were close to his home and decided to stop in for a parking lot chat. Unbeknownst to us, Jim Gordon was also on his way from Kitchener, but missed us.

We got to Point Pelee National Park at about 1:45 p.m. We rode back as far as we could, but to get to the point itself we would have to walk. We decided that we should get to the restaurant to meet Don and Timmy instead. As we were leaving, we stopped to get a picture and one of the security officers volunteered to take the picture for us.

Tim Yow and Alan Leduc at Point Pelee

My previous memory of Point Pelee was a family vacation through Detroit and Windsor, and a stay in Leamington. The hotel had an indoor swimming pool with a slide. The water was very shallow and the slide was only four or five steps high. My wife Brenda is terribly afraid of water, but the kids and I convinced her that if she went down the slide, we would catch her. Of course we didn't – she flew off the slide and went under water. Both the kids and I were in serious trouble for the rest of the trip, which included taking the ferry ride from Point Pelee to Pelee Island and then to Toledo.

Tim and I had lunch with Don and Timmy. Tim's wife Patty had considered making it to the lunch but decided against it. It was a good visit with familiar faces. Don had brought replacement parts for my speedometer since the temporary repair in Saskatchewan had not held up.

Chapter 14

We filled up with gas at about 2:30 p.m. and headed back north toward North Bay to finish the long "Y" detour to Point Pelee. We stopped for gas in Cambridge and Gravenhurst, getting into North Bay around 10:30 p.m. A sports bar was open next door to our Travel Lodge so we went there to have something to eat before going to bed.

Day 34
North Bay, Ontario to James Bay, Quebec
591 Miles

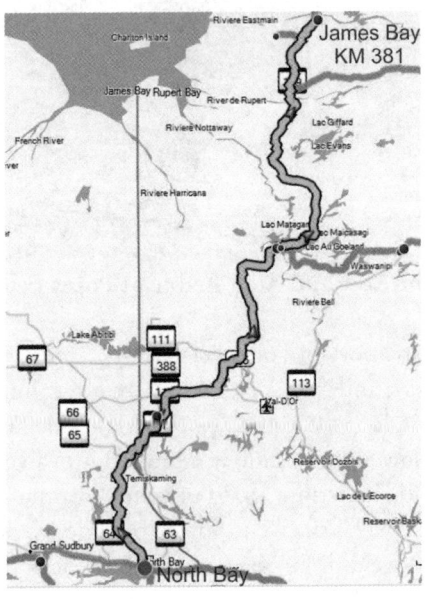

We left North Bay a little after 8:00 a.m. and made our first gas stop in Rollet around noon. We had been in Canada since Day 19, but now we were in Quebec where French is the primary language, including street signs. It now seemed more like we were in another country.

After Rollet, we stopped in Matagami for gas. It was only about 4:30 p.m. and we didn't want to stop for the day but we didn't know much about the road to James Bay. The gas station attendant told us there was a tourist center just outside of town. When we checked in at the tourist center they took our names, addresses, and telephone numbers and told us we needed to check in again when we came back out. This didn't quite make sense because there are other ways out of James Bay, but we gave them the information anyway.

The folks at the tourist center told us the only gas was at "KM381" on the Baie James Road (381 kilometers or 236 miles north). Our original plan was to travel to Eastman, which was the closest access to James Bay. This access was at KM350 (217 miles) with another 64 miles to Eastman. The road to KM350 was paved but the 64 miles on the Eastman access was gravel. We didn't think we would have enough gas to get all the way to Eastman and we thought we might run out of daylight as well. We decided we would be better off going to KM381 to spend the night, get gas, and then backtrack to the Eastman access the next day.

We got into the facilities at KM 381 at about 9:30 p.m. The place looked very similar to Coldfoot, Alaska: a pair of gas pumps, a restaurant, and dorm style housing. It was a little bit cheaper than Coldfoot; we only had to pay $121 for a room, and breakfast the next morning was reasonable. It ended up that we were the only people in our building so we had the place to ourselves. They had a lounge with a television, but we hadn't watched any television the whole trip so we went straight to bed.

Day 35
James Bay, to Mattagami, Quebec
616 Miles

After breakfast, we backtracked the 18 miles south along the paved road to the 64-mile-long Eastman access road. At the start, the access road was in good shape even though the gravel was 2-4" deep. The deep gravel was difficult but negotiable because it had a hard base. After about 10 miles, the access road turned to "crap" – the gravel was still deep but on a very

Chapter 14

soft sand base. This made riding extremely difficult, even when standing on the pegs. Tim and I fought these extreme conditions for about five miles and both of us had moments where we thought we were going to crash. We had no idea what the condition of the road was going to be for the remaining 50 miles to Eastman, but we knew that if it was like the last five miles, one or both of us were likely to be picking ourselves and our bikes up off the ground. We decided to return to KM381 and evaluate our options. Our morning adventure had resulted in a 69 mile detour.

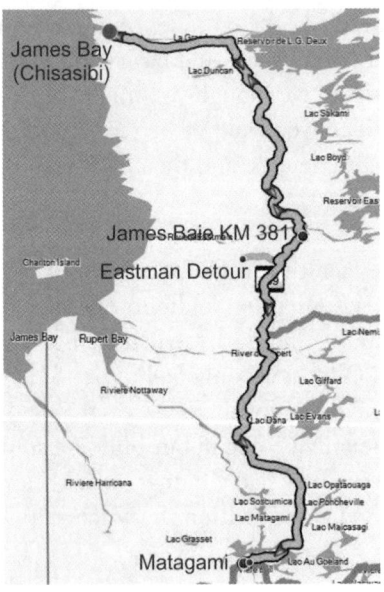

During trip planning, several people told us that they had taken the Baie James Road to Raddison, all the way to its end. Raddison is at the end of the road going east, but it is not on James Bay. We decided to turn west at the Raddison junction and travel toward James Bay another 54 miles to Chisasibi, which is on the bay. All but the last few miles to the water was paved.

Lunch with the Cree Nation. It was about 2:15 p.m. when we stopped for gas, so we inquired if there were any local restaurants. We were told that there was one at the community center – a large building with a tee-pee on top – in the center of town. The community center parking lot was full of newer vehicles, which was not what we were used to seeing in First Nation communities. It seemed odd.

Chisasibi Community Center

Inside the community center we found that the restaurant was closed for the day; however the community was having a bazaar and several families had prepared meals and were serving them in take-out containers. We looked around the bazaar hoping to find some hand-crafted souvenirs, which is something we had been unable to find to this point in the trip. But like most other places, most of the souvenirs were foreign made. Both Tim and I had a meat loaf dinner from one of the local families and sat in the middle of the bazaar eating a delicious meal as we absorbed the local culture.

We next backtracked toward the tourist center, making one more stop at KM381 for gas at about 6:30 p.m. There was a gravel road from Baie James Road east. However, given the time of day, it was likely that we would not get off the gravel before dark. We also didn't know anything about the condition

Chapter 14

of the gravel. We decided instead to go back to Mattagami for the night.

We stopped at the tourist center to tell them that we had returned. I parked my bike to the right of Tim's and got off. I had shortened my kickstand to accommodate the custom shock absorber, but after the rebuild my bike was now much higher and I had to be careful about parking. I thought I was on a level surface, but as I turned my back to the bike, it fell over, hitting me in the hips and knocking me forward. I was running trying not to fall but soon fell flat on my face. The bike continued to fall and hit Tim's bike, knocking it to the ground. Tim ran over to help me up and then we began picking up both bikes and all of the items that had fallen from our tank bags. The shock had held up after the rebuild, but I was once again cussing the manufacturer, Cogent Dynamics.

We got to the hotel in Mattagami a little past 11:00 p.m. It was late, but at least we avoided getting caught on gravel in the middle of the night.

Day 36
Mattagami to Alma, Quebec
371 Miles

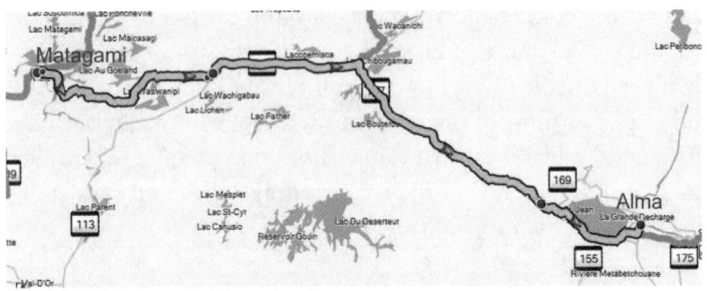

Our motel had a restaurant, so I got a hot breakfast and studied the maps for the best way to get to Labrador. We had elected to not take the gravel road on Baie James Road yesterday and

Northern Bay by Bay Part III

it would be out of our way to return to that road. It looked as if our choice was between backtracking to Amos and making a large south-east loop on pavement, or going a few miles north of town and taking Route 1055, which was 103 miles of gravel. Tim joined me for breakfast and we decided that we would save miles and take Route 1055.

Unexpected maintenance. I moved my bike to the front of the hotel and paid the bill. Tim came into the lobby and said, "I don't think I can go any further on that chain."

I went outside and saw it was kinked pretty badly. I asked, "What do you want to do? It's Sunday and there aren't any dealers in Mattagami." The last thing I wanted to do today was replace Tim's chain. I went back inside to the lobby. I had noticed a mechanic's shop next door and I asked the hotel attendant if the mechanic lived locally.

She said, "Yes, but he is closed today."

I explained that we had an emergency and that he might want to make some extra money and asked if she would call him. She did, but he was not at home.

Back outside, I noticed that there was a service station across the street with a garage. Tim investigated and found that they had a cut-off grinder – my chain breaker would not work on his chain – and would let us work on the bike in the garage.

I removed the rear wheel and told Tim to cut off the chain while I went outside to get some air. When I came back in, Tim had ground down the master link but had not cut the chain in half. "Why didn't you cut the chain in half?" I asked him.

"I thought I would just push out the master link and save this chain in case I need it later," Tim replied.

Chapter 14

Flabbergasted, I said, "What?" You just told me that you didn't think you could go any further on that chain. Why in the world would you want to save it?" I knew Tim's thriftiness was kicking in again. I grabbed the chain and told Tim, "Cut that in half!"

Tim only had about 8,700 miles on this chain and set of sprockets. His previous set had only lasted about the same miles and the guy in Fairbanks said it was because it was some kind of cheap ATV chain. The front sprocket looked okay, but the back sprocket was shot.

I asked Tim to give me his new rear sprocket. He handed me two sprockets, both of which were used. "I don't want those, they are used. Give me the new sprocket you bought in Saskatchewan."

"I didn't buy a new sprocket in Saskatchewan," Tim replied. I must have looked at Tim in both amazement and anger. I had told Tim in Saskatchewan that we would need to change the chain and sprockets one more time and suggested that he should buy a new chain and set of sprockets.

After a pause Tim said, "I had these two and didn't think I would need a new one."

I went to my bike and got my only remaining new sprocket. To make a point, I laid each of the old sprockets over mine and said to Tim, "Do you see how badly these sprockets are worn? If we put a new chain on this sprocket, it will just wear out your new chain." I then took my new sprocket and installed it on Tim's bike.

Tim promised me that he would order a replacement sprocket for my bike, and that he would always have a new chain and sprocket in his saddlebag on future trips like this. Tim immediately called Dual Sport Plus, a Canadian aftermarket dealer and made arrangements to have a chain and sprockets

Northern Bay by Bay Part III

shipped next day air to St. John's, Newfoundland for us to pick up at the FedEx office.

By noon, we had gotten Tim's bike put back together and were ready to head west, hoping the gravel road was in good shape.

The 103 miles of gravel was in good condition. At one point we came upon a saw mill and I stopped to take pictures. I noticed two young boys on small motorbikes riding toward us. They made a U-turn behind us and were waiting on me to go ahead. I motioned for them to come up beside me and they motioned back for me to go ahead. I motioned again, pointing beside me and they pulled forward. "You want to race," I asked.

"Nope," they both responded with big eyes.

I smiled at them and went ahead. You just knew that they could see themselves on bikes like Tim and I someday.

We stopped for gas in Waswanipi at about 3:30 p.m. and again at LaDore about 4 hours later. From LaDore we traveled around the south side of Lac St. Jean (Saint Jean Lake). This was a beautiful ride. Within the small villages along the lake were vintage cottages, side-by-side with newer cottages. I was also surprised to see traditional farms, complete with farm animals, within the limits of the villages. It was an odd mixture of urban and rural. I couldn't help but wonder at what point the "new urbanites" would begin to take over the farm land or complain about the smell of the animals.

We stopped at the Comfort Inn in Alma around 8:30 p.m. It was early but I was tired from starting the day off with maintenance work. We bypassed the fast food next door and went to the other side of the hotel to have pizza from a local restaurant.

Chapter 14

Day 37
Alma to Manic-5, Quebec
361 Miles

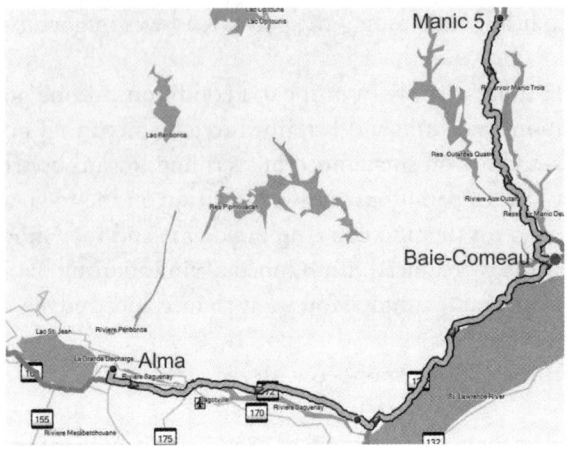

We had gotten to bed early and were awake a little after 5:00 a.m. However, we decided to have breakfast and do catch up on the internet, so we didn't leave until about 8:00.

Our first gas stop for the day was at Sacré-Coeur a little before 10:00 a.m. Tim's rear tail light had been working intermittently for the last several days, so we stopped at a motorcycle shop to see if they would be willing to work on the light. They said their mechanic was not available but told us there was a shop in Baie-Comeau.

A small repair turned big. We arrived in Baie-Comeau around lunch time and all the mechanics were gone to lunch. I showed the service manager where the taillight wires were and he agreed to work on it. Tim and I went across the street for lunch and when we returned they were still working on the bike. Tim went into the lounge and took a nap. I was wondering why it was taking them so long to fix the light and went around the back to the service area.

Northern Bay by Bay Part III

The service manager and the mechanic were both standing next to the bike with a look of "I don't know what to do now" on their faces. I asked if they were having problems and they said a wire was broken and they had spliced it, but it still wasn't working. They tried to tell me there was something wrong with the tail light. I told them I didn't think that was the case, as I had run a wire directly from the battery to test it in the parking lot and it was working. I asked if it was a fuse and they said the bike has some kind of aftermarket fuses and they all seemed to be okay.

The stock KLR has glass fuses. Most owners change the glass fuses to an automotive blade-type fuse and this was the situation with Tim's bike. The fuses they were looking at were for accessories.

I went in to ask Tim where he had located his primary fuses when he replaced the glass fuses. He responded, "I don't know. I had a dealer do that."

I went back to the service area and started checking the wiring and soon figured out that the mechanic had shorted two wires. While he was redoing the wire splices, I remembered that Tim told me he had bought some aftermarket stuff from a company called Totally Wired and that they had a fuse relocation kit that they put under the kickstand switch side cover. Sure enough, the main fuses were under the cover and the taillight fuse was blown. The mechanic replaced it and there were smiles on everybody's faces as the taillight came on.

It is not necessary for a rider to be able to do their own modifications. But if they are going on a trip like this they should at least understand what and how the modifications were done so they can communicate with a mechanic. Most mechanics will only know what the service manual tells them and do not want to work on aftermarket modifications of which they have no knowledge. A simple task turned into a big deal.

Chapter 14

Baie-Comeau was not originally a mandatory stop on our ride. However, as we thought about our route, it seemed someone could go to Goose Bay, Labrador (our next required location) by taking the new Trans-Labrador extension down the east coast. Since Baie-Comeau is a bay – Bay Comeau – we decided that we would include this as a mandatory stop, encouraging riders to do the entire Trans-Labrador loop.

Around 6:00 p.m. we arrived at Manic-5, also known as the Daniel-Johnson Dam, where the road turns from pavement to gravel. It was too late to continue toward Labrador City, so we inquired about a room. They only had worker dormitory-style rooms like many of the others we had stayed in. The price was only $65, which was cheap compared to what we had paid in other remote places. The building we were in was supposed to be non-smoking and had non-smoking signs posted everywhere, but the workers paid little attention and the smell of smoke almost made us gag. They didn't have a restaurant so I settled for a can of Pringles and a soda.

Day 38
Manic-5, Quebec to Goose Bay, Labrador
559 Miles

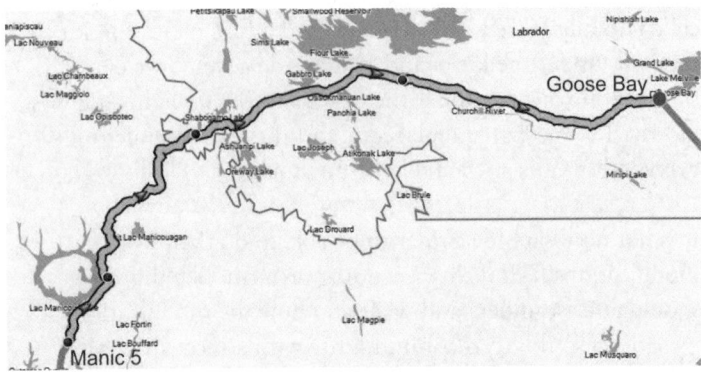

We got to Relais Gabriel, our first gas stop for the day, at about 9:15 a.m. There was a restaurant and the breakfast smelled so good Tim and I decided to have a sit down breakfast. I needed

Northern Bay by Bay Part III

something from my tankbag and noticed that Tim had left his bike parked at the pump. I was moving it over to a parking spot when the front tire dropped in a hole causing me to drop the bike. It is one thing to drop your own bike, but quite embarrassing when you drop your friend's bike. We had a terrific breakfast and went back to sucking dust on the gravel road.

Tim had done this portion of the Trans-Labrador highway in 2009 and had told me stories about the dust. It was bad, but the road was really in pretty good shape compared to the other gravel we had ridden, so I could deal with a bit of dust.

As we approached Labrador City, I noticed a large mill of some sort and the lake in front of it was a bright orange. It was really odd as the sun reflected off the orange lake. I would find out when we got to Labrador City that the orange color was from the iron ore mined in this area. Labrador has increased iron ore production and Labrador City was seeing something of a boom.

Tim got ready to pay for his gas in Labrador City and didn't have his credit card. After searching all pockets and his bike, he made a call to the restaurant in Relais Gabriel. Sure enough, he had left the card. He had them cut it up and then called his credit card company to cancel.

We had traveled 232 miles of gravel from Manic-5 to Labrador City and it had taken us about 8 hours, 40 minutes, including the breakfast stop at Relais Gabriel. We were riding 35 to 40 mph most of the time and slowing down periodically where there was loose gravel. It was about 4:00 in the afternoon, making it unlikely that we could make the 329 miles to Goose Bay today, so we set our target on spending the night at Churchill Falls, which was only 152 miles.

The gravel road follows the railroad pretty closely. However, the road twists and turns back and forth over the railroad track again and again. It seems that if the rail can follow a straight line, the road could, as well.

Chapter 14

Riding Gravel in the Dark. We got to Churchill Falls around 7:30 p.m. hoping to get food and some rest. Instead we found out there was no room at the inn. The construction boom had filled all of the rooms with workers.

We had averaged about 40 mph on this leg. It was another 177 miles to Goose Bay. If we could maintain the same pace, this would put us in Goose Bay around 1:00 a.m. Sunset would be around 9:30 p.m. so this meant we would have about three and a half hours of riding on gravel in the dark.

We went back inside to inquire if maybe we could find a sleeping room or anyplace at all that we might be able to spend the night, but were told that nothing was available.

It is very difficult to make reservations on a trip like this and we had been very lucky on our trip to this point, but now we were going to pay a price.

We headed toward Goose Bay, picking up the pace as much as was safe. Fortunately, the road was in good condition and there was little traffic. The remaining daylight hours went by far too fast and we still had about 90 miles of nighttime riding in the gravel to get to Goose Bay.

When it turned dark, Tim dropped his speed down to about 15 mph. The stock KLR headlight is like having a matchstick in a cave to guide you. Tim had some small "Eagle Eye" auxiliary lights, but they were not much help. I had converted my headlight to LEDs and had four-bulb LED auxiliary lights. However, the brackets were loose on my auxiliary lights and were not of much use. At 15 mph, it would take us six hours of riding on the gravel in the dark to get to Goose Bay.

I noticed that my dangling right auxiliary light was aimed such that it might benefit Tim if I could get up beside him. I pulled to a left track and found a spot where the light was giving Tim good light. At first he thought that I was trying to take the lead

Northern Bay by Bay Part III

and backed off. I held my position and he eventually figured out what I was doing. We were able to get our speed back up to about 35 mph and ended up getting to Goose Bay at about 12:30 in the morning. It had been a very difficult several hours.

Shock Failure Again. When I got off the bike, I noticed that I could barely touch my toes to the ground and almost dropped the bike. What is going on? My shock had failed again! This time it appeared as though I had lost all of the oil, but not the nitrogen. This pushed the shock to full extension and was the reason the bike was sitting so tall.

I was far too tired to deal with this issue. We had ridden 559 miles of gravel today and the last 90 miles was in the dark. I went to bed knowing that I had a big problem waiting for me the next morning.

Day 39
Goose Bay to L'Anse au Clair, Labrador
329 Miles

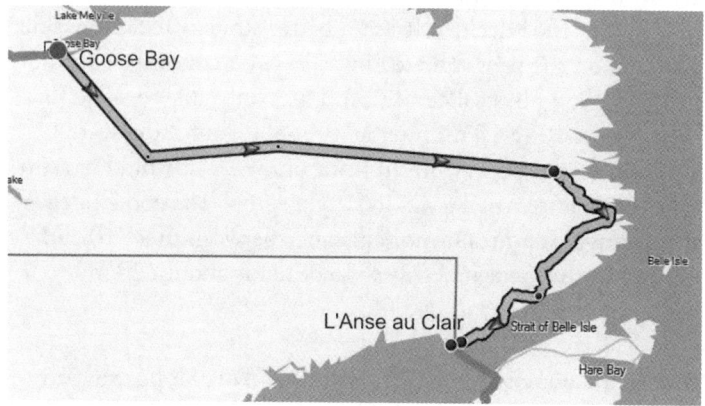

Given that my bike was sitting much taller after the rebuild in Inuvik than when I first installed the Cogent Dynamic shock at the beginning of the trip, and that now it was sitting taller yet, this seemed to confirm my suspicions that the shock had been

Chapter 14

shipped to me without any nitrogen and that was the likely cause of the original failure.

Having been frustrated by my dealings with Cogent Dynamics on the previous failure, I didn't think it made any sense to try to deal with them again. After the previous failure, they answered emails and on the surface appeared to be helpful, but they never sent complete information and couldn't seem to figure out any logistical solution. I decided that I would have my stock shock shipped to Bob Collin, a friend who lives in Maine, and would try to ride the bike the needed 2,500 miles with a broken shock. I only had about 350 miles of gravel remaining and I didn't believe there were any steep inclines that would cause me an issue. I had never ridden on a broken shock except for the few miles in Inuvik and really didn't know what to expect.

It took me most of the morning to make the necessary arrangements for getting my shock shipped to Maine, so we didn't leave Goose Bay until about 11:30. The shock with nitrogen and no oil to provide dampening was like riding on a semi-hard tail – sitting down was brutal on the one kidney that I have left. I decided it was a better strategy to simply ride standing on the pegs. The road was in good condition; but not being in good physical condition, I was only able to stand on the pegs for 10 to 15 minutes at a time. I would stop to rest and Tim would be way out in front of me and I would have to ride a little faster than I wanted, to keep up. The good part was that riding faster meant more distance between those 10 to 15 minute stops. I repeated this procedure for about 225 miles. It was quite fatiguing.

Ride-em Cowboy. About 20 miles from Port Hope the road turned to one continuous series of potholes and it was simply impossible to find a track without potholes. It only took about 10 minutes of this before I noticed a significant change in the bike's handling. I hit a very large pothole and the seat slapped me in the butt, crushing my spine. "Damn!" I thought,

Northern Bay by Bay Part III

"What's up with that?" I was only about 10 miles from Port Hope and decided I just needed to tough it out.

I pulled into the gas station at Port Hope, and when I put my feet down I noticed I was on the balls of my feet. It was obvious that I had now also lost the nitrogen from the shock and all that was remaining was the support provided by the spring. I pushed on the back of the bike and it just bounced. This is why the seat was hitting me in the butt.

It was about 5:45 p.m. and even with the starts and stops, I had averaged about 40 mph, so we were making decent time. However, I was not looking forward to the next 100 or so miles of pot-holed gravel to Red Bay.

Standing up was no longer an option, as the seat hitting me in the butt was brutally crushing my spine. I decided the best option was to try to just sit down. It was like riding a rocking horse as the bike constantly rocked. I wasn't having difficulty controlling the bike but it was still extremely fatiguing. I decided I would use the same "stop every 10 to 15 minute" strategy I had used previously.

My back was hurting so badly I decided that the least amount of time I spent on any one bump, the better off I would be – Speed became my friend! I would let Tim get way out in front and ride as fast as I possibly could to catch up. I never thought I would be riding this fast on gravel!

As we approached the Atlantic Ocean, we began to feel the ocean winds and they were swirling as they hit the mountain crests to our west. It had started misting, so the wet and the high, cold winds were making a miserable ride even more miserable.

I topped the hill to see the beautiful village of Red Bay. It was like something taken out of a picture book. I sat at the top of the crest just absorbing the view. It was like the view was telling

Chapter 14

my brain that the battering of my body was over. Pavement was just around the corner.

Entering Red Bay from Port Hope

We stopped at a convenience store in Red Bay and chatted with three ladies who were minding after the store and visiting. They were telling us that Red Bay was a dying town because there was very little commercial fishing, and that the younger generation was leaving town due to lack of work. What a shame to think that such a beautiful village might deteriorate due to lack of inhabitants.

We continued on to L'Anse au Clair, experiencing a beautiful coastal view with changing elevations. The views were breathtaking. I'm not sure if the views were truly that beautiful or if they just seemed so in comparison to the boring stretch across Canada; or if it was the relief that we were finished riding on gravel for the remainder of the trip; or that my body was no longer being brutalized.

Northern Bay by Bay Part III

We arrived in L'Anse au Clair at 10:05 p.m. and the bar had just stopped serving food. We hadn't had anything to eat all day, except for what was in our tank bags. With some begging we convinced the bartender to prepare some chicken wings. I normally don't drink at all but I decided that a Bloody Mary would make a good celebration of putting more than 2,700 miles of gravel roads behind us.

Day 40
L'Anse au Clair, Labrador to Gander, Newfoundland
427 Miles

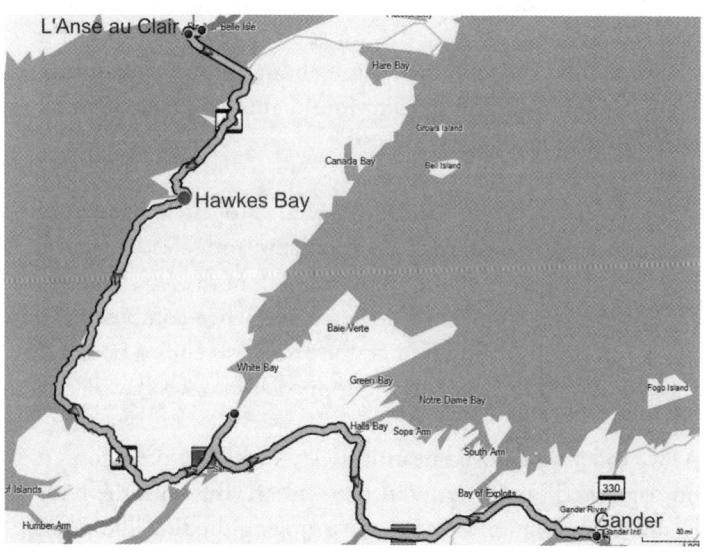

The ferry was scheduled to leave at 8:00 a.m. We didn't have a reservation and were told that we needed to be there at least an hour before boarding. Fortunately we were warned about the time confusion. The hotel was in L'Anse au Clair, Labrador, which is on Atlantic Daylight time (ADT). The ferry terminal is in Blanc-Sablon, Quebec, and all of Quebec is on Eastern Daylight time (EDT). But to make things even more confusing, the ferry runs on Newfoundland Time (NDT), which is one-half hour ahead of Atlantic Daylight Time.

Chapter 14

We arrived at the ferry about 6:30 a.m. and went inside the ticket office to get a ticket. We were placed in the "No-Reservation" line and were told that the ferry was full. There was a sign that said all people with reservations must check in one hour in advance of departure or their reservation would be cancelled. At exactly 7:00 a.m. one of the ladies working the ticket counter put a sign at the end of the reservation line and everybody that entered were told they had to go to the non-reservation line, reservation or not.

We got our tickets, which were only $11.50, and headed to the loading area. Unlike in Vancouver where motorcycles were the first to load, here we were the last to load and, as advised, the ferry was full. The ferry crossing is about 22 miles going from Blanc Sablon to St. Barbe, Newfoundland, and takes about 1 hour, 45 minutes.

While on the ferry, we decided we needed to add a mandatory stop on the eastern side of Newfoundland and selected Hawkes Bay, which was only about 50 miles south of the ferry landing. It was raining when we exited the ferry, and when combined with the winds coming off the water, the result was chilled bodies. It was about 11:00 a.m. when we stopped at Hawkes Bay.

As we rode, we enjoyed beautiful vistas with the ocean on our right and green mountains to our left. But with the on-again-off-again rain, we were not enjoying the ride like we had hoped. Around lunch-time we spotted a small restaurant serving moose burgers. We were the only two guests and took our time studying the menu of unique items: moose steaks, capelin (a smelt-like fish), seal, and seal flipper pie. Tim was interested in the capelin and I was interested in the seal. I asked the lady about the seal and she said, "I don't eat it. My mom wouldn't cook it. It smells." Both Tim and I decided to go the safe route and ordered a moose burger, which was very good.

We had two choices after getting to the mandatory stop in St. John's: 1) travel back across the island to Port aux Basques on

Northern Bay by Bay Part III

the eastern side of Newfoundland and take a 6-hour ferry ride; or 2) take the 14-hour Argentia ferry from the western side of Newfoundland. We had a schedule and decided, since it was raining and most of the return route to Port aux Basques was going to be the same as the route to St. John's, that we would take the Argentia even though it only ran every other day.

We had plenty of time, so we decided we would stop in Gander for the night and arrived about 6:30 p.m. after a short gas stop in Hampden.

Ride for Sight is a motorcycle charity event to raise money for vision research. The other riders we had met on the ferry were going to this event in Gander and there were several riders staying in the hotel. We fit right in. We had an upscale meal at the hotel restaurant and got a good night's sleep.

Day 41
Gander to Placentia, Newfoundland
297 Miles

The ferry didn't run until the next day, so we had plenty of time to ride the 300 or so miles to St. John's and then to Placentia to catch the ferry, so we got off to a lazy start at about 8:00 a.m. After sitting in the rain all night, Tim's bike did not want to start. After a lot of fiddling and almost running down the battery, it finally started.

We stopped at a Tim Horton's down the street and I yelled across the pumps to Tim that since we had plenty of time, we might as well eat breakfast. I pushed my bike away from the pumps and went inside to order. The next thing I know, Tim is leaving the parking lot. He is going the opposite direction from St. John's, so I figured he was just concerned about his battery and was charging it a bit. I got my food and found a seat where I could look out the window and watch for Tim. Just as I sat down, Tim pulled up to the parking area and just sat there in the rain. I finally walked out to see what he was doing. Tim

Chapter 14

said, "I'm not going to eat. I don't want to shut my bike off." I went back inside and gobbled down my donut and coffee.

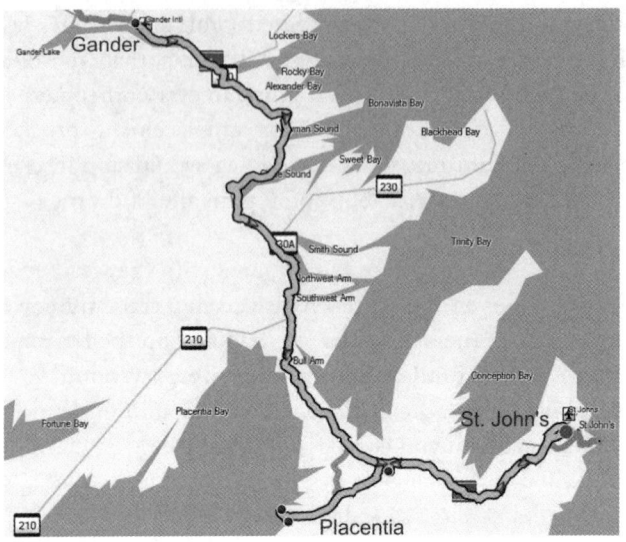

I was really disappointed with the weather in Newfoundland. I had never been there and was so looking forward to taking in the island, but all we had seen were water drops from the inside of our face shields. I asked one of the locals about the weather and they said the best time to visit Newfoundland was August. We were a month or so early.

Tim had made arrangements for Dual Sport Plus to deliver a chain and sprockets to the FedEx office in St. John's, which was a mandatory stop. We stopped at Whitbourne for gas around noon and arrived at the FedEx office around 1:00 p.m. The line was backed up out the door, as Canada was still involved in a postal strike which had overloaded all of the independent carriers. I waited outside as Tim waited in the line. When Tim came out he said, "They don't have the package and they say it won't be here until Monday. It was Friday and we had to board the ferry on Saturday.

Northern Bay by Bay Part III

Tim had ordered the parts four days earlier and had them shipped next day air. Tim called Dual Sport Plus to find that the owner was out of town and that they didn't seem to have any resolution. We couldn't really determine if the delay was caused by the overload from the Postal Strike or whether Dual Sport dropped the ball. This was going to create a problem for us, because I was counting on having a replacement sprocket – to replace the one I gave Tim in Matagami - when I changed my shock in Maine.

We went to lunch and were so frustrated with the weather and the FedEx experience that we decided to skip the short trip out to the point of Cape Spear, the westernmost point of Canada, and head straight to the ferry to make our reservation.

We made our ferry reservations at the Argentia terminal at about 4:30 p.m. When we were heading back to Placentia to look for a room, Tim made an unexpected left turn onto a road that was actually a staging area that led back to the ferry. I stopped, figuring he would turn around but after 10 minutes he had not returned.

I turned onto the staging road and continued to the top of the hill where I noticed that there was another road going to the right. My GPS indicated this road had no other exit so I decided to return to the point where Tim made the U-turn and wait as it seemed this was the only way out. Every time I saw a car I would stop them to verify that this was the only way out and each time they confirmed that it was. I waited nearly a half hour but never saw Tim.

I finally decided that I would just go to the small village of Placentia, figuring Tim would show up eventually. As I entered town Tim was coming out. Somehow he had gotten past me. I was sitting alongside the road and there was only one way out, but somehow I missed him and he missed me.

Chapter 14

The attendant at the Argentia ferry counter had told us that her mother-in-law worked at the Bridgeway Hotel in Placentia and it was a clean place to stay. It was not only clean it was very nicely decorated for a mom-and-pop hotel and our second floor room had a view of Placentia Bay. We went across the street and had Chinese food for dinner. I went to bed and Tim went to the bar next door to chat with the locals.

Northern Bay by Bay Adventure Complete

We began the **Northern Bay by Bay Adventure** in Prudhoe Bay, Alaska on June 1, 2011 at 7:29 a.m. AKDT (11:29 a.m. EDT). We ended the ride in St. John's, Newfoundland at 2:27 p.m. NDT (12:57 p.m. EDT) taking 23 days, 5 hours, 28 minutes to complete the ride.

My GPS showed that it took us 10,441 miles to complete the route, not including the six ferry rides. Our pre-ride estimate of 10,352 miles, which included the ferry rides, was computed by piecing together information from various mapping programs and internet sources. We decided to use 10,400 miles to estimate the allowed time for the **Northern Bay by Bay Adventure** rides.

The **Northern Bay by Bay Adventure** is based upon 300 miles per day over 10,400 miles, resulting in an estimated time of 34 days, 16 hours. A time of **35 days** is recommended for this ride.

The **Northern Bay by Bay Adventure Gold** is based upon 500 miles per day, resulting in an allotted time of 20 days, 19 hours, 12 minutes. A time of **21 days** is recommended for this ride.

Our time of 23 days, 5 hours, and 28 minutes puts us short of the **Northern Bay by Bay Adventure Gold** but well within the criteria for the **Northern Bay by Bay Adventure**.

15 Passion in the Wind
Eastern Bay by Bay

As we *approached the last leg of our ride it is hard to comprehend the number of miles we had ridden and the challenges we had overcome. We were not done yet and would still have to deal with some miscommunication and maintenance issues. However, those issues would soon take a back seat to the joy of meeting our friends along the route of this last leg and the joy we would share as we toasted our trip at the Key West buoy that marks the southernmost point in the U.S.*

The **Eastern Bay by Bay Plus** was the final leg of our ride, starting in North Sydney, Nova Scotia and ending in Key West, Florida with the following mandatory stops:

- North Sydney, Nova Scotia (Receipt)
- St. Margaret's Bay (Receipt from Peggy's Cove, Nova Scotia)
- Jordan Bay (Receipt from Lockport, Nova Scotia)
- St. Mary's Bay (Receipt from Digby, Nova Scotia)
- Cavendish, Prince Edward Island (Receipt)
- Bay of Fundy (Receipt from St. Martins, New Brunswick)
- Easternmost Point of U.S. (Receipt from Eastport, Maine)
- Penobscot Bay (Receipt from Belfast, Maine)

Chapter 15

- Cape Cod Bay (Receipt from Provincetown, Massachusetts)
- Delaware Bay (Receipt from Cape May, New Jersey)
- Chesapeake Bay (Receipt from Cape Charles, Virginia)
- Bulls Bay (Receipt from McClellanville, South Carolina)
- Kings Bay Naval Base (Receipt from St. Mary's, Georgia)
- Biscayne Bay, Florida (Receipt from Homestead, Florida)
- Southernmost Point of U.S. (Receipt from Key West, Florida)

MapSource calculates this route as 3,423 miles, requiring 2 days 14 hours, 35 minutes of actual riding time. Based upon the established criteria of 300 miles per day for the Plus level and 500 miles per day for the Power level, the calculated time would be 11 days, 9 hours, 50 minutes and 6 days, 20 hours, 18 minutes, respectively. Recommended time for the **Eastern Bay by Bay Plus Tour** is **11 days** and for the **Eastern Bay by Bay Plus Power Tour** is **6 days**.

Eastern Bay by Bay Gold

We elected not to include Newfoundland in our ride. However, Newfoundland can be included by adding the following two stops turning the **Eastern Bay by Bay Plus** into an **Eastern Bay by Bay Gold:**

- Port aux Basques, Newfoundland (Receipt from Ferry)
- St. John's, Newfoundland (Receipt)

MapSource calculates the route as 4,103 miles, including a 109 mile ferry ride from North Sydney, Nova Scotia to Port aux Basques, Newfoundland and requires 3 days, 9 hours, 17 minutes riding time. Based upon the Tour and Power Tour

Eastern Bay by Bay

criteria of 300 miles and 500 miles per day respectively, the allotted time would be 13 days, 16 hours, 14 minutes for the Tour and 8 days, 4 hours, 56 minutes for the Power Tour. Recommended time for the **Eastern Bay by Bay Plus Gold Tour** is **13 days** and for the **Eastern Bay by Bay Plus Gold Power Tour** is **8 days**.

Day 42
Placentia, Newfoundland to North Sydney, Nova Scotia
Argentia Ferry

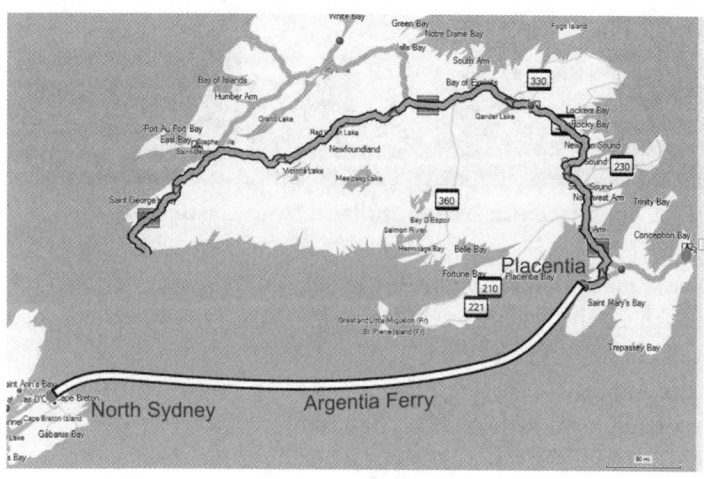

Rather than back-track across Newfoundland to Port au Basque, we elected to forgo the Gold version of the Eastern Bay by Bay ride and take the overnight Argentia Ferry, which is about a 14 to 15 hour ride to North Sydney, Nova Scotia. If we took the ferry from Port aux Basque, we would have had about a 6 hour ferry ride to North Sydney, Nova Scotia, but we would also have needed to ride back across Newfoundland, about 482 miles. The time required for each option is about the same.

We met a couple in the parking lot who were also taking the Argentia ferry, which was departing at 4:00 p.m. They were going to the Castle Hill National Historic Site just up the road

Chapter 15

from Placentia. We decided to go, as well. Fort Royal, built in the 1600's by the French, sits atop Castle Hill and provides a beautiful overlook of Placentia.

Placentia Newfoundland from Castle Hill

We went back to Placentia for lunch and then went to the ferry for check-in.

The Argentia Crossing. The ferry had an estimated arrival time in North Sydney, Nova Scotia at 6:00 a.m. We paid $163.50 for the ferry crossing and skipped the extra cost of a cabin. Upon boarding the ferry, we found a quiet area with comfortable reclining chairs and settled in. When the boat started moving, I went out onto the deck until we got out of the bay. The captain announced that a whale had been sighted off my side of the boat. I saw something, but it was too far away for me to claim that I saw a whale.

Once we reached the open water I went inside in search of some food. The choices were cold sandwiches, a buffet, and an upscale restaurant. The buffet was the most popular and had a long wait, so I settled for a not-so-appetizing sub and returned to my seat. It was really cold, even with my jacket. I tried to lie on the floor and sleep, but just shivered. I took a walk to warm up and the woman at the gift shop told me that the theatre had comfortable seating and was much warmer. I told Tim, but he was settled in for the night, so I went to the theatre on my own. I watched a couple of movies and then slept on the floor until morning, when I went back to Tim's "nest" to prepare for debarkation.

Day 43
North Sydney to Digby, Nova Scotia
552 Miles

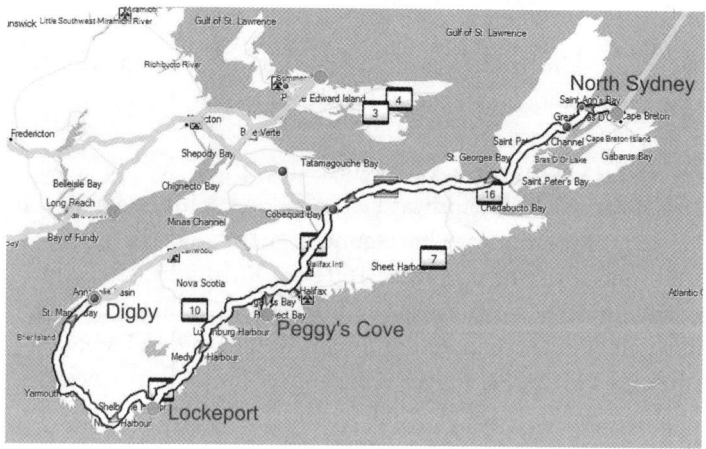

Our motorcycles were parked at the back of the ferry. In preparation for exiting the ferry, I unstrapped my bike and hit the starter, but it wouldn't start. I ended up pushing it out of the ferry and then Tim had to provide a jump start. This was the third time I had a battery issue. I had a battery monitor and it showed that the battery was charging, so cause of the problem was not clear; but it was frustrating to both Tim and me. I'm sure Tim was tired of dealing with my breakdown issues: first the carburetor, then the shock, and now, for the third time, the battery.

Our first planned mandatory stop was St. Ann's Bay. However, when we got there, we found that while it appeared as a town on the map, it didn't exist. We looked for an alternative, but

Chapter 15

there were no good options close by, so we elected to simply use North Sydney as the northernmost mandatory point for Nova Scotia.

The Cabot Trail circles around the northern part of Nova Scotia and is a popular motorcycle road. I had already ridden the Cabot Trail and Tim didn't want to add the extra miles, which would require some backtracking, so we elected not to include it. Riders who have not ridden the Cabot Trail and have the time should add it to their adventure.

We stopped in Baddeck around 9:00 a.m. for gas and breakfast and made another gas stop at Bible Hill around noon.

Ancestral Connection. I have ancestral ties to Nova Scotia and New Brunswick. My forbear Pierre Leduc left his home near Normandy, France with his regiment in 1691 on "Le Soleile d'Afrique," arriving on July 6, 1691 at Quebec. He served in Acadia, now New Brunswick and Nova Scotia, for nine years, likely under the command of Joseph Robineau de Villebon. After his service, Pierre received a concession of forty-one acres of land from the Montreal Sulpicians on what is now known as Ile Perrot, outside of Montreal. His heirs continued to live in this area, including my grandfather who lived in the area until he immigrated to Michigan.

Tim and I arrived at Peggy's Cove a little after 2:00 p.m. It was as magnificent as I remembered it. This was Tim's first time to visit Peggy's Cove and he was quite impressed with the rounded rocks leading to the lighthouse where it overlooks the Atlantic Ocean and guards the entrance to St. Margaret's Bay.

I love the small fishing villages on the east coast of Nova Scotia, and we traveled through several on our way out of Peggy's Cove to our next mandatory stop at Lockporte. We got gas around 5:00 p.m. and took a short ride down to view Jordan Bay.

Eastern Bay by Bay

Peggy's Cove
Photograph by Tim Yow

From Lockporte we would transition from the east coast of Nova Scotia to the west coast by traveling through Yarmouth at the southern tip. Yarmouth had been the docking point for the Cat ferry that ran between Nova Scotia and Bar Harbor, Maine. This ferry is now discontinued, but I had the opportunity to ride it in 2004 on the way to my start of the IBA's Tran-Canadian Gold ride.

We had originally selected Clare as the mandatory stop along St. Mary's Bay and turned off to look for a room. We only found one small motel and even though it was early in the evening, it was closed. We stopped at an ice cream shop for dinner and discovered that Clare is an Acadian village. While they spoke to us in English, the community was clearly French.

We decided that we would go north to Digby and use it as the mandatory stop instead of Clare. Digby is a popular destination since it has a ferry crossing from New Brunswick. It had a lot of motels and was a better choice. We stopped for the night at about 10:30. Our motel was right on the bay overlooking the ferry landing. Digby is known worldwide for its scallops but we got in so late we did not have the opportunity to enjoy them for dinner. We had to settled for food from our tankbag instead.

Chapter 15

Day 44
Digby, Nova Scotia to Woodland, Maine
616 Miles

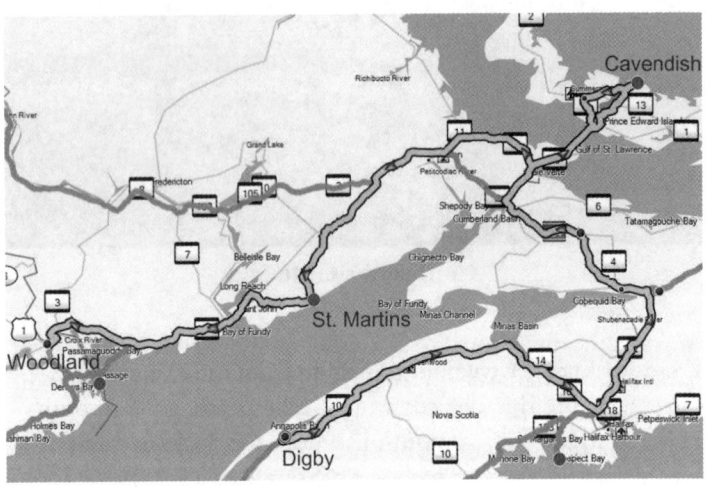

We traveled north along the Bay of Fundy with only occasional views of the water. The western side of Nova Scotia has a lot of farming, in contrast to the fishing villages on the eastern coast. We headed east toward Halifax before heading back north and then west on the toll road at Great Village. We stopped for gas around 1:15 p.m. at Thomson Station.

Our next mandatory stop was Prince Edward Island. You can enter the island by ferry from the east or by the Confederation Bridge from the south. We chose to take the bridge which is 8 miles long and advertised as the "World's Longest Bridge Over Ice Covered Waters." The bridge was built in 1997 with post-tensioned concrete and is an amazing work of construction.

We had difficulty deciding how to handle the mandatory stop for Prince Edward Island. We didn't want riders to have to document a circle around the entire island, so we decided on Cavendish as the mandatory stop. This would require riders to cross the island whether they took the bridge, ferry, or both to arrive and depart the island.

Confederation Bridge

We took the direct route to Cavendish and rode the western coast back to the bridge. What was most surprising about P.E.I. was the amount of farming, mostly new potatoes. The views of the lines of furrows in the potato fields were beautiful. Tim and I both agreed we wanted to return to Prince Edward Island someday.

A Lobster Treat. Next on the itinerary was a mandatory stop on the Bay of Fundy at St. Martins, New Brunswick. We arrived at about 8:30 p.m. While at the gas station, they told us we were just in time to see the lobster boats coming in. When we got to the dock they were just finishing up. I struck up a conversation with the captain. He started out rather gruff but opened up when he was convinced that I was really interested. He told me that the government was making it difficult on small fishermen by their policy of giving preference to boats run by larger corporations. Officials felt that smaller fisherman were selling their catch off the dock and not reporting the income for taxes.

On the way out of town Tim and I stopped at a lobster shanty and had a lobster roll and ice cream. The shanty was run by a grandmother and her 11-year-old granddaughter whose exuberance brought a smile to my face.

Chapter 15

Alan Leduc at Lobster Dock

Our GPS was routing us to the Letete-Deer Island Ferry. We thought it was likely too late to take the ferry and stopped several times to ask about the ferry schedule with no success. We wandered our way back on a dark twisty road to find that, in fact, the ferry was closed and then had to back track and go east around Passamaquoddy Bay.

Almost Back to the U.S.A. We were approaching the border on Canadian Highway 1, which is an interstate type highway. Suddenly a car passed me on my left, straddling the line between me and a car in the next lane. The car must have been going over 100 mph. It seemed like the car was inches from me and, as you might imagine, it scared the crap out of me. A minute later I saw another car zooming up behind me, weaving in and out of traffic. They must have been racing. I was in front of Tim at the time and asked Tim later when we stopped, "How close was that car to me.?"

"So close I couldn't see any gap. I thought he had you." Tim said.

Eastern Bay by Bay

We had no issues crossing the border into Calais, Maine. It was nearly 11:00 p.m. and we were definitely ready to stop for the night. There were two hotels in Calais but both of them were closed. We called the emergency numbers but no one would answer. I started checking my GPS and giving numbers to Tim to call and we finally found a room in Woodland, about 10 miles west. It wasn't a great room but at least it was a room. The owner said he got a lot of business because the hotels in Calais close at 9:00 p.m.

Eastern Bay by Bay Tour

The **Eastern Bay by Bay Tour** includes only the U.S. east coast mandatory locations, starting in Eastport, Maine and ending in Key West Florida. MapSource calculates the **Eastern Bay by Bay Tour** as 2,285 miles, requiring 1 day, 17 hours, 3 minutes riding time. Based on the 300 and 500 miles per day pace for the Tour and Power Tour designations, the required time would be 7 days, 14 hours, 48 minutes and 4 days, 13 hours, 40 minutes, respectively. The recommended time for the Eastern Bay by Bay Tour is **7 days** and the E**astern Bay by Bay Power Tour** is **4 days**.

Day 45
Woodland, Maine to Danvers, Massachusetts
388 Miles

We didn't leave the hotel until about 8:15 a.m. and made our first mandatory stop after returning to the U.S. at about 9:00 a.m. in Eastport, Maine, the easternmost point of the U.S. To stay close to the coast, we selected Belfast on Penobscot Bay as the next mandatory stop and arrived there about noon.

From Newfoundland, we had called ahead to Reynolds Motorsports in Buxton, Maine to see if we could schedule oil and tires changes and to order the replacement sprockets. My chain and sprockets would have about 13,000 miles on them by the time we got to Buxton and would need to be changed.

Chapter 15

I also wanted to get my shock changed at the same time. However, we were running late and when we called to confirm our appointment, we were told that they would not be able to get both of us in.

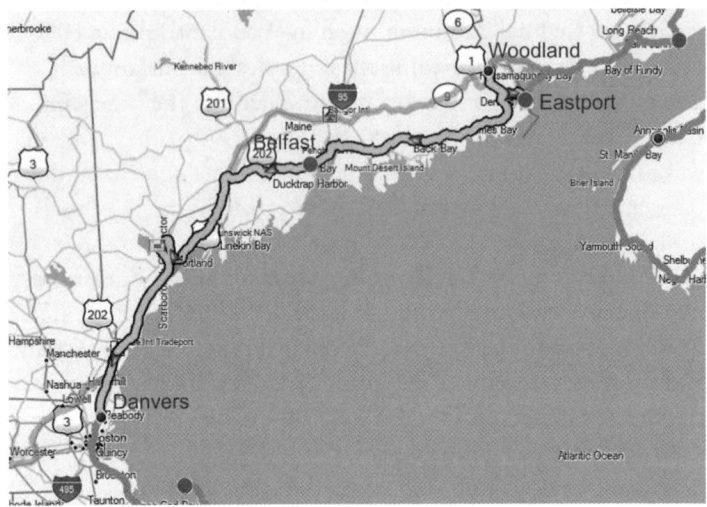

Splitting Up for Maintenance. Tim and I decided to split up for maintenance at Belfast. He would go directly to Reynolds in Buxton and I would go to Bob Collin's house in Cumberland Foreside, where Brenda had shipped my stock shock, and see if I could get maintenance done near there.

Bob was at the dentist, but his wife Sharon came out to meet me and told me that they had my shock and that Bob had the garage cleaned out and ready for me to work. I told Sharon I would take the shock and see if I could find someone who had sprockets and would install the tires and shock.

Bob had told me that Street Cycles in Falmouth, which was just around the corner, would not put on tires unless you had purchased them at their dealership. I decided I would buy another set of tires and have the tires I was carrying shipped home. Street Cycles had tires, but wouldn't be able to install them until next week. I made sure they understood I was on the road and was willing to buy the tires from them, but they still said, "It doesn't matter. We still can't get you in."

Bob mentioned that another option might be Moto Milano in Windham. I called, told them my situation, and they agreed to get me in. They made a point of telling me it would cost $75 per wheel, with me providing the tires. I called Tim to see if Reynolds could get me in, but they still couldn't so I decided that Moto Milano was the best option. My only other option was to change the tires by hand in Bob's garage, which would take most of the afternoon.

Moto Milano agreed to change my shock but they didn't have any sprockets and neither did any of the dealers in the area. I would just have to see how far I could get on my current chain and sprockets since the replacement sprockets Tim ordered were in Buxton.

Tim and I both got finished about the same time and agreed to meet at I-95 Exit 32, which was on our route south. I must have told Tim that this was north of Buxton instead of south, and Tim headed north on I-95 from Buxton. I waited at the exit for what I thought was too long, and started looking for Tim's Spot track on my smart phone. When I saw where he was, I called to tell him I must have given him the wrong directions and was still waiting at Exit 32.

We headed south after getting reconnected, stopping at the Comfort Inn in Danvers, Massachusetts around 9:00 p.m. After we got settled in our rooms, I decided that I would have a cup of coffee from the lobby. I had taken off my riding pants and only had on my LD Comfort tights when I decided that I could sneak downstairs and get coffee in this state of relative undress. I was in the lobby filling up my cup when a bus load of teenage girls arrived. It is hard to know who was more embarrassed.

Chapter 15

Day 46
Danvers, Massachusetts to Cape May, New Jersey
601 Miles

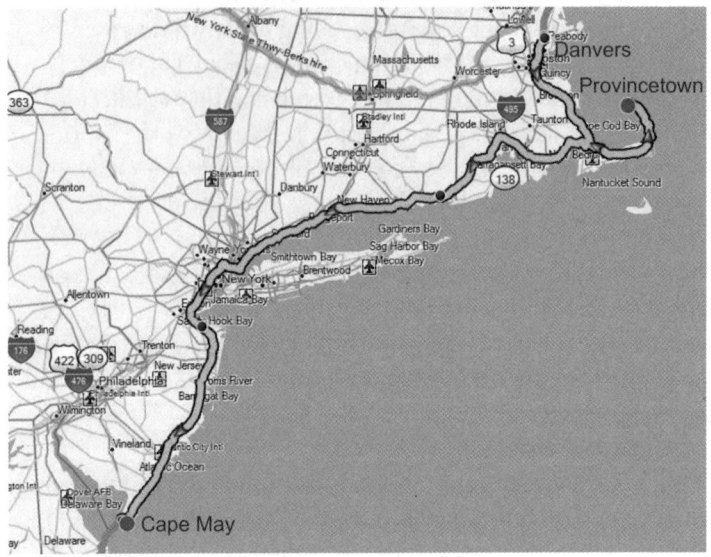

We had a good breakfast at the Comfort Inn and no young teenage girls or chaperones were giving me the evil eye, so maybe I had not made that big of an impression walking around the lobby in my tights the night before. We left the hotel at about 8:30 a.m., deciding to delay our start a bit to avoid the early morning Boston traffic, which we assumed would be ferocious.

We were on our way to Provincetown, Massachusetts on the tip of Cape Cod. The Boston traffic was not nearly as bad as we imagined and we averaged a little over 40 mph over the 135 mile ride, arriving in Provincetown a little before noon.

After taking the shoreline ride through Provincetown on the Cape Cod National Seashore, we were definitely pleased that we had added Provincetown as a mandatory stop. We looked

Eastern Bay by Bay

for a place to have lunch but the traffic was so insane we opted to just get gas and continue. Given the traffic, I'm not sure it would be high on my list to visit again; however, I recommend it as a must-do visit at least once.

We stopped for gas in Old Mystic, Connecticut around 3:00 p.m. and paused for a few minutes. Tim and I were both dreading the ride through New York City in rush hour traffic.

It took us over two hours to cross a 15 mile section of New York City, which included the George Washington Bridge. We were in full riding gear and under bright sun, so it was uncomfortably hot, not to mention having to breathe exhaust fumes. Traffic seemed to be constantly shifting lanes and Tim was doing his best to negotiate through the traffic. Since we didn't have any two-way communications, I had to keep him in sight, which proved to be a bit of a challenge. A couple of times when we came to a full stop, I split lanes between vehicles drawing some ugly stares. We stopped for gas on the Garden State Parkway in New Jersey at about 8:00 p.m.

Our plan was to ride to North Cape May, New Jersey so that we would be ready to catch the ferry across Delaware Bay the next day. Our friend Brian Hiley was planning to meet us there. All of the hotels in North Cape May were sold out, so we decided to stop at a McDonalds. It was about 10:00 p.m. and we hadn't had anything to eat but munchies since breakfast. Some folks at McDonalds told us that Cape May's beaches were a big tourist attraction and that they were sure we would find a room there.

Tourist attraction indeed! We rode past a marina as we entered town and multi-story hotels, one after the other, lined the beach. It was now nearly 11:00 p.m., yet there was still a lot of action on the streets. It definitely looked like a party town. It was my night to pay so I selected the Le Mer Beachfront Inn, away from most of the action, figuring we might have a chance to get some sleep. Talk about action, the room was $226!

Chapter 15

Day 47
Cape May, New Jersey to Andrews, South Carolina
551 Miles

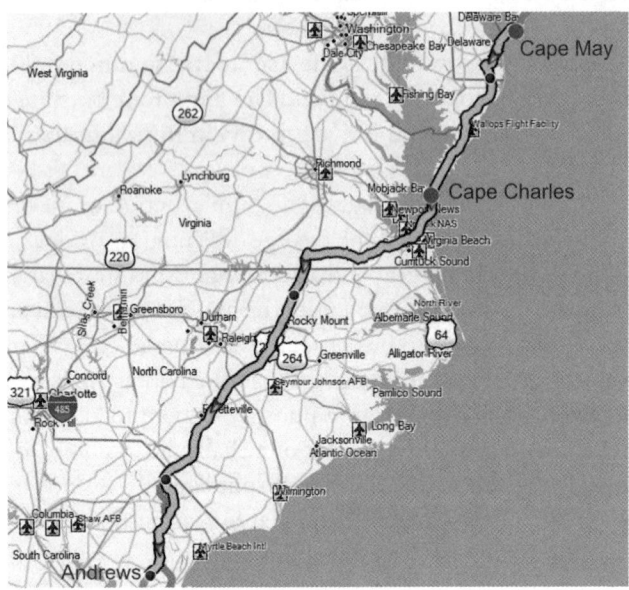

The next morning, our friend Brian Hiley was waiting for us in the parking lot. He had followed us by our Spot satellite trackers. We hugged and chatted for a few minutes and headed to the ferry. Brian was going to travel with us until we crossed the Chesapeake Bay.

Our timing was perfect for departure on the Cape May – Lewes Ferry which is a 17 mile, 85 minute cruise across Delaware Bay. Although Brian lives in Baltimore and Tim and I live in the Midwest, we see him quite often and it was good to share time with him once again.

We stopped for gas a little before 10:00 a.m. in Selbyville, Delaware near the Delaware / Maryland border before continuing through Maryland to Cape Charles, Virginia, where we would travel the Chesapeake Bay Bridge-Tunnel. At the Cape Charles gas stop Brian told us that he would break off after crossing the bridge and we said our good-byes until the next time.

I was confused about the geography in this area and realized I needed to do some review of my American history as to how the finger surrounded by the Chesapeake Bay to the west and the Atlantic Ocean to the right and dangling from the state of Maryland was divided. This finger is divided into three parts with some belonging to Maryland, some to Delaware, and some to Virginia.

Crossing Chesapeake Bay. I had long wanted to travel the Chesapeake Bay Bridge-Tunnel and think its website best describes my feelings as to why: "The Chesapeake Bay Bridge-Tunnel showcases the mighty surge of the Atlantic Ocean, the beauty of the Chesapeake Bay, and the soaring grace of an engineering marvel. The Bridge-Tunnel covers 20 miles: 12 miles of low-level trestle, 2 one-mile-long tunnels, 2 bridges, 2 miles of causeway, 4 man-made islands and 5-1/2 miles of approach roads."

After crossing the Chesapeake Bay, Tim and I targeted Bulls Bay in South Carolina. We were expecting to meet Harry Farthing, whom we had befriended in Inuvik. Harry had flown back to his home from Alaska and we had plans to have breakfast with him the next morning. He told us by email that he had in fact gone on to Prudhoe Bay and we were looking forward to hearing his story first-hand. We made gas stops in Enfield, North Carolina at about 4:30 p.m. and Dillon, South Carolina at about 7:30 p.m. We arrived in Andrews, South Carolina around 10:30 p.m. Tim was having difficulty with the dark and was concerned about wildlife so we decided to stop for the night. We searched the town for a hotel and finally found one that was a bit dumpy, but it would do. We were nearing the end of the trip and getting anxious to finish. We would have been satisfied with just about anything.

Chapter 15

Day 48
Andrews, South Carolina to Key West, Florida
830 Miles

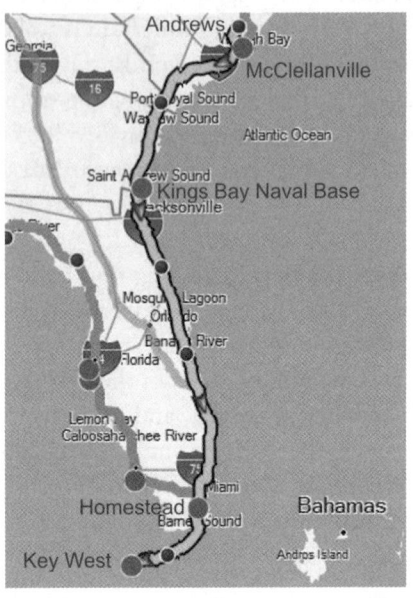

Bull's Bay was a mandatory stop and we documented it by stopping for gas in McClellanville, South Carolina at about 8:30 a.m. I had exchanged emails with Harry the night before and we agreed to meet him at the Isle of Palms between 9:00 and 10:00 a.m. As we crossed the bridge into town, Harry was waiting at the roadside. We stopped and chatted for a few minutes and Harry pointed us into town to Coconut Joe's Beach Grill and Bar overlooking beautiful sandy white beaches.

Harry's Circle to Circle. Harry told us that, after we split in Dawson City, he went to Fairbanks to change to knobby tires and then continued on to Prudhoe Bay. It was exciting to know that we had enabled Harry in such a way. Harry left Inuvik at 9:12 a.m. PDT (12:12 p.m. EDT) on Tuesday, June 7, 2011 and arrived in Prudhoe Bay at 3:14 p.m. AKDT (7:14 p.m. EDT), Friday, June 10, 2011. It took 79 hours, 2 minutes to complete the Circle to Circle ride from Inuvik to Prudhoe Bay.

Eastern Bay by Bay

Even after crashing on the Dempster Highway and having to make a tire change in Fairbanks, Harry completed the ride in less than the recommended time. He saved all of his receipts and got a witness form signed in Prudhoe Bay. It will be my pleasure to submit his ride to the Iron Butt Association as the first rider to complete this ride.

Tim and I had gone from Prudhoe Bay to Inuvik in 83 hours, 4 minutes which was just over the recommended cut off of 80 hours for the **Circle to Circle Insanity**.

After breakfast, Harry said he had a surprise for us. He pulled a bottle of champagne from his satchel and gave it to us to enjoy in Key West at the end of our ride.

Alan Leduc, Tim Yow, and Harry Farthing
Photo by Harry Farthing

Hearing about Harry's adventure and closing in on the end of our own journey gave us a good feeling about all that we had accomplished. We were looking forward to finishing this last leg of the ride and achieving our goal.

We stopped for gas at Port Wentworth, Georgia (near Savannah) around 1:00 p.m. and then traveled on to St. Mary's, which is the home of the Kings Bay Naval Base,

Chapter 15

arriving at about 3:30 p.m. During spring break several years ago, I found the base with a submarine sticking out of the ground and wanted to use it as a mandatory stop.

Tim Yow at Kings Bay Naval Base

It was 5:30 p.m. when we stopped for gas at Bunnell, Florida and we still had 442 miles to get to the end of our ride in Key West. That would be 7 to 8 hours if we could average 60 mph, putting us into Key West around 11:30 p.m. However, we would likely have two more gas stops and we could not travel at that speed on the two lane road from Homestead to Key West. This meant we likely would not get in until 1:00 a.m. or so.

The two lane road from Homestead to Key West can be very slow and it was Fourth of July weekend. I put a bug in Tim's ear about completing the ride tonight rather than fighting traffic tomorrow.

There was a mandatory stop in Homestead and we did not have the gas range to make the entire 300 miles from Bunnell. Before we left Bunnell, Tim and I discussed stopping at about the 150 mile point. Somewhere around 100 miles, Tim exited at West Melbourne. It was about 7:00 p.m. and I figured Tim was planning to stop for the night. When I got off the bike, he said we were in range of Homestead, so it didn't matter where we stopped and this looked convenient. We weighed the option of stopping for the night or continuing on and Tim agreed it would be okay to go ahead finish the ride.

I have been to Key West a few times and have never gotten a great picture at the buoy marking the Southernmost Point. I asked Tim if he would be willing to chip in to hire a professional photographer to take our picture at the end. Tim wasn't convinced that this was a worthwhile expenditure, but he agreed to do it. I called my friend Kevin Lechner and asked if he would do me a big favor and try to find a professional photographer that would meet us at the buoy around 1:00 a.m. Kevin agreed and said he would email me if he had any success.

Kevin's help was another example of the assistance and support we had experienced throughout our journey. Tim and I were fortunate to have friends all around North America that we could look to for help. In fact, Tim often commented along our ride, "We have friends we haven't used yet." This was so true, but we had racked up a lot of pay-backs.

Tim and I got a bag of ice to chill the champagne Harry had given us, so it would be cold at the finish. I was starting to have trouble with my chain slipping, which now had over 12,000 miles on it. I asked Tim to call our friend Tom Coppedge in Marathon, where Tim had left his truck and trailer, and see if he would be willing to meet us at the buoy with the truck and trailer, as I wasn't sure how long my chain was going to last. Tim called Tom and he was more than glad to meet us. He wanted to be a part of the finish anyway and we also wanted him to be a part of the finish. Tom also agreed to bring some champagne glasses.

We exited for gas at Homestead around 11:30 p.m., but somehow got on a section of road that took us right through town. We had to stop at nearly all of the many traffic lights.

Chapter 15

This was causing havoc on my chain. Every time I had to stop and start again, I could feel the chain slip and I still had about 135 miles to get to the end. I called the photographer. He didn't answer so I left a voice message and then sent an email telling him we were running late by about an hour.

There was virtually no traffic, even though it was Fourth of July weekend. That was good news, as even at a constant speed my chain was slipping. I finally figured out that if I dropped down a gear and kept the revs up, I was okay and I worked hard to hold a constant rpm.

We ended our ride with a gas receipt at 2:25 a.m., July 2, 2011. We then rode down to the buoy to get our pictures, hoping that the photographer was there. Sure enough as we pulled up Tony Gregory, a Key West Photographer, introduced himself and immediately began taking pictures.

Tony told us we could move our bikes inside the wall and close to the buoy. Once I got my bike placed and stepped away it fell over! One last victimization from my failed custom shock. I had shortened the kickstand since the custom shock lowered the bike. And now, with the stock shock installed it was too short and the bike fell over. As I bent over to pick up the bike, I laid my camera on the buoy.

Unfortunately, in my excitement, I left my camera on the buoy and the photographic documentation of my trip was lost. I advertised in as many resources as I could think of and checked with the police, but my camera was never recovered. (This explains why many of the pictures in this book are from other photographers or the public domain.)

Our friend Tom Coppedge was kind enough to get up in the middle of the night to bring the trailer down from Marathon and to share the end of the ride experience with us.

Eastern Bay by Bay

Alan Leduc, Tom Coppedge, and Tim Yow
Photograph by Tony Gregory

We started the **Eastern Bay by Bay Plus** ride at 6:00 a.m. ADT (7:00 EDT), June, 26, 2011 from North Sydney, Nova Scotia and ended in Key West, Florida at 2:25 a.m. EDT, July 2, 2011. It had taken us 4 days, 19 hours, 24 minutes to complete the ride, putting us well under the 6 day recommended time for the **Eastern Bay by Bay Plus Power Tour**.

We started the **Eastern Bay by Bay Tour** at 8:47 a.m. EDT, June 28, 2011 from Eastport, Maine and completed it in Key West, Florida at 2:25 a.m. EDT, July 2, 2011, taking 3 days, 17 hours, 38 minutes. We were well under the 4 day recommended time for the **Eastern Bay by Bay Power Tour.**

We shared the end of our ride with a champagne toast and reflected a bit on our journey. We had covered over 23,000 miles, including over 2700 miles of the most notorious gravel roads in the U.S. and Canada. We had faced adversity, overcome personal tensions, and met some great people along the way. We were now back where we had started 48 days earlier. ***We had done it!***

Chapter 15

Alan Leduc and Tim Yow End of Ride Toast
Photograph by Tony Gregory

16   Passion in the Wind
What a Ride!

Tim and *I committed to completing what we both thought might be our last "big ride." And what a ride it was! It was fraught with mechanical and maintenance issues, riding challenges, and personal tensions. It also included riding more gravel roads than I would ever have believed possible for me, and many amazing experiences – who would ever have imagined chasing a herd of buffalo? We met the challenges and achieved success, and we will have enough memories to stay with us for a lifetime.*

Refining the Vision

Tim had a vision of doing what he believed might be his last "big ride" by adding Inuvik, Northwest Territories to his 2009 Circumnavigation of North America Insanity, making it a Gold version of the ride. But Mike Kneebone, President of the Iron Butt Association, had a different vision for the Gold version of Tim's Circumnavigation ride and added Brownsville, Texas, as well. Adding Brownsville would encourage riders to hug the U.S./Mexico border as they rode through Texas.

Jack Gustafson had a vision for a ride that would force riders off the interstate by requiring them to visit 18 bays as documented stops. Tim decided that combining the Gold version of his ride and Jack's 18 bays into a single ride would put the cherry on the top of his long-distance riding career.

Chapter 16

Tim asked me if I would be interested in doing this ride with him. The idea of doing a big ride, completed mostly off the interstates and visiting the various bays of U.S. and Canada really intrigued me. The thought that this might be Tim's last big ride, and mine too, given recent health issues, and knowing that Tim had told his wife Patty that he would not do the ride alone, was all I needed to commit.

Taking the Gold version of Tim's ride as identified by the IBA and Jack's original 18 bays idea, we developed a ride we called 35 Bays – Ultimate Circumnavigation of North America. The IBA agreed to certify it as long as we completed it in less than 60 days. We targeted a 37 day completion time knowing it was a very aggressive schedule and we would not likely meet it.

The IBA requires that a rider validate mandatory stops for a proposed ride prior to offering the ride for certification by others, knowing that sometimes the best laid plans don't work out in practice. Tim and I would be the first to complete the ride and would have the additional responsibility of validating the mandatory locations. As we were doing so, some bays got dropped and some bays got added, but in the end there were still 35 bays. We renamed the ride the **35 Bay by Bay Adventure** and developed a whole series of component rides as documented in this book.

Staying in the U.S. with the 15 Bay by Bay

The **15 Bay by Bay Tour** includes only those bays and mandatory stops from the **35 Bay by Bay Adventure** ride that are located in the lower 48 United States. MapSource estimates this ride at 10,769 miles, requiring 7 days, 10 hours, 42 minutes. Using the 300 mile per day and 500 mile per day criteria for Tour and Power tour, the **15 Bay by Bay Tour** would require 35 days, 21 hours, 31 minutes and the **15 Bay by Bay Power Tour** would require 21 days, 12 hours, 54 minutes. Recommended times for the **15 Bay by Bay Tour**

What a Ride!

and the **15 Bay by Bay Power Tour** are **35 days** and **21 days**, respectively.

Staying on Paved Roads

The **29 Bay by Bay Tour** excludes all the mandatory stops from the **35 Bay by Bay Adventure** ride that would require the rider to travel on unpaved roads.

The following mandatory stops from the **35 Bay by Bay Adventure** are excluded for the **29 Bay by Bay Tour and Power Tour**:

- Prudhoe Bay, Alaska
- Little Gold Creek, Yukon
- Mackenzie Bay (Inuvik, NWT)
- Yellowknife Bay, NWT
- James Bay (Chisiasibi, Quebec)
- Baie-Comeau, Quebec
- Goose Bay, Labrador

MapSource estimates this ride at 18,820 miles. Using the 300 mile per day and 500 mile per day criteria for Tour and Power tour, the **29 Bay by Bay Tour** would require 62 days, 17 hours, 36 minutes and the **29 Bay by Bay Power Tour** would require 37 days, 15 hours, 21 minutes. Recommended times for the **29 Bay by Bay Tour** and the **29 Bay by Bay Power Tour** are **60 days** and **37 days** respectively.

35 Bay by Bay Adventure

The **35 Bay by Bay Adventure** requires completion of all of the mandatory stops in the following component rides:

Chapter 16

- Southern Bay by Bay Tour
- Western Bay by Bay Adventure
- Northern Bay by Adventure
- Eastern Bay by Bay Plus Tour

Current mapping software does not accurately calculate the route. But by piecing together various maps, it is estimated that this ride is about 23,100 miles. I recorded 23,144 miles on my GPS which does not include approximately 350 miles of ferry rides:

- Port Bolivar – Galveston Ferry : 2.7 miles
- Port Angeles – Victoria Ferry: 22.9 miles
- Victoria – Horseshoe Bay Ferry: 35 miles
- Dawson City Ferry: Less than 1 mile
- Dempster Peel Ferry: About 1 mile x 2
- Dempster Mackenzie Ferry: About 1 mile x 2
- Yellowknife Mackenzie Ferry: About 1 mile x 2
- Blanc-Sablon – St. Barbe Ferry: 23 miles
- Placentia – North Sydney Ferry: 299 miles
- Cape May – Dover Ferry: 16 miles

Our starting receipt from Key West was stamped 10:23 a.m., May 15, 2011 and our ending receipt was stamped from the same gas station at 2:25 a.m., July 2, 2011. It had taken us 47 days, 16 hours, 2 minutes to complete the ride, which included about 2,755 miles of gravel.

A **Gold level** of the **35 Bay by Bay Adventure**, based upon a 500 miles per day pace, would allow **47** days to complete the ride. We were beyond the 47 allowable days. Had we elected to ride the 50 miles from Marathon to Key West the morning of May 16 instead of doing only 15 miles on the first day of the trip, we would have been under 47 days. Or if I hadn't had a busted shock or any number of other "woulda-coulda-shoulda"

What a Ride!

moments, we would have met the Gold level of the ride. We completed the **35 Bay by Bay Adventure** with 22 days to spare, based on the 60 days negotiated in the original discussions with the IBA, and we are proud to be the first riders to do so.

"Would you do the ride again?"

The question we have been asked the most since completing the ride is, "Would you do the ride again?" My initial response is that it's hard to believe that I even did it at all! Had my core values not driven me, I'm sure it would have never happened. And even then, I don't think I really understood the magnitude of the ride until getting to Prudhoe Bay and realizing that we were less than 40% done.

The short answer is no. Harry Farthing, when telling us about the various mountains he had successfully peaked, commented that "once it was done, it was done." I feel the same way about long-distance rides. I don't have a desire to repeat rides that I have already completed.

Maybe the better question is "Knowing what you know now, would you have done the ride?"

My answer is, "Maybe."

It is not a ride I would enjoy doing by myself. Even with the differences in riding styles, Tim and I helped each other get through the ride. There is no denying the fact that having a partner avoided some of the homesickness that can occur on such a long ride. However, I have definitely learned some lessons and would have more serious discussions with my riding partner regarding riding styles and philosophies, to make sure we were on the same page.

Chapter 16
"Are you glad you did it?"

A popular follow-up question is, "Are you glad you did the ride?" Most definitely! It was an amazing experience! While I had previously traveled some sections of the route, there were many areas that I was able to explore for the first time. Even riding the areas in which I had ridden previously brought back fond memories of previous trips.

By riding more than 2,700 miles of gravel on some of the most notorious roads in the U.S. and Canada, I proved something to myself. I wouldn't consider myself a great off-road rider. I wouldn't even consider myself a good off-road rider. However, I had done something that I couldn't imagine I would ever be able to do.

Final Thoughts

Independent – Dreamer – Single Focused. These core values should have been evident, from the time I started considering to commit to this ride with Tim through to the conclusion of this book. I have often dreamed of writing a book and began thinking of documenting this ride after dealing with the broken shock in Inuvik. Once I returned home, I began to write furiously, setting aside all but those events in my life that were very high priority.

Dedication – Self Initiative – Perseverance. There were many times that I could have quit. My wife Brenda consoled me and encouraged me to continue during Tim's and my first conflict in Texas, and I dedicated myself to finish no matter what. When I crashed, I never even thought of quitting. When my shock failed, I had no idea how a shock was built, but had enough self-initiative to figure it out and kept at it until I was successful. I was really concerned about Tim's superior abilities in riding on gravel, but strived to improve my skills and feel that I did so.

What a Ride!

Challenge – Achievement. This ride was an amazing challenge and completing the ride was an equally amazing achievement! Throughout my life I have simply refused to let a task beat me. Tim has the same core values. Together, despite our differences, we pushed each other to complete an epic ride and life challenge.

My world has changed many times in my life. Completing this ride brought yet another change. I would never have imagined that a few years after I quit riding in 2008, I would be completing a ride such as this.

I also confirmed that, at heart, I am a loner. I think this is why I've never had the successful family life that I desire. And why mild disagreements with Tim were blown out of proportion in my mind. It is odd how I can enjoy the company of others yet at the same time not fully appreciate it.

Joseph Juran in his autobiography, written at age 98, noted that he was not often liked by his peers. He realized, at that late age, that it was due to the circumstances of his youth and he could have corrected it by his actions, but chose not to do so. I'm only 60, and I acknowledge that I need to be much better at appreciating others. But I have difficulty being consistent at it. I hope it is something I will learn before leaving this earth.

I do not think that Tim or I would have ever completed this ride individually. We owe each other a big debt of gratitude for working through the conflicts and pushing each other to the end. Tim is an amazing rider and completing this ride at age 68 is an inspiration to me and others.

Living a Song

Barb Smith, who served as editor for this book, sent me the lyrics to Lee Ann Womack's song, *I Hope You Dance* and said I had certainly danced in my life and rarely sat it out.

Chapter 16

Lyrics by Tia Sillers and Mark D. Sanders

I hope you never lose your sense of wonder
You get your fill to eat but always keep that hunger
May you never take one single breath for granted
God forbid love ever leave you empty handed
I hope you still feel small when you stand beside the ocean
Whenever one door closes I hope one more opens
Promise me that you'll give faith a fighting chance
And when you get the choice to sit it out or dance

I hope you dance
I hope you dance

I hope you never fear those mountains in the distance
Never settle for the path of least resistance
Livin' might mean takin' chances, but they're worth takin'
Lovin' might be a mistake, but it's worth makin'
Don't let some Hellbent heart leave you bitter
When you come close to sellin' out, reconsider
Give the heavens above more than just a passing glance
And when you get the choice to sit it out or dance

I hope you dance
I hope you dance
Time is a wheel in constant motion always rolling us along
I hope you dance
I hope you dance
Tell me who wants to look back on their years and wonder,
where those years have gone?

I hope you still feel small when you stand beside the ocean
Whenever one door closes I hope one more opens
Promise me that you'll give faith a fighting chance
And when you get the choice to sit it out or dance

Dance...
Time is a wheel in constant motion always rolling us along
I hope you dance
I hope you dance
Tell me who wants to look back on their years and wonder,
where those years have gone?

What a Ride!

I have always been passionate. After dealing with cancer at age 42, and coming face-to-face with the fragility of life, I decided that I would live life to its fullest.

When Tim and I were standing by the ocean taking in the view of the elephant seals, we definitely felt small. When we looked at the mountains in the distance we proceeded with joy. When there was an opportunity to give up on our trip, we did not yield to the path of least resistance. Many feel that motorcycling is dangerous, particularly long distance riding, and would view that Tim and I were "takin' chances," but they were worth takin'.

When you look back on the years, don't wonder where the years are gone!

This was an amazing experience and one that I hope will be duplicated by many other riders in the future. If not the whole ride, then the components of the ride as we have developed them.

Ordinary people can do extraordinary things, if they only dream, believe, and strive to achieve!

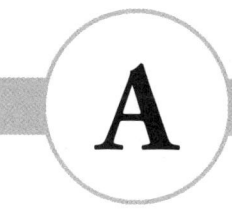

Passion in the Wind
Appendix A

Alan's Long-Distance Accomplishments

At the time of this writing the Iron Butt Association lists certified rides as:

- SaddleSore 1000
    * 05/05/2001 Honda Shadow Spirit
    * 03/29/2003 Honda ST1100
    * 03/05/2008 BMW F650 GS Dakar IBA Party Ride-in
    * 03/10/2011 BMW F650 GS Gator 1000
    * 06/16/2007 GL1800 Goldwing Rhode Island 1000
    * 09/13/2008 Honda Silverwing Scooter Indy 1000
    * 06/01/2007 Suzuki V-Strom 650 Alaska Insanity Gold
- BunBurner 1500 05/06/2001 Honda Shadow Spirit
- BunBurner 1500 Gold
    * 10/06/2001 Honda GL1800 Goldwing
    * 09/21/2002 Honda GL 1800 Goldwing Minnesota North Stars Group Record Ride

- 50CC JAX to SDO 05/18/2002 Honda GL1800 Goldwing

Appendix A

- 50CC SDO to JAX 03/08/2006 Honda GL1800 Goldwing
- 100CCC Honda GL1800 Goldwing 03/2003
- Great Lakes Gold 5/25/2002
- Trans-Canadian Gold 06/2004 Honda GL18000 Goldwing
- Ride Around Texas (RAT) Insanity Gold 05/2006
- Burn Burner 3000 Gold 01/03/2002
- Border to Border to Border from Hell 05/16/2007 Suzuki V-Strom 650
- Ultimate Coast to Coast 06/2004 Kawasaki KLR 650
- 48 States – 3 Countries 05/2005 Honda GL1800 Goldwing

Long-Distance Rallies:

- Palmetto Ramble
    * 2003 GL1800 Co-Champion with Bob Moore
    * 2004 GL1800 Goldwing 5th Place
    * 2002 GL1800 9th Place
- 2002 Feast in the East GL1800 4th Place
- 2003 Minnesota 1000 Honda GL1800 Goldwing 5th Place-Expert Class
- 2002 Buckeye 1000 Honda GL1800 10th Place-Expert Class
- Iron Butt Rally 2003 DNF (Accident)

Passion in the Wind
Appendix B

Tim's Long-Distance Accomplishments

At the time of this writing certified Iron Butt Association rides are:

- SaddleSore 1000
    * Most SaddleSore 1000's on different motorcycles
    * 2003 Most SaddleSore 1000's in 30 days on different motorcycles
    * 05/23/02 Honda GL1800 Goldwing
    * 10/05/02 Harley Davidson Heritage
    * 04/13/03 Yamaha Virago
    * 06/01/03 Honda ST1100
    * 06/10/03 Yamaha Road Star
    * 06/21/03 Honda Goldwing
    * 06/28/03 Honda Valkyrie
    * 07/14/03 Honda Helix
    * 07/20/03 Harley Davidson Road King
    * 09/06/03 Honda Magna V-45
    * 06/26/04 Harley Davidson Heritage
    * 08/08/04 Harley Davidson Softail
    * 08/18/04 Harley Davidson Road King
    * 10/10/04 Kawasaki KLR 650
    * 06/11/05 Honda VTX 1800
    * 07/09/05 BMW R1200 GS
    * 03/09/06 1969 Moto Guzzi 750 Oldest SaddleSore 1000 Motorcycle
    * 04/15/2006 Kawasaki Vulcan

Appendix B

- * 05/05/06 Suzuki V-Strom 650
- * 05/09/06 Yamaha FJR 1300 Indiana 1000
- * 05/11/06 Suzuki Boulevard
- * 08/20/06 Kawasaki KLR 650
- * 06/09/2007 Kawasaki Concours Illinois 1000
- * 04/26/2009 Kawasaki 1400
- * 06/25/2009 Kawasaki KLR 650
- * 06/28/2009 Kawasaki KLR 650

- BunBurner 1500 08/26/06 Kawasaki KLR 650
- BunBurner Gold
  - * 08/18/02 Honda GL1800 Goldwing
  - * 04/19/04 Honda GL1800 Goldwing
  - * 04/04/05 Honda GL1800 Goldwing
- 50cc Quest 04/19/04 Honda GL1800 Goldwing
- 100ccc Insanity 04/2005 Honda GL1800 Goldwing
- SaddleSore 5000 04/2005 Honda GL1800 Goldwing
- Ultimate Coast to Coast to Coast Insanity
  - * 08/06 Kawasaki KLR 650
  - * 07/09 Kawasaki KLR 650
- Bay to Bay 07/09 Kawasaki KLR 650
- Ultimate Coast to Coast to Coast Insanity 07/09
- The 5 Coasts of North America Insanity 07/09 Kawasaki KLR 650
- Circumnavigation of North America Insanity 07/09 Kawasaki KLR 650
- National Parks Tour Traveler Gold 2009
- Tim was selected as a member of the Iron Butt Association Mile-Eater Gold Club – Most Extreme Riders – in 2008.

Passion in the Wind
Appendix C

Proposed Ride List

- 35 Bay by Bay
    * Adventure Gold - 47 days
    * Adventure - 60 days

- 29 Bay by Bay
    * Power Tour - 37 days
    * Tour - 60 days

- 15 Bay by Bay
    * Power Tour - 15 days
    * Tour - 35 days

- Southern Bay by Bay
    * Power Tour - 6 days
    * Tour - 11 days

- Western Bay by Bay
    * Power Tour - 3 days
    * Tour - 5 days

- Western Bay by Bay Plus
    * Power Tour - 8 days
    * Tour - 14 days

Appendix C

- Western Bay by Bay Adventure - 11 days

- Northern Bay by Bay
    * Power Tour - 12 days
    * Tour - 20 days

- Northern Bay by Bay Plus
    * Power Tour - 13 days
    * Tour - 23 days

- Northern Bay by Bay
    * Adventure - 21 days
    * Adventure Gold - 35 days

- Eastern Bay by Bay
    * Power Tour - 4 days
    * Tour - 7 days

- Eastern Bay by Bay Plus
    * Power Tour - 6 days
    * Tour - 11 days

- Eastern Bay by Bay Gold
    * Power Tour - 8 days
    * Tour - 13 days

- Circle to Circle
    * Insanity Gold - 55 hours
    * Insanity - 80 hours

Key West Start

Passion in the Wind
Dream, Believe, and Achieve the Extraordinary

Golden Gate Bridge

Dempster Highway

Passion in the Wind
Dream, Believe, and Achieve the Extraordinary

Peel Ferry